CSR Image Discursive Construction of Banks and the Effects on Capital Markets

Muchun Wan

CSR Image Discursive Construction of Banks and the Effects on Capital Markets

Comparative Study of China and US

Springer

Muchun Wan
School of English Language, Literature
and Culture
Beijing International Studies University
Beijing, China

This work was supported by the Beijing International Studies University 2022 Annual Academic Work Publishing Funding

ISBN 978-981-19-6014-7 ISBN 978-981-19-6012-3 (eBook)
https://doi.org/10.1007/978-981-19-6012-3

Jointly published with Social Sciences Academic Press
The print edition is not for sale in China (Mainland). Customers from China (Mainland) please order the print book from: Social Sciences Academic Press.

This Springer imprint is published by the registered company Springer Nature Singapore Pte Ltd.
The registered company address is: 152 Beach Road, #21-01/04 Gateway East, Singapore 189721, Singapore

About This Book

The comprehensive opening-up pattern in the financial field has been advocated since the 19th National Congress of the Communist Party of China. Thus, it is necessary and urgent for Chinese banks to establish an international corporate image in order to attract more foreign investment and improve China's international image in the financial sector. CSR reports provide banks with good platforms to establish relationships with stakeholders and construct responsible corporate images by disclosing their CSR information.

Previous studies of CSR reports and corporate image in business discourse studies have focused on the discursive interpretation and explanation of a language's functions in business discourse with few studies exploring a language's actual effects on corporate governance and economic practice. Previous studies in management, economics and finance have noted a language's importance in organizational discourse and corporate performance. However, without a linguistic perspective, these studies fail to fully explain a language's discursive functions in economic practice. In order to fill this gap and in light of Biber's register analysis, the theory of discourse and institutional identity, and corporate identity system (CIS), this study attempts to establish an inter-disciplinary discourse evaluation framework to analyze multi-dimensional discursive features along four dimensions in Chinese and American banks' CSR reports: sentiment, readability, CSR keyword and visualization, in order to help Chinese banks improve their CSR disclosure and construct international CSR images along three dimensions: mind image, behavior image and visual image. Then, guided by signaling theory and behavioral finance, the influencing mechanism of CSR reports' discursive features on capital market reaction will be illustrated, which aims to further analyze and verify a language's functions in economic practice. The multi-dimensional discourse evaluation framework of banks' CSR reports for the refinement of banks' CSR disclosure system, CSR image construction and corporate value enhancement is an inter-disciplinary attempt and an integration of linguistics, management and finance theories. It promotes the cross-disciplinary research into business discourse and sheds light on the research into organizational discourse, institutional identity and corporate governance.

To help Chinese banks' CSR reports better comply with international contexts, quantitative analysis based on corpus and computational linguistic tools (Antconc, WordSmith, DICTION and Coh-Metrix) is conducted to explore the various multi-dimensional discursive features in Chinese and American banks' CSR reports. The results indicate that (1) In general, Chinese banks' CSR reports show a significantly higher sentimental tendency than American banks' CSR reports; (2) American banks' CSR reports show comparatively higher readability than Chinese banks' CSR reports; (3) Chinese banks disclose more CSR contributions to society and the public, whereas American banks disclose more CSR information about employees, the environment and corporate governance; (4) American banks prefer to employ pictures in their CSR reports to persuade and interact with their stakeholders.

In order to help Chinese banks better establish an international CSR image and transmit banks' CSR images with Chinese characteristics, this study analyzes Chinese and American banks' different discursive construction of CSR images based on the corporate identity system. The findings are as follows: (1) Chinese banks construct an authoritative, national strategy-oriented, society and public-oriented CSR image, while American banks show a pragmatistic and individual-oriented CSR image; (2) American banks show objective and factual construction of CSR image; Chinese banks, besides showing objective and factual construction of CSR image, also express prospective construction of their CSR image. (3) Chinese banks convey an active, innovative and positive CSR image, while American banks convey a stable and conservative CSR image. Guided by stakeholder theory and legitimacy theory, accounts for Chinese and American banks' different CSR images are explained in terms of their different political, economic, social, cultural and regulatory contexts.

In order to examine the actual effects of CSR reports' discursive features on capital markets and to improve Chinese banks' awareness of using CSR reports' discursive features to construct CSR images and enhance corporate value, empirical research of event study and gray relational entropy analysis is conducted. The results show that (1) discursive features in both Chinese and American banks' CSR reports may bring significant cumulative abnormal returns to banks' stock prices within 30 days after the release of their CSR reports. Discursive features in American banks' CSR reports bring more influence to the capital market compared with Chinese banks; (2) readability indicators in both Chinese and American banks' CSR reports contribute the most to capital market performance.

Based on the findings, several suggestions are proposed. Chinese banks may emphasize the function of CSR reports' discursive features in stakeholder engagement, CSR image construction and corporate value enhancement. Regulatory organizations need to strengthen the regulation and guidance of Chinese banks' CSR information disclosure. As for Chinese banks, they need to reconstruct their English version of CSR reports. Recontextualization is suggested in order to better comply with international stakeholders' reading habits and to promote banks' CSR images with Chinese characteristics to international stakeholders in a concise and straightforward way. This can be accomplished by improving the reading ease, disclosing more CSR contributions to an inclusive group of stakeholders, and using pictures to interact with stakeholders.

This study contributes to the improvement of Chinese banks' awareness of CSR disclosure and the establishment of Chinese banks' international images. Since more and more Chinese companies in different sectors are choosing overseas listings, findings in this study also have practical implications for their information disclosure, international image construction and corporate value enhancement through corporate narratives, such as annual reports and IPO prospectuses. In other words, this study contributes to the internalization of Chinese companies from the discourse perspective, thus more effectively telling "Chinese stories" and spreading China's national image.

Contents

Abbreviations

BI	Behavior Identity
CAR	Cumulative Abnormal Return
CBIRC	China Banking and Insurance Regulatory Commission
CIS	Corporate Identity System
CPC	Communist Party of China
CSP	Corporate Social Responsibility Performance
CSR	Corporate Social Responsibility
CSR-A	Corpus of American Banks' CSR Reports
CSR-C	Corpus of Chinese Banks' CSR Reports
ESG	Environment, Social and Governance
GREA	Gray Relational Entropy Analysis
IPO	Initial Public Offerings
MD&A	Management Discussion and Analysis
MDA	Multidimensional Analysis
MI	Mind Identity
MSCI	Morgan Stanley Capital International
R&D	Research and Development
SEC	U.S. Securities and Exchange Commission
STTR	Standard Type/token Ratio
VI	Visual Identity

List of Figures

List of Tables

Chapter 1
Introduction

This chapter introduces the research orientation, rationale, research objectives and questions, and organization of this dissertation.

1.1 Research Orientation

The fulfillment of corporate social responsibility (CSR) of commercial banks as the most important allocators of financial resources has a radical effect. Commercial banks can affect their customers' and related industries' CSR performance through credit policies, such as green credits and inclusive finance. Thus, the improvement of banks' CSR performance and banks' CSR images deserves further study.

Also, the comprehensive opening-up pattern in the financial sector has been advocated since the 19th National Congress of the Communist Party of China (CPC), as China's economy is integrated into the world economy. As the leading force in China's economic development, Chinese banks have the responsibility to increase the supply efficiency of financial resources and promote China's financial reform. Thus, it is crucial for Chinese banks to establish an international corporate image in order to attract more foreign investment and enhance China's international image in the financial sector.

CSR reports provide banks with good platforms to establish relationships with stakeholders and to construct good corporate images by disclosing their CSR information on economic, environment, social and governance performance (ESG performance). Also, more and more international investors are considering companies' CSR performance when making investment decisions. Companies with better CSR performance will have a higher return on investment than the ones with lower performance (ICBC Green Finance Research Group, 2017; UNEP-FI & Mercer, 2007).

Due to banks' irreplaceable role in China's financial opening-up policies, their radical role in CSR performance as well as Chinese banks' limited experience in publishing English versions of their CSR reports, it is necessary and meaningful to

M. Wan, *CSR Image Discursive Construction of Banks and the Effects on Capital Markets*,
https://doi.org/10.1007/978-981-19-6012-3_1

examine the discursive features of Chinese banks' CSR reports in order to help them effectively communicate with their stakeholders and establish good international images.

Under this background, this research (1) describes the multi-dimensional discursive features in Chinese and American banks' CSR reports; (2) analyzes Chinese and American banks' different discursively constructed CSR images via the employment of various discursive features in CSR reports within their different contexts; (3) examines the effects of Chinese and American banks' discursively constructed CSR images on capital markets, with an inter-disciplinary approach of linguistics, management and economics.

1.1.1 CSR Image Construction Via Discursive Features in CSR Reports

Firms can construct good CSR images via disclosing CSR information and adopting suitable discursive features in CSR reports.

Corporate image is divided into two categories: the image of corporate economic responsibility and CSR image. CSR image is the direct result of CSR behavior based on companies' "soft" strength (such as corporate governance, corporate strategy, corporate culture, business ethics, and social concerns) (Liu, 2008). A CSR report, which mainly consists of the non-financial aspects of business performance is the reflection of corporate social responsibility as well as an important way for companies to communicate with their stakeholders.

Non-financial information, such as CSR reports, is a kind of voluntary disclosure containing many words, leaving companies a significant amount of space to manipulate the linguistic features such as the tone, readability, content and visual expression. Doing so can be a means for impression management. Smith and Taffler (2000) have conducted a survey of 109 listed British companies and found that the percentage of non-financial information disclosed in the company's annual reports had increased from 45 to 57% during the period from 1996 to 2000. The amount of information provided for investors by non-financial information disclosure was twice as much as that in the financial information disclosure section. Thus, content analysis of CSR reports provides stakeholders with an increasingly important approach to address more incremental information than do financial statements.

Case studies and extensive overviews of non-financial reporting come from multiple perspectives in social sciences such as accounting (Li, 2008), management (Rezaee & Tuo, 2017), business communication studies (Gazdar, 2007) and recently also in linguistics and discourse studies (Wang & Bu, 2018; Aiezza, 2015a; Catenaccio, 2012; Fuoli, 2012).

As for CSR reports, they are the generic hybrid: the combination of informational and promotional elements (Bhatia, 2004). A CSR report is used partly to pass environmental, social and governance information to internal and external stakeholders, and partly to build and maintain a good corporate image (Kushal, 2011). This enhances the company's "positive face", and the self-image that firm wants to claim for itself (Brown & Levinson, 1987). Thus, interpreting discursive features that CSR reports adopt, and exploring how companies construct CSR image via discourse features warrant inquiry from an interdisciplinary perspective.

1.1.2 Corporate Performance Via Discursive Features in CSR Reports

Adopting suitable discursive features in CSR reports can bring a firm good performance in both financial development and in capital markets.

Discourse is an important form of social existence. There is an inseparable relationship between discourse and institutions: discourse both reflects institutions and builds institutions. These institutional identities are used by their members in understanding the institutions (Richards, 2006). CSR reports, the typical type of institutional discourse, are a reflection of corporate CSR values. They are the vital ways for companies to communicate with stakeholders. The suitable employment of discursive features in CSR reports enables companies to present a good image in corporate social responsibility performance (hereinafter CSP). CSR reports are constructed by companies. At the same time, they are also influenced by various aspects such as corporate culture and corporate governance. CSR reports help companies establish corporate images, interpersonal relationships, knowledge systems and values which are correlated with their operation performances as well as the capital market performance. A survey conducted by KPMG in 2005 found that one motive for companies to issue CSR reports is to build their brands and reputations. Vilanova et al. (2009) have established a model of the relationship between CSR information disclosure and corporate competitive advantages. This model indicates that corporate reputation and corporate image are the link connecting CSR and competitive advantage. To be specific, information disclosure of CSP will affect a company's image identification and improve interpersonal relationships with stakeholders. This, in turn, affects the competitive advantage of the company.

Non-financial textual information has been found to influence companies' future earnings releases (Li, 2008), security prices and stock returns (Tetlock, 2007; Davis et al., 2012), trading volumes (Das & Chen, 2007) and ROA and ROE (Li & Wang, 2017). The discursive features in non-financial information, such as CSR reports, do convey much more incremental information than financial information does. They might influence companies' performance, since companies can use suitable linguistic features to construct good corporate images via impression management.

Research on corporate performance in the disciplines of management, accounting, and finance has experienced a "linguistic turn". Due to the inseparable relationship between discourse and institutional identities, language's function in corporate image construction and corporate performance needs to be explored and verified by an inter-disciplinary approach.

1.1.3 Chinese Banks' Internationalization Via Discursive Features in CSR Reports

The contrastive analysis of discursive features in Chinese and American banks' CSR reports can help Chinese banks achieve internationalization.

Stones from other hills may serve to polish this jade. American companies have a more complete system of CSR performance and disclosure, due to their mature CSR-related theories and concepts. A comparative analysis of discursive features used by Chinese and American banks' CSR reports can help the Chinese banks establish a better CSR discourse disclosure system in line with international standards. With Morgan Stanley Capital International (MSCI)'s inclusion of A shares in the emerging market investment index and an increasing number of companies choosing to list overseas, Chinese companies, including banks, need to learn from foreign companies' CSR disclosure strategies in the process of information disclosure. MSCI's ESG survey has shown that Chinese companies' ESG scores lag behind other global companies by an average of 25%. In environmental factors, scores are lower by more than 50%. Therefore, the Chinese banks should pay more attention to CSR performance and CSR information disclosure in order to achieve internationalization and to attract more foreign investment.

Discourse can help companies construct and spread their corporate images. The promotion of suitable discursive features in CSR reports is of great significance to the international communication and the construction of banks' international images. To a degree, Chinese banks' images represent China's national image in the financial sector due to their significant position in China's financial reform and opening-up. Therefore, a cross-disciplinary study on the Chinese banks' international image construction from the perspective of linguistics, management, and economics is vital for more effectively spreading China's national image and telling "Chinese stories".

1.2 Rationale

Under the background of China's financial opening-up policies since the 19th National Congress of the CPC, it is necessary for the Chinese banks to establish an international CSR information disclosure system and CSR image in order to promote China's national image in the financial sector.

Current studies about banks' CSR and image construction are primarily confined to the management and economic level, and they have already noted language's importance in organizational discourse, corporate image construction and corporate performance. However, these studies cannot explain language's discursive function in economic practice without a linguistic perspective. The amount of research about banks' CSR reports and corporate image construction from the linguistic perspective is small. It has mainly focused on the discursive interpretation and explanation of language's function in business discourse based on qualitative and corpus-based analysis from single dimensions and single approaches. Thus, studies from the linguistic perspective have been unable to explain language's functions in corporate image construction and economic practice, comprehensively or scientifically.

In order to help Chinese banks improve their CSR disclosure and construct international CSR images, this study integrates Biber's register analysis, the theory of discourse and institutional identity, and corporate identity system (CIS) into an interdisciplinary discourse evaluation framework to analyze various discursive features in Chinese and American banks' CSR reports along the dimensions of sentiment, readability, CSR keyword and visualization, via corpus and computational linguistic tools. The corporate identity system (CIS) from the perspective of management provides an "entry point" to analyze banks' discursive image construction. It is used to examine how the multi-dimensional discursive features in CSR reports construct banks' CSR images on 3 levels: mind image, behavior image and visual image.

Language use varies with situational context: core and pervasive linguistic features are always functional; certain features are used in association with the situational context of the text (Biber & Conrad, 2009). The multi-dimensional evaluation framework in this study is a further application of Biber's register analysis and multi-dimensional analysis (MDA). It expands Biber's MDA to lexical, syntactic, semantic, textual and discourse level, and also applies Biber's register analysis to business discourse research.

Discourse reflects an institution's values and operations. At the same time, it also constructs institutions. Linguistic features such as positive and negative sentimental words, high lexical density, and connectives, are functionally used by managerial groups in CSR reports. This reflects corporate values, development strategies and managerial groups' preferred corporate governance concepts. Identity construction has always been a focus of research in different disciplines such as philosophy, linguistics, sociology, politics, psychology, and anthropology (Xiang, 2009). However, the theory and research methods of any discipline alone are insufficient to explain the problem of institutional image construction. This study is a cross-disciplinary attempt at the discursive construction of banks' CSR images. It also contributes to the development of inter-disciplinary research in institutional identity.

Guided by signaling theory and behavioral finance, the influencing mechanism of CSR reports' discursive features on capital market reaction is proposed in this study in order to examine the actual effects of banks' discursive construction of CSR images on capital market performance. It also aims to further analyze and verify language's function in economic practice. Discursive features in CSR reports serve as signals that can transmit, as well as influence, information about banks' CSR concepts, strategies and CSR behaviors to their stakeholders. Stakeholders' attitudes towards corporate image and evaluations of corporate value, as well as investors' investment decisions, will be influenced. Thus, signaling theory and behavioral finance validate the influence of CSR reports' discursive features on banks' CSR image construction and investors' expectations of corporate value in capital markets.

The multi-dimensional discourse evaluation framework for discursive construction of banks' CSR images and the influencing mechanism of discursive features on capital market reaction proposed in this study contribute to the integration of linguistic theories, management theories and financial theories. This study is a cross-disciplinary attempt at the discursive construction of institutional identity. It contributes to the development of institutional identity's cross-disciplinary research. Additionally, this study reveals the problem-solving function of discourse. This sheds light on theoretical research into both corporate governance and business discourse.

Different from previous studies' qualitative methods from the perspective of business discourse, the research in this study employs various corpus and computational linguistic tools to extract the multi-dimensional discursive features along lexical, syntactic, textual and discourse dimensions of CSR reports. It overcomes the deficiency of one-dimensionality in previous research.

Also, this research uses event study in the financial area and gray relational entropy analysis in the mathematical field to examine discursive features' effects on capital markets. This provides Chinese banks with more practical implications in CSR image construction, internationalization and corporate value improvement. It also provides more inter-disciplinary research methods and data processing methods for business discourse analysis.

Therefore, theoretically, practically and methodologically, the present research can make its due contributions to the inter-disciplinary research on business discourse, and institutional identity construction, and corporate governance as well as to the realization of Chinese banks' internationalization.

1.3 Research Objectives and Questions

The present study aims to explore Chinese and American banks' different discursively constructed CSR images and their linguistic realization of the multi-dimensional discursive features in CSR reports, as well as their effects on capital market performance from the inter-disciplinary perspective of linguistics, management and economics.

To achieve such an end, this study integrates a multi-dimensional discourse evaluation framework of banks' CSR reports based on Biber's register analysis, the theory of discourse and institutional identity and the corporate identity system (CIS). This framework analyzes and contrasts various discursive features in Chinese and American banks' CSR reports along the 4 discursive dimensions of sentiment, readability, CSR keywords and visualization. This will help Chinese banks improve their CSR disclosure systems and promote their international CSR images along 3 dimensions: CSR mind image, CSR behavior image and CSR visual image. Corpus and computational linguistic tools are used to explore the multi-dimensional discursive features in Chinese and American banks' CSR reports in order to provide more practical implications for Chinese banks to improve their CSR disclosure systems.

With the aim of helping Chinese banks establish international CSR images and spreading CSR images with Chinese characteristics to foreign stakeholders, this study explains and compares Chinese and American banks' discursive construction of CSR images in CSR reports based on the multi-dimensional discourse evaluation framework from the inter-disciplinary approach of linguistics and management. Reasons behind Chinese and American banks' different discursively constructed images are explained under their different social, cultural, economic, political and regulatory contexts.

Additionally, in order to further analyze and verify language's function in economic practice, the influencing mechanism of CSR reports' discursive features on capital market reaction (banks' stock price trends) is proposed in this study, guided by signaling theory and behavioral finance. It will also provide additional suggestions for Chinese banks to achieve internationalization and corporate value improvement.

With these clear objectives of exploring the multi-dimensional discursive features in Chinese and American banks' CSR reports, analyzing the discursive construction of Chinese and American banks' CSR images and examining its actual effects on capital market performance, this study's 3 research questions are proposed as follows:

(1) What are the differences of the multi-dimensional discursive features between Chinese and American banks' CSR reports?
(2) How do Chinese and American banks construct their CSR images via the multi-dimensional discursive features in CSR reports and what are the differences between their discursively constructed CSR images?
(3) What are the effects of banks' discursive construction of CSR images on capital markets based on the multi-dimensional discourse evaluation?

1.4 Organization of This Dissertation

This dissertation consists of eight chapters.

This chapter is the introduction. It introduces the research orientation and explains the rationale of this research. Then, it discusses the research objectives, questions and organization of this dissertation.

Chapter 2 is the literature review. It first reviews and defines the key concepts germane to this research. Then, it reviews previous studies of business discourse, the evaluative studies in business discourse analysis, studies of CSR and CSR reports, studies of corporate image construction and studies of the economic effects of CSR reports. The limitations of previous studies are pointed out, and the significance of this study is highlighted.

Chapter 3 explains the theoretical foundations of this research which includes the theoretical foundations behind the multi-dimensional discourse evaluation framework for banks' CSR reports: Fairclough's three-dimensional model, Biber's register analysis, discourse and institutional identity, linguistic theories behind discursive features, as well as theories concerning corporate image construction (corporate identity system and information asymmetry). Signaling theory and behavioral finance are introduced to support the influencing mechanism of CSR reports' discursive features on capital market reaction. Then, with an inter-disciplinary approach of linguistics, management and economics, this study's analytical model for banks' international image construction and corporate value improvement is proposed based on the multi-dimensional discourse evaluation framework and the influencing mechanism of CSR reports' discursive features on capital market reaction.

Chapter 4 illustrates the research methods. It contains corpus data, research tools, data selection and processing, and research procedures.

Chapter 5 answers the first research question and conducts a corpus and computer-assisted descriptive and contrastive study of Chinese and American banks' CSR reports by the multi-dimensional discourse evaluation framework.

Chapter 6 answers the second research question and identifies how Chinese and American banks construct their CSR mind image, CSR behavior image and CSR visual image, respectively, via the adoption of multi-dimensional discursive features in CSR reports. Then, reasons for their different constructed images are explained by legitimacy theory and stakeholder theory under their varying political, economic, cultural, social and regulatory contexts.

Chapter 7 conducts empirical research using the method of event study and gray relational entropy analysis to examine banks' CSR reports' discursive features' effects on capital market performance.

Chapter 8 contains the conclusions, suggestions, implications and limitations of this research.

Chapter 2
Literature Review

In this chapter, the key concepts in this research are illustrated. Before an analytical model is constructed, a broad review of what have been going on with regard to business discourse, organizational discourse, evaluative studies in discourse analysis, CSR and CSR reports, corporate image construction, the economic effects of CSR reports and discursive construction of corporate image in the field of linguistics, management and economics will be conducted in this chapter. Additionally, the limitations of previous studies are pointed out.

2.1 Key Concepts in This Research

The key concepts in this research are: CSR, banks' CSR, CSR reports, CSR report's multi-dimensional discourse evaluation indicators, discursive strategies and features in bank's CSR image construction, corporate image construction, and the effects of bank's discursive CSR image construction. The connotations of these concepts in this research are as follows.

2.1.1 CSR

Corporate social responsibility (CSR, also called corporate sustainability, sustainable business, corporate conscience, corporate citizenship or responsible business) is a type of international private business self-regulation (Sheehy, 2015). It was first proposed by Oliver Sheldon in 1923 as the need of a company manager to meet the needs of various human beings outside the enterprises (Sheldon, 1923). According to Carroll (1991), CSR is what enterprises do for society. The cognition of society to enterprises is different from that of insiders, and it is expected that they can abide by the law, establish ethics, and donate to charity. Therefore, a complete CSR

M. Wan, *CSR Image Discursive Construction of Banks and the Effects on Capital Markets*,
https://doi.org/10.1007/978-981-19-6012-3_2

includes corporate economic responsibility, legal responsibility, ethical responsibility and philanthropic responsibility (Carroll, ibid). One way to devise CSR is the voluntary commitment of companies to contribute to sustainable economic development by integrating social and environmental concerns into their operations and interactions (Banerjee, 2008). Thus, CSR contains not only the moral and social responsibilities of a company, it also conveys the economic aspects. Included in this are corporate governance and corporate sustainable development.

Corporations may shoulder CSR for either ethical or strategic aims. From the perspective of strategic development, the purpose of taking responsibility for corporate actions is to get long-term profits and win shareholder trust. CSR strategies encourage companies to make a positive impact on the environment and stakeholders such as consumers, employees, investors, and communities. From the ethical perspective, some corporations will conduct CSR policies and practices due to the ethical beliefs of their management group. Most CSR concepts in this research are strategic CSR: companies' investment in CSR is a strategic choice for maintaining a good corporate image and gaining competitiveness in order to achieve sustainable development and good corporate performance.

2.1.2 Banks' CSR

Compared with general enterprises, commercial banks' fulfillment of CSR has a radial effect. Banks can affect their customers' and related industries' CSR performance through green credit policies and investment concepts. In addition, while performing CSR, commercial banks can realize the optimal allocation of social financial resources, the control of risk, environmental protection and the reduction of energy consumption through their capital's leading function—green finance, thus achieving sustainable development of society's economy and environment. Fundamentally, commercial banks promote harmonious development and mutual benefit among the banks themselves, the environment, and the economy, by fulfilling CSR. This directly or indirectly affects the economic stability and overall security of the entire country. For example, banks' credit supply for the real estate industry will affect the price of real estate assets, and the loosening level of the commercial banks' credit policy will also indirectly affect the consumer price index by affecting the money supply. Additionally, along with China's financial liberalization, Chinese banks need to emphasize their CSR performance in order to establish a good corporate image within international capital markets. Thus, banks' fulfillment of CSR has three radical effects that deserve inquiry.

2.1.3 CSR Reports

CSR reports, also referred to as sustainability reports, or ESG reports, are organizational reports that provide information pertaining to economic, environmental, social and governance performance. CSR reporting refers not just to those reports generated from collected data; instead, they are a method to internalize and improve an organization's commitment to sustainable development in a way that can be demonstrated to both internal and external stakeholders (Aiezza, 2015a). Non-financial reporting, including CSR reporting, becomes the trend which has expanded over the last two decades in western countries. Research has revealed the positive function of CSR reporting discourse in improving a company's reputation, corporate financial performance, capital market performance based on the reputation theory, stakeholder theory, and signaling theory (Shen et al., 2011). However, it was not until 2006 that Chinese corporations begin to publish their CSR reports normatively. Many firms now release an annual sustainability report, and there are many different kinds of ratings and standards, such as the Global Reporting Initiative (GRI). Companies produce these reports for a variety of reasons, but at their core, they are intended to be "vessels of transparency and accountability" (Carroll, 1991). They also strive to improve internal processes, engage stakeholders, and persuade investors (ibid). This research focuses on how banks discursively construct their images through CSR reporting, and capital markets' reactions to banks' discursively constructed CSR images, as realized by functions of various discursive features of banks' CSR reports.

2.1.4 CSR Reports' Multi-dimensional Discourse Evaluation Indicators

Corporate image construction, including the CSR image, is a management concept. Several related studies exist in the field of management. However, since language plays an important role in institutional business communication and image construction, it is not enough to focus only on the management mechanism. We need to uncover the discourse mechanism underlying corporations' negotiations. The research on the discursive features of companies' CSR reports can help them build a good CSR image among stakeholders, and facilitate sustainable development.

The discursive indicators of CSR reports' multi-dimensional discourse evaluation framework are sentiment evaluation indicators, readability evaluation indicators, CSR keyword evaluation indicators and visual evaluation indicators. Each dimension consists of many linguistic features that are from the register level and can help evaluate companies' CSR image construction on the level of situational context. Sentiment evaluation and readability evaluation can be considered implicit evaluation since they help companies persuade their stakeholders to identify with their corporate culture and strategy and construct their CSR mind images. CSR keyword evaluation indicators help reveal companies' CSR activities in explicit content. This is the company's CSR behavior image. Visual evaluation indicators are the explicit indicators which can spread companies' CSR visual images.

2.1.5 *Discursive Strategies and Features in Banks' CSR Image Construction*

Banks' CSR image construction is a type of institutional image construction. Banks' corporate images can be constructed, managed, manipulated and transmitted by discourse. The discourse-historical approach, one of the mainstream of critical discourse analysis, posits that discourse analysis needs to be conducted along 3 dimensions: (1) The theme of the discourse; (2) the discursive strategies of the discourse; (3) the linguistic devices or features which can realize the theme and discursive strategies of the discourse (Reisigl & Wodak, 2014). The theme of discourse (i.e. the core objective) is on the macro level, and in this study, it refers to banks' CSR image construction under different contexts. The discursive strategies are along the meso level, and they serve to construct the discourse system. In this study, they refer to the 4 dimensional discursive evaluation indicators (sentiment, readability, CSR keyword, visualization) which help banks construct their CSR images discursively. The specific discursive features on the micro level in this study are the discursive components which realize the discursive strategies and themes. They refer to various sentimental tendencies, mean word length, type/token ratios, etc. in CSR reports.

2.1.6 *Corporate Image Construction*

The differences between corporate identity and corporate image are defined. Corporate identity is the manner by which a company presents itself to the public (such as customers and investors) as well as the definition of company for itself. The essence of corporate identity is the definition of the company which answers the question of what the company is. Corporate image refers to the impression and evaluation of the public and employees of the company as a whole. The corporate identity and corporate image are related, but different. Both are expressions of "what the enterprise is", but corporate identity refers to the views of internal members, while corporate image refers to understandings of the enterprise's external stakeholders (Liu, 2008). Many scholars have equated the two in their research. This study focuses on banks' discursive CSR image construction via CSR disclosure and its corresponding effects on capital markets, as well as stakeholders' perception of banks' discursively constructed images.

Corporate behavior can be divided into social behavior and corporate economic behavior. These are vital bases for recognizing and evaluating corporate value and important factors in the formation of corporate image. Based on this, corporate image can be broken into two categories: the image of corporate economic responsibility and the image of CSR. The former is companies' ability to create perceptions of profits or "hard" economic strength; the latter is the perceptions of "soft" strength (such as corporate governance, corporate strategy, corporate culture, business ethics, or social concerns) (ibid).

According to the connotation of the concepts of corporate image and CSR, Liu (ibid) defines CSR image as: impressions of a company's attitudes and behaviors when they deal with stakeholders other than shareholders and a wide range of social issues, or attitude and evaluation of a company's CSR concept and behavior. A CSR report, which discloses the all-round corporate concept and CSR performance, is an important strategic choice for corporations to construct their CSR images. Numerous studies have addressed corporate image, in fields such as management, economics, communication, psychology, and the arts. This research focuses on how banks construct CSR image discursively via CSR reports from the inter-disciplinary perspective of linguistics, management and economics.

2.1.7 *The Effects of Banks' Discursive CSR Image Construction*

Since CSR performance is tied to corporate reputation and corporate image, CSR disclosure serves as a signal to convey referential information for capital markets and investors when they evaluate corporate value. CSR performance and CSR report disclosure may bring a company financial development, such as profitability, asset operating level, solvency and subsequent development capabilities (Shen et al., 2011); they are connected to capital market reaction (Song & Gong, 2007).

In this study, CSR disclosure is regarded as an event which influences stakeholders' perceptions of corporate image and capital markets after banks release CSR reports. The cumulative abnormal return, the most obvious and commonly adopted indicators for market reaction, will be used as the effect of discursive construction of banks' CSR image via adopting multi-dimensional discursive features in their CSR reports. The cumulative abnormal return is measured by event study, and the event period is 30 days after banks release their CSR reports.

2.2 Studies on Business Discourse

2.2.1 *Studies on Business Discourse in Linguistics*

The CSR report is a genre of business discourse. Business discourse is all about how people communicate in commercial organizations, either orally or in writing, in order to accomplish their work (Bargiela-Chiappini et al., 2007). Business English research focuses on the application of business English language, the contextual characteristics in business environment, business discourse, as well as issues concerning business English education research (Wang & Zhang, 2016). Recently, business English researchers have advocated a discursive turn (from language to discourse) in business English research (Bhatia, 2002, 2005; Wang & Zhang, 2016). Shi and Wan (2018) use quantitative content analysis to compare and analyze the research methods in Business English studies published in CSSCI and SSCI from 2007 to 2017. In terms of business English discourse studies, there are significant differences in the number of published articles and topical journals, both in China and abroad. Both the number and proportion of business English discourse studies in international journals are significantly larger than those of Chinese journals. Although the depth and breadth of domestic research are different from those of studies outside of China, the importance of business English discourse studies has increased among Chinese scholars over the past three years. As such, the number of published papers has increased. Topics include business discourse evaluation modeling research (Li, 2016; Li & Wang, 2017), conflictive discourse in business communication (Hu & Fan, 2016), metaphors in business discourse (Hu, 2014) and Chinese and American banks' annual report discourse structural relation (Wang & Bu, 2017). Corpus-based evaluation of different aspects in business discourse is a trend in current studies. Several studies have focused on the multi-dimensional evaluation of business discourse. Li and Wang (2017) have established a three-dimensional appraisal framework to study the appraisal patterns of UK and US companies' CEOs' risk discourse. Wang and Bu (2017) have used a multi-dimensional sentimental evaluation framework to analyze the sentimental tendencies of Chinese and American listed companies' annual reports. The multi-perspective analysis of discourse can elucidate how business activities are discursively conducted. However, there is still scant multi-dimensional evaluative research in business discourse. As for the disciplinary background, most studies of business English, both in China and abroad, from 2007 to 2017, have been based on single subjects. However, researches in other countries have been more interdisciplinary (Shi & Wan, 2018). Recent years have seen the proliferation of interdisciplinary studies based in fields such as "Linguistics + Management" and "Linguistics+Psychology". This shows that Chinese scholars have begun conducting interdisciplinary business English studies. However, the quantity of this research remains small, and some simply convey linguistic theories to business texts, rather than establishing a "linguistic+management" or "linguistic+economics" approach.

In terms of specific data processing methods, domestic studies have used corpus analysis tools, but there is still room to diversify the analytical tools used (Shi & Wan, ibid). Due to the development of artificial intelligence and machine learning, some computer-assisted language processing tools can help extract textual features more scientifically, such as sentimental tendency and text complexity (Li, 2011). Also, in recent years, domestic business English researchers have begun to use statistical methods, such as structural equations and linear regression, to explore quantitative relationships between business linguistic features and financial factors in business contexts (Li, 2016; Li & Wang, 2017).

Empirical research on the correlation between linguistic features and financial indicators has also taken a linguistic turn: "language to practice" and the "functional" nature of language is used to explain and solve practical problems discursively. However, such empirical studies, with inter-disciplinary "linguistic+" approaches, are rare among business discourse research in China.

2.2.2 Studies on Business Discourse in Corporate Governance

Corporate governance is an inseparable component of information disclosure. Research on business discourse analysis from the perspective of corporate governance has included content analysis of organizational discourse's non-financial information from the perspectives of management, accounting and economics. These studies conduct empirical research on the relationship between textual features and corporate performance indicators to highlight the importance of organizational discourse in corporate governance and performance. As stated in the Concepts of Statement No. 1 of the FSAB, investors need information to predict companies' future cash flow. This includes financial information (or non-narrative information such as income statements and balance sheets); and non-financial information such as CSR reports, CEO letters, Management discussion and analysis (MD&A), and earnings release conferences (Li, 2008). Non-financial information in CSR reports may also consist of voluntary information disclosure (i.e. strategic information such as corporate culture, products, competition and customers). Li (ibid) suggests that textual information can provide a more independent test of market efficiency than number-based measures. More generally, textual analysis can provide an important approach to address pivotal questions in behavior science by explaining the discursive and social practices behind text. Also, due to the discursive and social practices behind a text, non-financial information can convey incremental information that transcends the language itself.

According to Xiao et al. (2016), there are 9 quantified textual features in non-financial information. These are then divided into two categories according to whether they are related to the content. Tone (sentiment), readability, repeatability and manager's characteristics are not related to content. Risk, competition, forward-looking, falsehood, R&D information and financing constraints are related to content. Among these, tone (Davis et al., 2012; 2015; Henry, 2008; Loughran & McDonald, 2011; Wang & Bu, 2017), readability (Li, 2008; Loughran & McDonald, 2014, Wang & Li, 2018) and risk (Loughran & McDonald, 2011; Wang & Li, 2017) in business texts have been analyzed the most in terms of their relationship to stock price (Das & Chen, 2007), security prices and returns (Tecklock, 2007), and future earnings (Li, 2011; Huang et al., 2014). Other research on discourse and corporate performance have focused on keywords (Beattie et al., 2004; Abraham & Shrives, 2014; Leung et al., 2015; Yekini et al., 2015), personal pronouns (Clatworthy & Jones, 2006), passive voice (ibid), and visual emphasis (Courtis, 2004, Ji et al., 2016). These studies have found that companies have significant differences in the above discursive indicators based on profitability. From the management and accounting perspectives, tone, readability and keywords and visual emphasis are vital textual features in non-financial information. They can reflect corporate governance, and can influence corporate performance, stock price, and capital markets.

In summary, most researches on non-financial information from the perspective of corporate governance are from management, accounting and economics perspectives. Due to the lack of linguistic expertise, their research has been confined to descriptions of textual features—conducting empirical research between textual features and financial indicators. These studies have covered a multi-dimensional level of lexis, semantics, syntax and text. Thus, the discursive and social contexts behind these textual features can be interpreted and explained from a linguistic paradigm, instead of management or finance theory alone.

An inter-disciplinary approach of "linguistic+management" or "linguistic+accounting" into the discursive features of non-financial information disclosure can push content analysis research from management or accounting to the discursive level. Textual features' function on the financial level can be explained and corroborated discursively. It can also make the research method and outcome of discourse analysis more convincing and comprehensive, from the perspective of linguistics.

2.3 Evaluative Studies in Discourse Analysis

2.3.1 Studies on Discourse Evaluation from Multi-dimensional Perspective

Based on the above review of studies on business discourse, discourse evaluation is an important approach in business discourse analysis in the field of linguistics, management, and finance.

Evaluation is a complicated issue that has been frequently addressed across disciplinary boundaries. Linguistic approaches are increasingly interested in evaluation expressed in language (Tang, 2015). Lemke (1998) emphasizes the interpretive skill in the analysis of evaluation, and identifies seven categories of evaluative attributes of propositions and proposals. Additionally, he points out the value orientation of texts, which develops along the axes of goodness, modulation/mood, and modality (Tang, 2015). Hunston and Sinclair (2000) differentiate evaluative categories (opinion: adjectives indicating an evaluative quality) and evaluating responses (emotion: adjectives indicating personal reactions). "Evaluation" is then adopt since it is a broad term to express speaker or writer's viewpoint on, stance towards, or feelings about the entities or propositions about which he or she is talking (ibid; Tang, 2015).

Many linguistic features have appeared together to achieve situational contexts (Biber, 1988), and other previous studies have addressed separate opportunely selected linguistic features. Thus, it is necessary to evaluate a large number of business texts multi-dimensionally. The multi-dimensional analysis (MDA) approach to register analysis was developed to compare written and spoken registers in English (Xiao, 2010; Biber, 1998). Biber uses 67 functionally-related linguistic features to explain the register variation in 6 major discourse functional dimensions (Biber, ibid). It has then been used in various range of language variation research (Xiao, 2010), including synchronic analyses of specific registers and genres and author styles; diachronic studies describing the evolution of registers (Xiao & McEnery, 2005); register studies of non-western languages and contrastive analysis (Jiang & Xu, 2015); research of university English and course material development (Pan, 2012). Gui (2009) has adopted 46 linguistic features of MDA in a comparative study of English linguistic corpus and FLOB, and has found that academic papers are different from interactive discourse. Lei and Yang (2001) have compared a corpus of JDEST with LOB and have found that academic English focuses on informational production which has a non-narrative concern and is less persuasive. MDA can help evaluate linguistic features in a large quantity of discourse in various situational contexts. However, linguistic features in the above studies are largely confined to lexical and grammatical levels.

According to discourse appraisal theory, appraisal resources can be divided into explicit (grammatical and lexical level), and implicit (rhetoric, prosody, textual level) (Martin & Rose, 2007). Li and Wang (2017) have built a three-dimensional appraisal framework of appraisal markers, metaphors and semantic prosody to investigate CEO risk discourse. Their appraisal framework covers lexis, semantic, collation, and cognitive levels of discourse evaluation. Wang and Bu (2017) have established a multi-dimensional evaluation framework of discourse sentimental tendency to investigate sentimental tendency and sentimental keywords in Chinese and American companies' annual reports. Aiezza (2015b) has analyzed keywords and appraisal theory's engagements in corporations' CSR reports, and has found that those linguistic features construct discourses and views, persuade investors, and promote corporate image.

As for evaluative research in content analysis from management, accounting and economics perspectives, Muslu et al. (2019) have developed a disclosure score based on the sentiment, readability, length, and the numerical and content of CSR report narratives, and has examined the relationship between CSR disclosure scores and analyst forecasts. Li (2008) has analyzed readability and lexical properties concerning writing styles: the relative frequencies of self-referential words, exclusive words, causation words, and future tense verbs in annual reports, and examines the relationship between textual features with firm performance and those with earnings persistence.

According to the above review of business discourse and discourse evaluation from multi-dimensional perspectives in various disciplines, various textual features such as tone, readability, keywords and visual emphasis function in implicitly and explicitly conveying corporate visions, strategies and reflecting corporate governance, corporate image and capital market performance. Sentiment, readability, CSR keyword and visualization are evaluative indicators covering lexical, syntactic, semantic, textual levels of discourse. In order to further explore the multi-dimensional linguistic realization of banks' CSR image construction in CSR reports, a review of related studies pertaining to those 4 kinds of evaluative indicators follows below.

2.3.2 Studies on Sentimental Evaluation

Sentiment analysis is the study of emotions, opinions, and appraisals and attitudes regarding "services, products, individuals, organizations, issues, topics and their attributes" (D' Andrea et al., 2015). Studies of the evaluation of sentimental features have received wide attention from the disciplines of linguistics, natural language processing and management.

In computational linguistics, sentimental analysis involves the extraction of topics and opinions, presentation choices, and evaluation word extraction and sentimental tendency recognition. The most common content analysis methods in the textual sentiment literature are dictionary-based approaches and machine-learning (Kearney & Liu, 2014). The former uses dictionaries and word lists such as General Inquirer (GI) (Stone, 1966), LIWC, DICTION, L&M lists (Loughran & McDonald, 2011), and the latter uses machine learning such as Navive Bayesian algorithm, k-nearest neighbor, and Rainbow package (Loughran & McDonald, 2014; Lo et al., 2017; Wang & Bu, 2017). These form the core of today' s artificial intelligence. Textual sentiment analysis of foreign natural language processing revolves around product reviews, online news, Weibo, and media comment digging, conduct public opinion analysis of the Internet and media and political news analysis.

In management, sentiment analysis has focused on business textual tones' influence on capital markets performance and corporate financial performance such as the abnormality of stock prices, trading volumes, IPO overvaluation, and future earnings. (Kothari et al., 2009; Davis et al., 2012; Price et al., 2012). Some studies have indicated that negative tone in corporations' annual reports has the most significant predictive effect on financial performance (Twedt & Rees, 2012). Sentiment analysis can provide valuable information for various organizations across many fields, especially business, regarding products and services (Liu & Lei, 2018). It can also be applied to political science and sociology, concerning issues and policies (Feldman, 2013).

In linguistics, most studies of sentimental evaluation are from the viewpoints of appraisal theory, metaphor, or pragmatics. These examine appraisal features in the discourse and its reflected discursive strategies and functions. (Fuoli, 2012; Wang & Bu, 2017). Genres of discourse analysis on sentimental evaluation focus on advertising, product comments, fiction, political speech and news reports. Liu and Lei

(2018) investigate Hillary and Trump' s speeches during the 2016 presidential election to identify their sentiments and discourse themes, and discourse strategies, by using machine-based methods.

Emotions, opinions, and appraisals and attitudes in firms' financial discourse are subjective, and thus can reflect firms' objective situations, principles and the values behind them (Fuoli, 2012). Thus, many studies have focused on what kind of sentiment a text conveys through the analysis of appraisal features in specific contexts. They have then explained the social practices behind them. However, few studies have investigated CSR reports' sentimental tendency and sentimental features through artificial intelligence and computer-assisted tools. Additionally, few studies have looked into corporate image construction by manipulating sentimental tendency and its correlation with a company's financial performance or influence on capital markets (Wang & Bu, 2017).

2.3.3 Studies on Readability

Readability refers to the extent to which a document is easy to understand in terms of its composition and text-based style (Courtis, 2004; Merkl-Davies & Brennan, 2007). The management obfuscation hypothesis argues that managers are incentivized to obfuscate information when firm performance is poor. This is because the market may react with the delayed incorporation of information contained in complicated disclosures (Bloomfield, 2002).

After the U.S. Securities and Exchange Commission (SEC)'s enactment of the Plain English Rule, most international studies have assessed the readability of annual reports and their components, such as MA&D (Management Discussion and Analysis) (Li, 2008; Laksmana et al., 2012; Wang & Li, 2018). The measurements of readability include the Fog index, Bog index, file length, and file size (Drago et al., 2017). An increasing number of recent studies propose that the readability of an annual report is a key element of communication between managers and stakeholders (Lang & Stice-Lawrence, 2015; Lo et al., 2017). Li (2008) measures readability of listed firms' annual reports by the Fog index from the computational linguistics literature and document length. He finds that: (1) firms' annual reports with lower earnings are harder to read; and (2) firms with annual reports that are easier to read have more persistent positive earnings. You and Zhang (2009) use the number of 10-K words as a measure of firm complexity, and find that firms above the annual median word count have a delayed stock market reaction over the ensuing 12 months. Franco et al. (2015) find a positive relationship between analyst report readability (measured by a combination of Fog, Flesch-Kincaid, and Flesch Reading Ease) and the trading volume reaction to the report. Other studies indicate that financial issues such as corporate performance, managers' characteristics and investors' expectations, are connected with corporate non-information disclosure readability (Stone, 1966; Leung et al., 2015; Hwang & Kim, 2017; Lahtinen & Shipe, 2017). Studies of readability from the management, economic perspective exhibit a scientific measurement of a business text' s readability; they conduct convincing empirical research on the relationship between readability and corporate financial activities. However, due to the lack of linguistic expertise, they neglect the discursive function behind those readability indicators and the situational and social context behind managers' employment of readability strategies, such as how readability indicators discursively affect belief transfer and social interaction between corporations and stakeholders.

Studies of readability in linguistics have focused on the combination of syntax complexity and readability, and most studies have been about second language acquisition and English teaching. Jiang and Xu (2015) use Coh-Metrix, a computer program used for textual cohesion, syntactic complexity, and readability, to examine 54 lexical and grammatical and semantic features of 60 students' translations. They investigate the linguistic features of student writings and shed light on English language teaching and textbook compilation. Du and Cai (2013) conduct a Coh-Metrix-based study on linguistic features that influence the argumentative writing quality of English majors. They have devised a predictive model of argumentative writing quality for EFL learners. Wu (2017) examines the syntactic complexity and readability of international journal articles by Chinese scholars, and finds wide variation in the syntactic complexities of journal articles across disciplines; articles in the natural sciences are more readable than those in the social sciences, and syntactic complexity is an influencing factor in text readability. Liu (2017) investigates the different readability between original and translated versions of Chinese classical literature from the lexical, syntactic and textual level, and analyzes the reasons for these differences.

The above review shows that research on readability from the linguistics perspective is mature in the field within English language teaching and translation. The readability of corporate disclosure is the outcome of corporate communicating styles. This style is, in turn, influenced by the governance principles and corporate values of management groups. However, few studies have focused on the readability of business discourse from the perspective of linguistics, nor have they conduct empirical research into the correlation between readability indicators and corporate financial performance (Wang & Li, 2018) or capital market reaction.

2.3.4 Studies on Keyword Analysis

Through the corpus tools WordSmith or Antconc's keyword function, researchers can compare frequency wordlists with others in order to obtain a keyword list of words that occur more often than expected in one corpus than another (Baker, 2006).

Keyword analysis is one of the most common methods used in corpus linguistics. Scott is the pioneer to define keywords as those whose frequencies are unusually high in comparison with a norm (Scott, 1996). The keywords are worked out by first making a wordlist for the corpus, and a wordlist for a reference corpus, and then comparing the frequency of each word in the two lists (Hu, 2015a). A keyword does not simply mean high frequency, but unusual frequency relative to a reference corpus (Baker, 2006). Business discourse studies have been influenced by critical discourse analysis, pragmatics, conversation analysis, ethnography, genre theory, systemic functional linguistics, cognitive linguistics, and corpus linguistics. And one of the core technology of corpus linguistics, keyword analysis can help researchers dig into different aspects of language information and business information contained in business discourse (Hu, 2015a). Hu (2015b) analyzes the keyword features of business contracts in order to examine their stylistic features. He finds that besides using excessive professional jargon, literary words, and archaisms, business contracts also make excessive use of conjunctions and modal verbs. Koller (2009) examines the keyword features in corporate mission statement; O' Keeffe et al. (2007) analyzes different keyword features of business oral English, academic oral English and daily conversation. Aiezza (2015b) finds that keywords are a useful tool for highlighting significant discursive differences in companies' CSR reports which can be linked to their CSR performance.

Studies of keywords from the perspectives of management and accounting have focused on the relationship between the thematic content of corporate non-financial information and corporations' financial performance. Rutherford (2005) analyzes the frequencies of 90 keywords in "Operations and Financial Review" sections of corporate annual reports in order to find their relationship with firm performance. Henry (2008) studies the relation between keywords in firms' press releases and corresponding market reaction.

The above review shows that keyword analysis has been applied to business discourse research due to its unique style and genre. However, as a genre of "hybridity" (Bhatia et al., 2008; Bhatia, 2012), keyword features in CSR reports which can reflect companies' CSR activities on the content level, and CSR intentions, have not been analyzed systematically. Studies of keywords from the perspectives of management and accounting have focused on the corporate narratives, keywords' function in corporate performance. However, these studies fail to explain the discursive reasons behind different keyword features in corporate information disclosure without linguistic theories.

2.3.5 Studies on Visualization

Visualization refers to the technique of creating images, diagrams, or animations to communicate a message (Merkl-Davies & Brennan, 2007). Visualization by visual images is an effective way to communicate both abstract and concrete ideas (Kress & Van Leeuwen, 1996).

Studies of visualization from the perspectives of management and accounting have elucidated the importance of the visualization and the structures in corporate information disclosure. These have been connected with firm performance. Visual emphasis occurs when firms use visual effects to make information obvious to readers (Merkl-Davies & Brennan, 2007); Courtis (2004) has found an association between change in color and change in profitability in firms' annual reports, and that color influences investor perception and judgment. Ji et al. (2016) find that colorful covers and number of pictures in CSR reports influence their readability. This is then connected with firms' performance. The above review shows that multimodality in firms' information disclosure does influence investors' perceptions and firms' profits. However, the discursive functions behind these semiotic resources and their correlation with firms' profits have yet to be explained within either situational or social contexts, from the perspective of linguistics.

In linguistics, visual representation is a non-linguistic symbol which conveys and constructs discourse along with linguistic symbols (Forceville, 1999). If a discourse contains more than one type of semiotic, we may call it a multimodal discourse. Multimodal discourse analysis originated from systemic functional linguistics. It uses non-linguistic symbols such as images or sound movements as part of social symbols to emphasize the construction of the meaning of linguistic and non-verbal symbols. Information structure, rhetorical structure, genre structure, and layout structure are the research focuses of multimodal discourse studies (Yang & Miao, 2017). Multimodal discourse analysis studies the construction of meaning through the integration of different semiotic resources (Cheng & Zhang, 2017). This has been applied to language instruction (Hu, 2007; O' Halloran, 2005), reader's cognitive reaction (Muller et al., 2012; Meng, 2011), media press releases (Rohdin, 2009), TV commercials (Feng & Wingnell, 2011), and multimodal metaphors in political discourse (Zhao, 2011). Multimodal analysis provides a good perspective to analyze the interpersonal function behind semiotic resources in business discourse.

Due to the promotional nature, CSR reports contain many visual images. However, few studies have focus on the functions of these visual images in stakeholder interaction, corporate image construction and corporate value improvement.

2.4 Studies on CSR and CSR Reports

2.4.1 Studies on CSR and CSR Reports in Management and Accounting

CSR reports are the means for companies to disclose to stakeholders their values, strategies, methods of implementing CSR, the influence of its business activities on the economy, environmental and social areas, achievements it has gained and existing deficiencies (Drago et al., 2017). CSR reports are the crucial conduit for non-financial information disclosure and the vital communication media between firms and stakeholders. CSR is generally used to refer to the obligation of the firm to use its resources in ways to benefit society (Carroll, 1991). CSR reporting practices have been adopted by companies via releasing CSR report or sustainability report annually, complementing the information disclosed in financial accounts and enabling stakeholders to estimate the intangible value drivers and the overall sustainability-related achievements (Gazdar, 2007).

Information about companies' CSR performance will be useful for analysts and investors if CSR activities affect firms' financial performance (Bakar & Ameer, 2011; Muslu et al., 2019). Margolis and Walsh (2003) analyze the positive link between CSR activities and firms' financial performance by empirical studies. Recent studies have also explored the relationship of CSR activities and financial performance. For example, firms with more CSR activities receive more favorable financing from banks (Goss & Roberts, 2011); charitable contributions enhance sales growth (Lev et al., 2010); companies with more CSR activities perform better in their mergers and acquisitions deals (Deng et al., 2013); and CSR activities improve financial performance, especially for R&D firms (Mishra, 2017).

Additionally, CSR activities and disclosures also facilitate companies to focus on and improve their relationships with stakeholders. Investors have increasingly considered CSR activities and CSR disclosure when they make investment decisions, and appropriate social information also promotes investors' decision-making behaviors (Shen et al., 2011). Thus, many companies have begun releasing CSR reports. While providing details about CSR activities to investors, these reports bring significant capital market benefits to the firms (Lys et al., 2015). For example, issuing CSR reports is closely connected with analyst forecast accuracy (Dhaliwal et al., 2012; Muslu et al., 2019). Hooghiemstra (2000) notes that firms use CSR as a means to influence public perceptions. CSR acts as a tool to legitimize firms' actions, and to protect and enhance their reputations and images. The information contained in CSR reports varies in both quantity and format due to the lack of an enforced CSR reporting framework (Perrini, 2011; Sethi et al., 2017). What's more, the opportunistic incentives of managers to positively skew corporate information, coupled with the voluntary nature of CSR reporting, can hamper the credibility of CSR reports (Ramanna, 2013). For example, for the sake of syntactic complexity, the readability of a CSR report of Malaysian listed companies correlates their corporate performance and management with that of poorly performing companies who deliberately choose difficult language in their CSR reports (Bakar & Ameer, 2011). Firms are challenged to increase their credibility, and thus capital markets impact of their CSR reports (Chen et al., 2016).

In summary, the above literature shows that research on CSR and CSR reports and disclosure began with a period of investigating the relationship between corporate CSR disclosure and corporate financial performance. Later, focus shifted to evaluating narratives in CSR reports in order to help corporations disclose their corporate narratives in a more effective way. There is no denying that research on CSR and CSR reports, from disciplines such as management, accounting and economics, has experienced a "linguistic turn". However, research into CSR and CSR reports in these fields only focuses on the pivotal role of language by conducting empirical research—the discursive context behind why language has such power, and how corporations manage discursive features to build reputation, and to stimulate financial growth and capital market performance has been neglected. That is to say, effort must also be taken from linguistic perspective.

2.4.2 Studies on CSR and CSR Reports in Linguistics

CSR reports cover the non-financial aspects of business performance. They utilize more language resources than do corporations' other public reports. Due to it being a hybrid between the informational and promotional genres, many studies have explained the intentions of CSR reports, the professional performance they enact, and the social reality they construct, from the perspective of genre analysis (Bhatia, 2004; 2005). CSR reports is a discourse of promotion, goodwill and self-justification, socially and pragmatically co-constructed within an interdiscursive space (Bhatia, 2012).

Wang and Han (2015) contrast Chinese and American CSR reports' generic features and explain their findings through intercultural differences. Livesey (2002) analyses "salient themes, metaphors, modes of expression, and argument structures" employed in Shell's CSR reports to explore how the company reshaped its public discourse after the increasing public pressure of major environmental controversies. Livesey's (ibid) research verifies discourse as a "practice not just representing the world, but of signifying the world, constituting and constructing the world in meaning" (Fairclough, 1992). Some research has used Halliday's systematic functional grammar and Martin's appraisal theory to evaluate linguistic resources and corporations' hidden communicative purposes behind CSR reports. Aiezza (2015a) uses a corpus-assisted discourse analysis of CSR reports issued by energy companies to unveil how words are subjectively used to construct discourses and ethical images. Her study focuses on the modality makers of forward-looking statements and finds that self-promotion is enacted through optimistic projections; they stress a constant commitment and communicate an already optimal performance, while relativizing risks (ibid). Fuoli (2012) employs appraisal theory in comparative analysis of BP's and Ikea's 2009 CSR reports to find how they construct their corporate identity and relationship with their stakeholders, and to explain their image construction under legitimization theory. He finds that while BP deploys interpersonal resources to portray itself as a trustworthy and authoritative expert, IKEA discloses itself as a sensitive and caring corporation, engaged in a continual effort to improve. Fuoli's (ibid) research explains the discursive mechanism of corporate legitimacy intention of CSR activity through appraisal theory, which supplies the current debate over the social responsibilities of businesses (Carroll & Shabana, 2010). Huang and Zhu (2017) examine Chinese corporations' conceptions of sustainable development based on an innovative view of corpus analysis of CSR reports. They suggest that Chinese companies should enhance their concept of sustainability in business transactions.

In summary, the above review shows that only a handful of studies on CSR reports have focused on the discursive strategies of CSR reports in corporate image construction via corpus analysis. Also, few have focused on cross-disciplinary image construction. Additionally, it is worth mentioning that linguistic research on CSR reports has evolved from qualitative to quantitative analysis—the latter adopts corpus-based evaluation methods. However, with the development of artificial intelligence and natural language processing, some computer-assisted techniques have been used in textual analysis. This can help explore the multi-dimensional discourse features of CSR reports (Kearney & Liu, 2014). Furthermore, research from management, economics, and accounting have indicated the predicative function of textual features in terms of corporate financial performance and the correlation between them. They have done so by conducting empirical research. Current research on CSR reports from linguistic perspectives also can contribute to this interdisciplinary research, such as Wang and Li (2018). Furthermore, linguistic theory can help explain the discursive mechanisms behind the predicative functions of linguistic features.

2.5 Studies on Corporate Image Construction

Identity is playing an increasingly vital role in people's lives. The process of identity construction or image construction has also received growing attention from many disciplines including management, communication, linguistics, psychology, anthropology, and philosophy. Corporate image refers to the impression of a company in people's minds, or people's perceptions and evaluations of the company. The essence of corporate identity is the definition of the company and answering the question of what the company is. The corporate identity and corporate image are related, but different. Both are expressions of "what the enterprise is", but corporate identity refers to the views of internal members, while corporate image refers to understandings of the enterprise's external stakeholders. This study focuses on stakeholders' discursive identification of banks' CSR image construction via CSR disclosure and its corresponding effects on capital markets. The target readers of banks' CSR reports are their stakeholders. Banks uses CSR reports to influence public perception of their corporate reputation and image. Thus, this study will use the concept of corporate image construction.

2.5.1 Studies on Image Construction in Linguistics

Studies on identity from the perspective of linguistics focus the on identity construction in discourse. Ron Scollon's theory of discourse identity refers to the identity constructed in intercultural communication. Identity in discourse is an intricate issue that transcends the question of either the social or the personal identities of the participants (Scollon, 1996). Scollon (ibid) conducted an ethnographic study of public discourse in Hong Kong and found that within any discourse there are specific discourse identities which are expected to be adopted by the participants. These discourse identities are not the same as the social identities of the participants in the discourse. Based on his field study, Scollon (ibid) defines discourse identity as: the persona along with the degree or range of power a particular person can claim in a specific discourse. It consists of the range of production/reception format roles intersecting with the social interactive roles over which one has the power, right, or obligation to enact, in any particular discourse (ibid).

Critical discourse analysis also focuses on identity and the relationship between discourse and identity. Scholars from this perspective regard identity as socially shaped, constructed by ideology and power relationships under a social context. Social identity exists in power, and the relationship and can be constituted through the power relationship.

Identity construction from the pragmatic perspective explores how communicators can communicate meanings by constructing identities based on contexts at moments of communication, and what kind of interpersonal relationships they have consolidated, and established. They also explore what specific communicative effects are gained (Chen, 2014). Li and Ran (2015) establish several theoretical principles for identity construction in interpersonal pragmatics.

The construction of institutional identity concerns the co-construction of institutional discourse and institutional identity. Discursive construction of institutional identity explains how discourses are presented in institutions and the relationship between discourse and institutional interaction and mutual influence by describing and analyzing discourses in specific workplaces (Chen, 2016). Institutional discourse, including companies' public disclosure, institutions' news reports and websites, political speeches, and media discourse, is becoming increasingly important in the field of linguistics. Sun and Zhang (2013) have written a literature review on current research on institutional discourse and have highlighted its practical and theoretical significance. Chen (2016) integrates a comparative research framework for universities' discursive institutional image construction from 3 levels: macro, sub-macro and micro, based on the 3 context level of Discourse-Historical approach between Chinese universities and American universities. This is done in order to improve the mentorship and internationalization of Chinese universities.

Corporate image as an important institutional image also arouses researchers' interests in linguistics. Zheng (2018) has studied the CSR reports of American banks and insurance companies in Fortune 500, based on the Attitude system of appraisal theory. She finds that these linguistic features' function in image construction and discursively constructed images: the banking industry establishes a confident, progressive, positive, corporate image, whereas, insurance industry establishes a reliable and caring corporate image. Wu and Zhang (2019) combine Chen's (2017) analytical framework on the discursive strategies for institutional identity construction with the Discourse-Historical Approach to analyze different discursive strategies that Huawei and Apple use in their corporate annual reports for discursive image construction.

Thus, existing studies have pointed out the significance of discourse, and discursive features for corporate image construction. However, most of those studies have been confined to the discourse level. Since discursive corporate image construction is an interdisciplinary issue, language's function in corporate image construction still needs to be explored from other disciplines such as management and economics.

2.5.2 Studies on Corporate Image Construction in Other Disciplines

Corporate image has been followed by scholars from various disciplines such as management, economics, and communication. They have explained the concept and values of corporate image, within their own perspectives.

Based on corporate identity system (CIS), corporate identity includes mind identity, behavior identity and visual identity. This indicates that companies can identify, construct and transmit their identities through corporate minds, behaviors and at the visual level. Sun (2013) analyzes the visual identity construction and development of Chinese brands from the perspective of design and communication. Li et al. (2009) find that corporate image influences customer-company identification via customer satisfaction from the perspective of marketing. CIS has been used in to improve corporate image, national image (Fan, 2013), university image (Zhou, 2004), and city image (Zhang, 2004). It has thus developed into an image construction framework in many disciplines.

In the field of management and economics, corporate image is a comprehensive manifestation of all past behaviors and results of a company. It reflects the ability of enterprises to provide valuable output to various stakeholders. It is a certain emotion, attitude and evaluation of stakeholders towards a company, which may influence cooperation between stakeholders and company, consumer's purchasing behavior, employee's employment behavior, work behavior, investor's investment behavior, the government's regulatory behavior, and so on (Rindova & Fomburn, 1999; Liu, 2008). Fomburn (1998) outlines 6 aspects of corporate image: (1) financial performance; (2) product quality; (3) employee relationship; (4) community participation; (5) environmental performance; (6) organizational issue. The concept of corporate image is connected with stakeholder theory, and the 6 aspects of corporate image coincide with Carroll's 5 dimensions of CSR. Shen et al. (2011) empirical research of A-shares listed companies also indicates that CSR performance and disclosure can improve corporate image.

Additionally, CSR reports transmit a company's CSR activities and enhance the positive correlation between CSR and corporate image. Many theoretical studies (Carroll, 1991; Mahon & Wartick, 2003) have recognized the CSR activities' function in establishing and improving corporate image and reputation. Gray and Balmer (1998) highlight the importance of communication in corporate reputation management. They define communication as the collection of informal and formal information which transmits corporate characteristics to stakeholders via different means. Hooghiema (2000) regards CSR reports as an important means of corporate communication, as well as a strategy which can influence public perception of a company and improve corporate image. Liu (2008) explores the inner relationship between CSR and corporate image, then he advocates the concept of CSR image and two approaches of CSR image construction: CSR mind image construction and CSR behavior image construction. Several studies use content analysis to evaluate the quality of CSR disclosure and their correlation with corporate image and investor decisions (Song & Gong, 2007; Zhang, 2013).

In summary, the above review shows that much research in management and economics has noted CSR activities' positive function in corporate image improvement, as well as CSR report's signaling function in corporate communication and image construction. However, according to research on the textual analysis of non-financial disclosure, the linguistic features, such as tone, readability and passive voice, convey incremental information. This is due to information asymmetry between corporations and stakeholders, as well as managerial groups' impression management motives. Thus, besides the content of CSR reports, the non-content elements (the discursive features in CSR reports) and their function in corporate image construction and influence on capital markets still need to be further analyzed from a linguistics perspective.

2.6 Studies on the Economic Effects of CSR Reports

Since the 1980s, evaluation standards for companies have undergone profound changes. In the past, companies were evaluated based on whether their products are good, whether their services are comprehensive, and whether the quality is superior and the price cheap. Now, people only regard these corporate evaluation factors as the surface value provided by a company. It is not enough to evaluate only these surface values, so it tends to explore the essence behind the surface value. Developed countries have seen the emergence of "socially-responsible consumers", and the decisions they make are influenced by companies' CSR performance. Studies have shown that in the eyes of consumers, a "good company" must not only be economically profitable, but also obey the law, emphasize morality and have a sustainable development plan. More and more companies are using CSR as an image construction strategy and are trying to build positive CSR images among their stakeholders via CSR activities and CSR reports. Correspondingly, much research has examined the effects that a good CSR image, CSR performance and CSR report will have on corporate financial performance from within, as well as exterior influence on capital markets.

As for the CSR report and discursive CSR image's influence on capital markets, scholars have associated CSR disclosure with capital markets, and have examined the usefulness of decision-making and the impact on capital markets caused by publishing social responsibility information or CSR reports. They have explored this through different indicators and role paths including stock prices, stock returns and stock liquidity. CSR reports bring significant capital market benefits to the firms, since they provide details about CSR activities to investors (Lys et al., 2015). In terms of stock prices, Dhaliwal et al. (2011) show that CSR disclosure has a positive effect on stock prices, and this effect is transmitted and realized by generating investor attention in the stock market. CSR information disclosed by listed companies in China is correlated with corporate value (Shen & Yang, 2008). They use content analysis to get the social disclosure index and find the significant positive correlation between the quantity and quality of CSR disclosure and stock returns. Song & Gong (2007) have used a questionnaire survey of professionals to analyze information related to CSR issued by companies along with annual reports. They explore whether the CSR disclosure is useful for investor decision-making. The conclusions show that CSR disclosure does not cause investors to pay much attention, and the usefulness of the decision-making is low. The possible reason is that the CSR information is scattered throughout the complicated financial information when companies disclose CSR information along with their annual accounting reports. The quantity and quality of the CSR information have not been received enough attention, and this needs to be improved. Xu and Huang (2014) examine the impact of CSR reports on cumulative abnormal return. They use event study to analyze and evaluate CSR reports' disclosure content and quality issued by listed companies over the past two years. Their study finds that the higher the quality of social responsibility reports, the higher the cumulative abnormal rate of return, and the greater the market response. Muslu et al. (2019) develop a disclosure score based on the tone, readability, length, and the numerical and content of CSR narratives. They use this to examine the relationship between the CSR disclosure scores and analyst forecasts. They find that CSR reports with high disclosure scores are associated with more accurate forecasts.

As for the influence that CSR disclosure and discursive CSR image bring to corporate financial performance, scholars associate CSR performance and CSR reports with future earnings, profitability, and costs of equity. This is connected with corporate reputation and corporate value. Malaysian listed companies with poor management and financial performance deliberately chose difficult language in their CSR reports (Bakar & Ameer, 2011). Eccles et al. (2014) have found that firms who perform better CSR tend to outperform their counterparts over the long terminology, in both the stock market and profitability. Also, there is a positive association between non-financial CSR performance and financial performance, and their integrated effect on cost of equity (Rezaee & Tuo, 2017). Lys et al. (2015) find that companies may commit to good CSR and disclose CSR information in the current period when they anticipate future financial performance. Hummel and Schlick (2016) find that firms with good CSR performance use high-quality CSR reports to signal their good CSR performance. This coincides with the signaling theory. Ji et al. (2016) find that a colorful cover and number of pictures in CSR reports influences their readability and are connected with firms' performance. Wang and Li (2018) find there is no significant correlation between complexity of banks' CSR reports and financial performance, as measured by net profits, earnings per share and ROA.

In summary, a significant amount of research has focused on CSR reports and CSR's influence on capital markets and corporate financial performance. Most of this research indicates a positive relationship between them since both CSR reports and CSR activities serve as signals that improve stakeholder's perceptions of corporate image and expectations of corporate value. However, the linguistic features of CSR reports in those studies has been under-explored, thus corpus and computational linguistics processing tools and linguistic theory are needed. Also, language's function and influences on capital market performance still requires further explanation with the perspective of linguistics.

2.7 Limitations of Previous Studies

(1) Previous studies of business discourse evaluation and CSR reports have focused on the qualitative analysis of specific linguistic features. They are usually driven by specific linguistic theories, and few studies have employed cross-disciplinary approaches to corporate image construction via CSR reports. However, when faced with certain complex business phenomena, it is difficult to interpret, explain and solve these phenomena discursively with specific linguistic theory by analyzing several linguistic features in business discourse. Corporate image construction is a complicated phenomenon which includes many aspects, such as mind image construction, and behavior image construction. If companies want to construct good images, efforts need to be taken in their daily operations and CSR information disclosure. Thus, multi-dimensional perspective and inter-disciplinary approaches are suggested to help companies discursively construct and promote good images via CSR reports.
(2) Previous studies of CSR report and corporate image from the perspective of linguistics have focused on the discursive interpretations and explanations of linguistic features and discursive strategies in business discourse. A handful of studies have explained the relationship between those linguistic features and their influential effects on corporate financial performance and capital markets via empirical studies. Linguistic features' economic function in corporate performance, capital market performance hasn't been analyzed and verified.
(3) Previous studies of CSR reports and image construction from perspective of management, economic, finance have already noted language' importance in organizational discourse and corporate performance through both theoretical and empirical research. However, these studies fail to explain language's discursive function in economic practice comprehensively without linguistic perspective. They focus on the relationship between textual features and corporate performance via empirical methods in econometrics and connect linguistic features to corporate performance without micro-level discursive analysis. That is, the discursive functions of textual features in banks' image construction and their correlation with firms' financial performance, as well as capital market reaction haven't been discursively explained within either situational or social contexts.

To fill this research gap, this study attempts to establish an inter-disciplinary discourse evaluation framework to analyze multi-dimensional discursive features in Chinese and American banks' CSR reports in 4 dimensions of sentiment, readability, CSR keyword and visualization based on Biber's register analysis, the theory of discourse and institutional identity and corporate identity system, in order to help Chinese banks refine their CSR disclosure and improve international CSR images in 3 dimensions: mind image, behavior image and visual image.

Then, influencing mechanism of CSR reports' discursive features on capital market reaction is proposed to probe and verify the language's discursive and economic function in banks' CSR image construction and capital market performance guided by signaling theory and behavioral finance. Event study is adopted to examine the significance of cumulative abnormal return 30 days following the release of CSR reports. Gray relational entropy analysis will be conducted to analyze the contribution degrees of the CSR reports' multi-dimensional discursive features to capital market performance in order to offer more practical suggestions for Chinese banks' to improve the international CSR image and corporate value.

Chapter 3
Theoretical Framework

Based on the literature review in Chap. 2, this chapter illustrates the theoretical background and theoretical foundation of this study. Then, this study's analytical model of multi-dimensional discourse evaluation of banks' CSR reports for CSR disclosure improvement, CSR image construction and corporate value enhancement is proposed.

Since this study attempts to establish a cross-disciplinary and multi-dimensional discourse evaluation framework of Chinese and American banks' CSR reports in order to help Chinese banks to discursively improve their CSR disclosure system, international CSR image and corporate value, various theories and concepts in linguistics, management and economics are inter-disciplinarily integrated to valid the reasonability and feasibility of the multi-dimensional discourse evaluation framework and the integrated analytical framework of this study.

3.1 A Theoretical Background for the Multi-dimensional Discursive Construction of Banks' CSR Image

The theoretical framework of multi-dimensional discursive construction of banks' CSR image is in light of Fairclough's three-dimensional model and Biber's register analysis.

Fairclough's three-dimensional model analyzes the interactive relationship among text, discourse and society. Discursive practice serves as a bridge between text and social practice (Dai, 2012). Under such background, it is workable and reasonable for us to explain the multi-dimensional discursive features in CSR reports, discursive practice (CSR image construction), and social practice behind banks' discursive CSR image construction. Fairclough's three-dimensional model also provides this study with a complete analytical framework: description, interpretation and explanation.

Biber's register analysis claims that language use varies within situational contexts, and that certain linguistic features are used in association within different

M. Wan, *CSR Image Discursive Construction of Banks and the Effects on Capital Markets*,
https://doi.org/10.1007/978-981-19-6012-3_3

situational contexts in the text. Under this background, it is workable to conduct a multi-dimensional discourse evaluation of banks' CSR reports to investigate how multi-dimensional discursive strategies realized by commonly occurring patterns of discursive features with the same function are employed in situational contexts: banks' CSR image construction.

3.1.1 Fairclough's Three-dimensional Model

Fairclough's three-dimensional model of text, discourse and society suggests that the analysis of texts should not be artificially isolated from the analysis of institutional and discursive practices, within which texts are embedded and textual analysis within discourse is a kind of social research in various disciplines (Fairclough, 1995). "Text" is used for both written texts and transcripts of spoken interaction, and a text is regarded as a form of social practice; "Discourse" refers to the use of language as a form of social practice. This underlines a dialectical relationship between the microstructure of discourse like linguistic structures and the macrostructures of society such as social structural and ideology (ibid).

The analysis of the discursive event as a social practice may refer to different levels of social organization—the context of a situation, the institutional context, or the wider societal context or "context of culture" (Malinowski, 1923; Halliday & Hasan, 1985). Viewing language use as social practice implies, first, that it is a mode of action (Austin, 1962) and, secondly, that it is a socially and historically situated mode of action; it is in a dialectical relationship with other facets of social context, and thus it is socially shaped, but it is also socially shaping, or constitutive (Fairclough, 1995). Language use is simultaneously constitutive of (i) constitution (establishment, reproduction, negotiation) of identities of participants, (ii) social and personal relationships between them and (iii) and systems of knowledge and belief (ibid). Thus, the linguistic features in banks' CSR reports are shaped by the social contexts behind the CSR reports. Those linguistic features also constitute banks' CSR image in situational contexts.

According to Fairclough's three-dimensional conception of discourse, and a corresponding three-dimensional method of discourse analysis, discourse, and any specific instance of discursive practice, is seen as (i) a language text, spoken or written, (ii) discourse practice (text production and text interpretation), (iii) sociocultural practice. The method of discourse analysis includes linguistic description of the language text, interpretation of the relationship between the (productive and interpretative) discursive processes and the text, and explanation of the relationship between the discursive processes and the social processes (ibid). A feature of the approach is that the link between sociocultural practice and text is mediated by discourse practice (Dai, 2012) (Fig. 3.1).

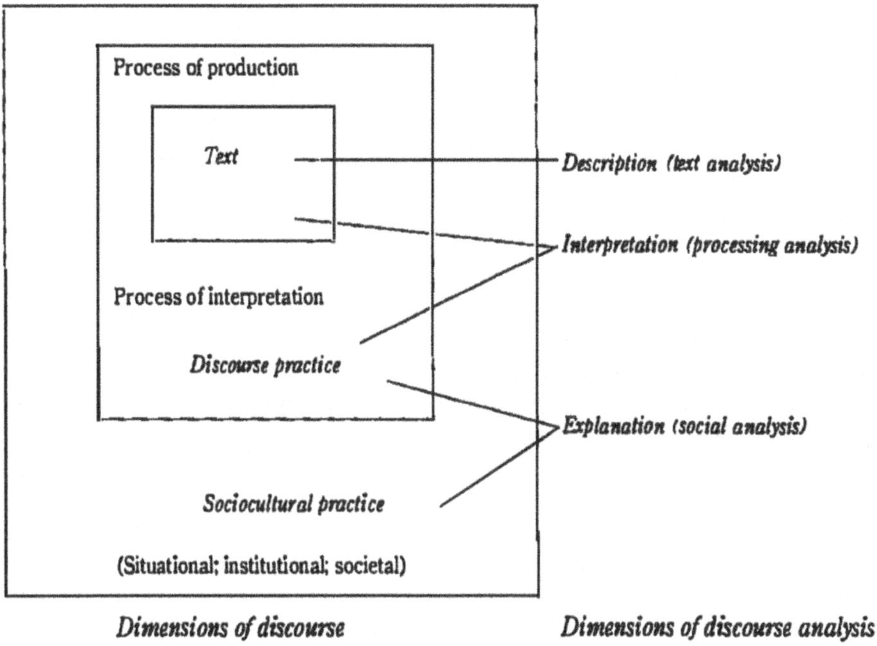

Fig. 3.1 Fairclough's three-dimensional model of discourse and discourse analysis (Fairclough 1995: 98)

3.1.2 Biber's Register Analysis

A register can be defined as "a functional variety of language—the patterns of instantiation of the overall system associated with a given context (a situation type)" (Halliday & Matthiessen, 2004). Biber defines a register as a language variety associated with both a particular situation of use and with pervasive linguistic features that serve important functions within that situation of use (Biber & Conrad, 2009). According to Biber & Conard (ibid), language use varies with the situational context: core and pervasive linguistic features like lexical features (e.g., type-token ratio, word length, hedges, emphatics), grammatical features (e.g., nouns, prepositional phrases, adjectives), and syntactic features (e.g., relative clauses, adverbial clauses) are functional—certain features are used in association with the situational context of the text (Fig. 3.2).

Fig. 3.2 Components in a register analysis (Biber & Conrad, 2009: 6)

As shown, a register is a variety of linguistic features associated with a particular situation of use (including particular communicative purposes). In addition, the description of a register covers three major components: the situational context, the linguistic features, and the functional relationships between the first two components (ibid). Some linguistic features coexist to convey communicative purposes in their situational contexts. Since linguistic features in Biber's register analysis are functional, linguistic features tend to occur in a register because they are suited to the purposes and situational context of the register (ibid). Language usage is different within different situational contexts and the linguistic features, such as the verbs, adjectives, conjunctions, pronouns, word length, compound sentences and visual mode are functional. Thus, the linguistic features and the discourse function interact and influence each other. Just as Halliday (1988) said, "The register is a series of interrelated, linguistic features with a co-occurrence frequency higher than the random probability." Linguistic features are usually tied to communicative purpose in situational contexts (Biber & Conrad, 2009). As for banks' CSR reports, linguistic features such as lexical words which have meanings similar to "tenacity, collectiveness, [or] insistence" (Henry, 2008) may appear together as a discursive strategy to convey one of the communicative purposes of CSR reports—establishing an image of "certainty" among stakeholders.

In order to uncover different registers' characteristics realized by numerous co-occurring linguistic features among a large body of texts, the multi-dimensional approach to register variation was developed by Biber for comparative analysis of spoken and written registers in English (Biber, 1988). Methodologically, the approach uses computer-based text corpora, computational tools to identify linguistic features in texts, and multivariate statistical techniques to analyze the co-occurrence relations among linguistic features, thereby identifying the underlying dimensions of variation in a language (ibid). The analytical goal of the Multi-dimensional approach is to provide comprehensive descriptions of the patterns of register variation having two components: (1) identification of the underlying linguistic parameters, or dimensions, of variation; and (2) specification of the linguistic similarities and differences among registers with respect to these dimensions (bid). Dimensions are defined by distinct groupings of linguistic features that co-occur frequently in texts. Dimensions are subsequently interpreted in terms of the communicative functions shared by the co-occurring features (bid; Jiang & Xu, 2015).

Language forms and textual functions are interrelated, that is, language forms reflect interpersonal, cognitive, and other language functions, and a textual function is often coordinated by a set of related, co-occurring language features (Biber & Conrad, 2009). Different discourses have different functions, and different functions are implemented by different linguistic feature patterns. However, Biber's multi-dimensional analysis (MDA) of the linguistic features in the register level stays micro. This level only focuses on the lexical and grammatical level which may neglect other significant linguistic phenomena at the syntactic, semantic and discourse levels.

Thus, enlightened by Biber's register analysis and MDA, this study expands Biber's register analysis and conducts a multi-dimensional evaluation of various co-occurring linguistic features which exist in lexical, syntactic, semantic, textual and discourse levels in banks' CSR reports (sentiment, readability, CSR keyword and visualization). This is done in order to analyze the various and pervasive co-occurring linguistic patterns in situational contexts (CSR reports' various communicative purposes). Additionally, the functions or themes of the discourse (image construction) that these co-occurring linguistic patterns achieve in CSR reports will be analyzed in specific sociocultural contexts. The multi-dimensional evaluation framework in this study is a further application of Biber's register analysis and MDA. It expands Biber's MDA to other levels of language, while also applying Biber's register analysis to business discourse research.

3.2 The Theoretical Foundation of Multi-dimensional Discursive Construction of Banks' CSR Images

The construction of corporate image is of great significance to the company itself. It not only influences the stakeholders' evaluation of the company, but also the ability of company to obtain resources and achieve sustainable development. Corporate image, including CSR image, is an important category of institutional image. With the "discursive turn" of identity research in recent years, more and more scholars have begun to study the discursive construction of corporate identity, image based on social constructivism, and institutional identity. Institutional identity theory may shed light on banks' discursive construction of CSR images from the perspective of linguistics.

The corporate identity system (CIS) is a mature and commonly used theory which corroborates that corporations can identify, construct and transmit their identities through corporate mind, behavior and visual level. The multi-dimensional discursive features of CSR reports in this study (sentiment, readability, CSR keywords and visualization) may reflect and construct the concept of corporate CSR, CSR behavior, and CSR visualization, respectively. Thus, CIS theory may provide the integration of multi-dimensional discursive features and the analysis of banks' discursive image construction with an "entry point" from the perspective of management.

The theoretical framework of multi-dimensional discourse evaluation of banks' CSR reports has also been enlightened by some mature multi-dimensional corporate narrative evaluation frameworks. These have aided in selecting evaluation indicators and integrating evaluative framework, including Merkl-Davies and Brennan's (2007) framework of disclosure strategies in corporate narratives for impression management, Muslu et al.'s (2019) disclosure score of CSR narratives, Li and Wang's (2017) three dimensional appraisal of CEO's risk discourse as well as the linguistic theories behind those indicators: discourse appraisal theory, readability theory, and corpus linguistics' keyword analysis.

3.2.1 Discourse and Institutional Identity

Social constructivism is the philosophical foundation of institutional identity construction. Scholars who espouse these theories think that language can construct social identity, social relation and mankind's understanding of the world. Under this background, it is reasonable to analyze banks' discursive image construction via the discursive features in CSR reports.

The concept of identity in social constructivism is relative to the traditional concept of identity. The latter believes that identity is a fundamental, persistent self, and the former emphasizes the exploration of multiple identities, with fluidity, impermanence, complexity, and context sensitivity (Chen, 2014). The latter represents the traditional view of identity, while the former represents the contemporary view of identity. Research on the relation between language and identity has transitioned from the study of the static relationship between language and identity to the study of the dynamic construction of discourse and identity (Kroskrity, 1999; De Fina et al., 2006; Gu & Li, 2007; Hall, 2011). Social constructivism focuses on the positive process of discourse and the potential production and transformation of social reality (Chen, 2016). They explore how people use language strategies to communicate and construct their identities in social situations. Identity is considered to be implemented, executed and embodied in discourse through various linguistic or non-verbal means (Chen, 2014).

Institution and discourse are also interrelated. Discourse reflects an institution's value, mind concepts and operation. At the same time, it also constructs institution. Institutional identity needs to be achieved through discourse. Linguistic features such as positive and negative sentimental words, high lexical density and connectives are used by managerial groups in CSR reports. These features can reflect corporate values, development strategy and managerial groups' preferred corporate governance concepts. Studies of the discursive construction of institutional identity are crucial to understanding the mechanisms of institutions. Studies of institutional discourse and identity focus on how institutions dynamically construct, negotiate, manage and transmit their multi-dimensional identities via discourse.

Chen (2016) examines the theories and methods of the construction of institutional identity research, and proposes a comparative research framework of discursive the construction of institutional identity. This is applied to Chinese and American universities based on the 4 dimensions of context of Wodak's Discourse-Historical Approach. By introducing the theory of higher education, Chen (2017) develops a three-dimensional analytical framework for the of discursive construction of institutional identity: macro, sub-macro and micro levels, as well as the discursive strategies of institutional identity on the micro level based on contrastive analysis and Chinese and American universities' different modes and strategies for discursive construction of institutional identity.

At the macro level, this framework focuses on the social, political and historical context in which institutional discourse is located: the analysis of the historical context (social, political and historical background) which reflects and constructs

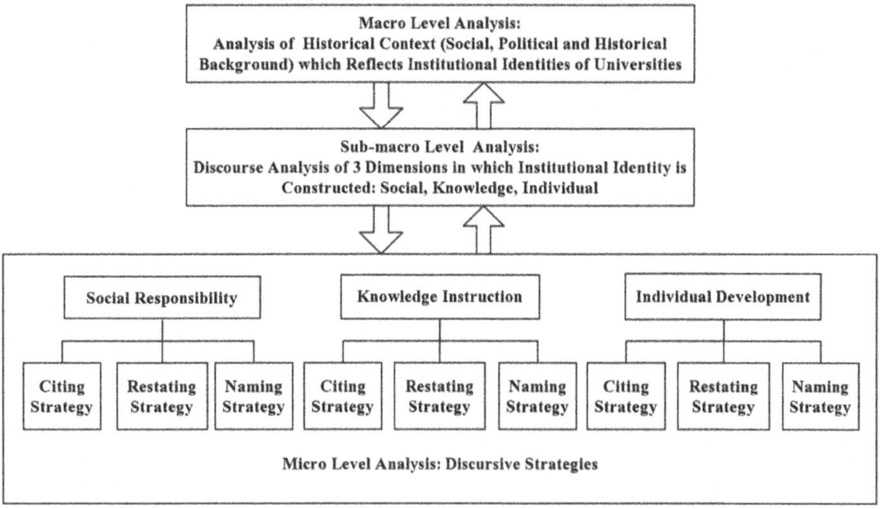

Fig. 3.3 Discursive construction model for Universities' Institutional identity and its discursive strategies on the micro level (Chen, 2017: 27)

the institutional identities of universities. At the sub-macro level, this study focuses on the discourse analysis of 3 dimensions by which an institution's identity is constructed: social responsibility, knowledge instruction, and individual development. These 3 dimensions on sub-macro level provide an observational dimension for the micro level's discursive strategies: intertextuality—that are citing strategy, restating/reporting strategy and naming strategy (Fig. 3.3).

Chen's (2017) framework provides an authoritative and workable analytical framework for studies of the discursive construction of different institutional identities. The multi-dimensional discourse evaluation framework for Chinese and American banks' CSR image construction in this study is in light of Chen's (ibid) framework. On the macro level, this study analyzes different social, cultural, economic, and political backgrounds for Chinese and American banks' CSR image construction. On the sub-macro level, this study analyzes Chinese and American banks' CSR image along 3 dimensions (CSR mind image, CSR behavior image and CSR visual image). On the micro level, it analyzes CSR reports' various discursive features on 4 dimensions of sentiment, readability, CSR keyword, visualization which reflect and construct Chinese and American banks' 3 dimensional CSR images. Wu and Zhang (2019) also expand this framework to analyze the different discursive strategies in Chinese and American company's corporate identities, based on the 3 dimensional analytical framework of the discourse-historical approach.

Identity construction has always been a focus of research in different disciplines such as philosophy, linguistics, sociology, politics, psychology, and anthropology (Xiang, 2009). However, the theory and research methods of any discipline alone are not sufficient to explain the problem of institutional identity construction. Therefore, it is necessary to conduct interdisciplinary research on corporate image construction, such as discursive construction of corporate image via CSR reports from the perspective of linguistics and management.

3.2.2 Corporate Identity System (CIS)

A corporation's identity refers to what an organization stands for and the mix of elements that give the organization its distinctiveness (Balmer, 2008). Corporate identity is a primary goal of corporate communications in order to build and maintain an identity which accords with and facilitates their business objectives. To be specific, corporate identity is the manner by which a corporation, firm or business presents itself to the public (Liu, 2008).

The corporate identity and corporate image are related, but different. Both are expressions of "what the enterprise is", but corporate identity refers to the views of internal members, while corporate image refers to understandings of the enterprise's external stakeholders. Many scholars have equated the two in their research. This study focuses on banks' CSR image construction via CSR disclosure and stakeholders' perception of banks' discursively constructed images. Companies' images are transmitted to stakeholders via various elements: corporate communication, physical architecture and location, corporate visual identity, corporate behavior, management behavior, employee behavior, goals/philosophies/principles, nationality, organizational imagery/history, and nature of the industry and corporate/marketing strategies (Melewar & Jenkins, 2002).

Corporate Identity System (CIS) provides this study an "entry point" to integrate the multi-dimensional discursive features of banks' CSR report as well as to identify and analyze banks' discursive CSR image construction in 3 dimensions: CSR mind image, behavior image and visual image. CIS which includes corporate mind identity (MI), corporate behavior identity (BI) and corporate visual identity (VI) refers to a company that consciously and systematically presents and transmits its various characteristics of business to the public. It does this so that the public, in the market environment, has a standardized, differentiated impression and understanding of a particular company (Liu, 2008). CIS theory was first proposed by Paul Rand in the 1930s in the United States under the background of the United States' commodity economy. Its development has been a starting point, and has promoted research into private enterprise organization and management. The competition has intensified, and the competition for product quality has evolved into a competition in the field of corporate brand image.

Firstly, CIS theory pays more attention to the identification at the concept level, such as corporate philosophy and strategies. Secondly, it implements the concept level through behavior identification, that is, corporate behavior. Finally, it integrates corporate identity through visual recognition. This trinity can enhance its dissemination effect, enabling companies and other organizations to quickly increase their visibility, improve their reputations, and promote public recognition. The relationship

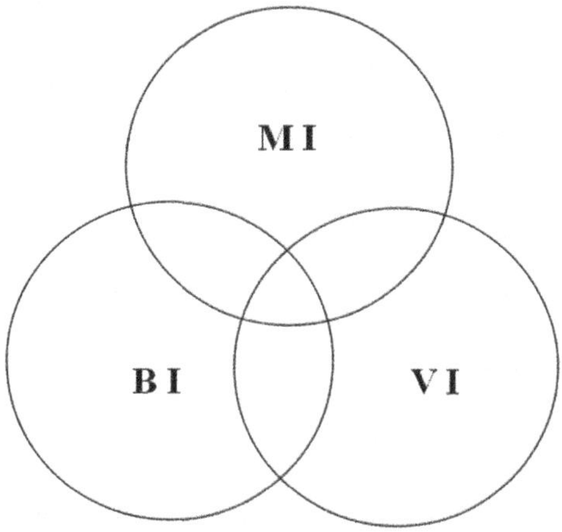

Fig. 3.4 The corporate identity system (CIS)

between the three can be explained with MI as the conceptual level of CIS strategy and the soul of the enterprise; BI is the concrete operation level of CIS strategy and is the behavior of the enterprise; VI is the visualization of CIS strategy and the face of the company. The three complement each other and are indispensable (Fig. 3.4).

CIS provides a company with overall business strategy and comprehensive, strategic public relations measures. It is an effective means of communication between a company and the public. A company's identification system is unified, standardized, personalized and transmitted based on specific concepts and unique behavioral activities through the overall design, control and dissemination of all visible aspects of the company in order to form or strengthen its image in the public mind. The introduction of CIS by a company is to shape and spread the corporate image to the public, and to enhance corporate image power. CIS system provides an "entry point" to integrate the multi-dimensional discursive features and analyze banks' discursive image construction in this study. It is used to examine how the multi-dimensional discursive features in CSR reports construct banks' CSR images on 3 levels: mind image, behavior image and visual image.

Liu (ibid) proposes the foundation of a company's CSR image constructions in Fig. 3.5. This indicates that corporate image includes corporate economic image and corporate social image, based on the characteristics of corporate organization and corporate behavior. Liu (ibid) also defines CSR image as: "impressions of a company's attitudes and behaviors when they deal with stakeholders other than shareholders and a wide range of social issues, or people' attitudes and evaluation of the company's CSR principles and behavior". A company's CSR image can be constructed via its CSR performance which may be transmitted through CSR disclosure. Based on the 3 dimensions of corporate image construction and the connotation of CSR and corporate image, Liu (ibid) proposes a theoretical approach for a company's CSR image construction: CSR image construction can be realized by CSR mind concept construction and CSR behavior construction, based on the CSR mind identity system and the CSR behavior identity system (Fig. 3.6). Based on Carroll's

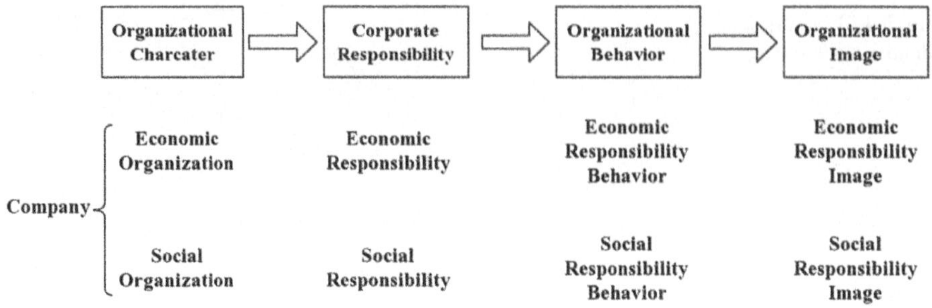

Fig. 3.5 Foundation of a company's CSR image construction (Liu, 2008: 84)

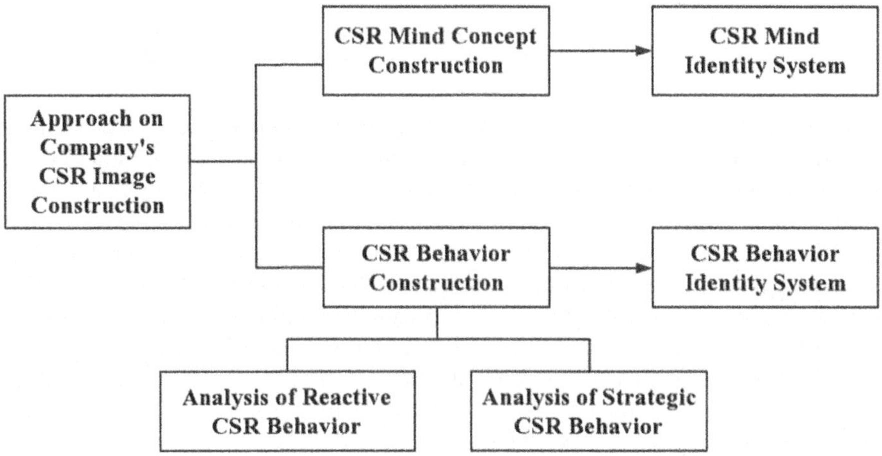

Fig. 3.6 Approach to a company's CSR image construction (Liu, 2008: 11)

(1991) classification of CSR and the qualities of CSR behaviors, Liu (2008) also divides CSR behavior into 2 categories: reactive CSR behavior and strategic CSR behavior.

A company's CSR mind concept includes corporate culture and strategy. This is the connotation of the company's core CSR values. Corporate mind concept is a company's commitment to its stakeholders. Once the corporate mind concept is established, it becomes the guiding ideology for the construction of corporate CSR behavior image and CSR visual image. Corresponding and continuous CSR activities need to be conducted to fulfill these commitments in order to construct a responsible and sustainable corporate CSR image among stakeholders.

This study is enlightened by Liu's (ibid) concept of companies' CSR image: a company's CSR image can be transmitted through company's CSR disclosure of CSR performance. His approach to companies' CSR image construction also shed light on banks' construction of CSR images in this study: company's CSR image construction is realized by CSR mind concept construction and CSR behavior construction. Liu's (ibid) approach to CSR image construction is based on corporate identity system. However, CSR visual image construction: visualization of company's CSR mind concept and CSR behavior based on visual identity system haven't been focused.

3.2.2.1 Mind Identity

The corporate mind identity recognition system in CIS, abbreviated as MI or MIS, also known as the corporate ideology identification system, refers to a company's unique positioning and cognition of its own business philosophy. It uses this to distinguish itself from similar companies. It is the overall planning and definition of the business objectives, business ideas, and marketing methods for the current and future periods. The main contents of mind identity include corporate culture, corporate spirit, corporate mission, corporate values, corporate creeds, corporate slogan, corporate vision, corporate objectives, operating value, social responsibility and development planning. Mind identity belongs to the ideological category of corporate culture which reflects company's managerial group's understanding of the nature of the company and the characteristics of the corporate activities. Corporate mind concept is the basis for the company to formulate and implement corporate strategy.

Correspondingly, a company's CSR mind identity refers to corporate's concept and value in performing CSR. The mind concept of CSR is formulated based on a company's managerial group and employees' understanding of the nature of the company and the relationship between the corporation and society, especially the understanding of the relationship between its stakeholders including the philosophy of CSR, CSR declaration, goals and guidelines of CSR behavior (Liu, ibid). CSR mind concept is an important part of corporate culture. Corporate CSR mind concept guides the development orientation of CSR activities and decides the level of CSR performance. The construction and transmission of CSR concept is also an important means for a company to communicate with stakeholders.

According to Zhu's (2009) mechanism and standard for commercial banks' CSR performance, commercial banks should establish and enhance CSR value in their business operations in order to improve their CSR contributions. CSR value in Zhu's (ibid) research is realized and established via banks' corporate strategy and corporate culture; it has the same connotation as CSR mind concept.

CSR mind concept/value, including corporate culture and strategy, are contained in CSR reports, both implicitly and explicitly. Corporations use CSR reports to express their attitudes towards stakeholders, corporate development, and other CSR information. However, they also use them as an opportunity to persuade stakeholders to accept their CSR concept. Sentiment analysis is the study of emotions, opinions, and appraisals and attitudes regarding "services, products, individuals, organizations, issues, topics and their attributes (D'Andrea et al., 2015). According to Systemic Functional Linguistics and appraisal theory, language is functional and persuasive (Martin & White, 2005).

We may conduct sentimental analysis on a company's CSR report to analyze how its CSR mind image is constructed by expressing its CSR concept. CSR concept includes the company's attitudes towards stakeholder relationships and corporate development. This can be conveyed via sentimental words (discursive features) in CSR reports. Additionally, a company persuades its stakeholders to accept their CSR concept through sentimental words in CSR reports.

Thus, a CSR report's sentimental tendency can influence stakeholders' attitudes towards the company's CSR mind concept, and then the perception of corporate mind image. A company's CSR concept, corporate culture and strategy are transmitted via the sentimental words in CSR reports.

The readability of corporate disclosures, the complexity of the wording and sentence structure of the text in a CSR report, is connected with the management's incentives and values of corporate governance. This may influence corporate financial performance and capital market reaction based on the management obfuscation hypothesis, the theory of impression management, information asymmetry or signaling theory. The management obfuscation hypothesis argues that managers have incentives to obfuscate information when firm performance is poor. This is because the market may react with the delayed incorporation of information contained in complicated disclosures (Bloomfield, 2002). Due to information asymmetry between management and stakeholders, management has the incentives and opportunities to manipulate the complexity of corporate disclosures in order to transmit "manipulated" or "modified" concepts to their stakeholders.

According to signaling theory, the readability of a CSR report may serve as a signal for investors. The readability of a CSR report may influence stakeholders' perceived efficiency of the company's CSR value. Then, stakeholders' different perceptions or attitudes towards the company are constructed via the discursive features of readability.

Also, CSR report readability is the outcome of a company's writing/communication style with their stakeholders. Companies with different CSR values, corporate culture and strategies may use different communicative styles in their CSR reports. Thus, the readability of a CSR report can convey a company's unique CSR value. Stakeholders' attitudes towards a company's CSR values and mind image will be influenced by the reading ease of its CSR reports.

The co-constructive mechanism between CSR mind image and sentiment, readability of CSR reports is illustrated in Fig. 3.7.

3.2.2.2 Behavior Identity

The corporate behavior identification system (BI), also known as the corporate activity identification system, refers to the process by which corporations identify different goals according to their concepts of MI. It also addresses how they formulate a series of specific corporate behaviors to demonstrate corporate values and business missions through series of actions. BI can make a company form a specific business style, and thus distinguish itself from other companies. BI includes two

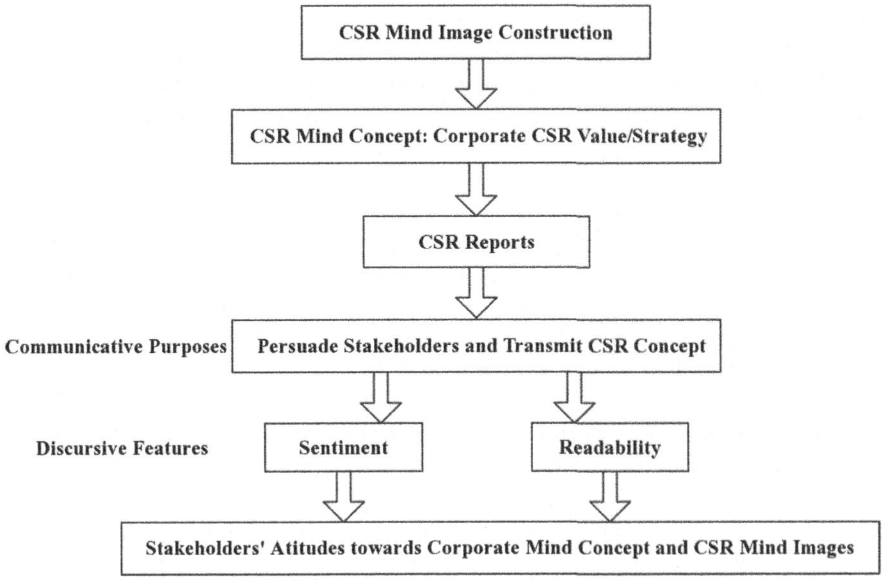

Fig. 3.7 Co-constructive mechanism between CSR mind image and sentiment, readability of CSR reports

levels of content: firstly, based on the business philosophy of the agreement of MI, BI will standardize and harmonize basic corporate behaviors (internal production and external services); the second refers to embodying the business philosophy in terms of norms and specific behaviors, and forming a unique impression and specific image concept among stakeholders.

Internal BI includes production and operation management, employee skills training, enterprise rules and regulations, distribution of benefits, improvement in working conditions, and the maintenance of production equipment. The company's external BIS includes market status surveys, product development and upgrades, market information feedback, public relations planning, promotional activities, distribution strategies, advertising, large-scale social activities, public benefit organizations, and marketing campaign planning.

Similarly, a company's CSR behavior image refers to its CSR activities. This includes all corporate activities in which a company behaves in order to maintain and improve stakeholder relationships, based on the company's CSR mind concept. According to Carroll's Construct (1991), CSR can be divided into 4 categories: economic responsibility, legal responsibility, ethical responsibility and philanthropic responsibility. Economic responsibility is a company's prior and basic responsibility. This refers to the products and services that need to be provided in market transactions and the profits returned to shareholders. Activities that control employee productivity or monitor consumer complaints are examples of companies fulfilling their economic responsibilities. Legal responsibility refers to the observance of the law, and companies have the obligation to sacrifice profits according to law. For example, a company that invests in environmentally friendly equipment that is not part of its own production still gets credit for reducing pollution. Ethical responsibility means that in a fair and responsible market transaction, especially when not legally required, the company's behavioral model and treatment of its stakeholders comply with ethical standards. Ethical responsibility implies a legal spirit that helps guide a company's business practices in decision-making areas where regulations and laws are either unsound or non-existent. Philanthropic responsibility means that the company voluntarily guides its activities with higher corporate responsibilities and expectations higher than what is stipulated by law (Carroll, ibid). Companies need to contribute to society with their own resources, and promote the improvement of human society.

The above 4 aspects of CSR are hierarchical, and economic responsibility is the primary responsibility of the company. All other functions of the company are derived from this fundamental assumption; second is legal responsibility which must be observed by a company in order to become established in a society; third is ethical responsibility which reflects the public's expectations of the company; finally, there is philanthropic responsibility. In Carroll Construct, CSR has clear contents, and highlights the important role of economic factors in CSR. Based on the content of CSR, CSR behavior or CSR activity can also be divided into 4 categories: economic CSR behavior, legal CSR behavior, ethical CSR behavior, and philanthropic CSR behavior.

Based on Carroll's (ibid) classification of CSR and the qualities of CSR behaviors, Liu (2008) divides CSR behavior into 2 categories: reactive corporate social responsibility behavior and strategic corporate social responsibility behavior.

Reactive CSR behavior refers to a company's reactions, responses based on common social issues. The basic principle is to be a good social citizen. Under the reactive CSR behavioral model, companies focus on understanding and sympathizing with social requirements and expectations and their changing trends, such as issues of environmental protection, education and social problem. The advantage of reactive CSR behavior is that it is flexible, adaptable to situations, and timely. It is also conducive to rapid adaptation and meeting social expectations. The disadvantage is that it lacks a long-term outlook and is not conducive to synergies with business activities and strategies.

Strategic CSR behavior combines CSR with a company's business operations. This improves and solves social responsibility by giving full play to the strategic capabilities of the company. The strategic CSR behavioral model can internalize social issues into corporate strategic issues, translate social responsibility costs into corporate strategic investments, and (companies hope) obtain compensation from strategic investments, thus enhancing the initiative of CSR.

As a special public enterprise, commercial banks rely on both capital investments from shareholders and the efforts of customers, employees and other stakeholders to utilize different bank resources. As for banks' CSR behavior, based on the connotation of CSR and reasons for banks' CSR performance, Zhu (2009) proposes that commercial banks should bear specific social responsibilities which can be summarized as five types: social responsibility to the community and the public, social responsibility to customers, social responsibility to employees (management and employees), social responsibility to suppliers and competitors, and to investors (owners, shareholders, or the social responsibility of creditors). Commercial banks should actively undertake these social responsibilities, which not only benefit the public and all stakeholders, but also benefit themselves.

Similar to the mechanism behind commercial banks' CSR performance in Zhu (ibid), the famous database CSRHub has set up 4 CSR focus areas for commercial banks: Communities, Employee relationships, Environmental problems and Corporate Governance. These are based on stakeholder theory. CSRHub is an investment research company specializing in commercial banking, community, environmental, corporate governance and employee assessments. It collects and adjusts data from all aspects of government, NGOs, publications and social networks, making it the world's largest and most comprehensive CSR and sustainability database. Enlightened by CSRHub's classification of CSR performance, Xiao and Shao (2014) propose 4 approaches to banks' CSR performance: the community approach, the employee approach, the environmental approach and the corporate governance approach. They conduct an empirical study and find a positive relationship between banks' CSR activities in 4 areas and banks' financial performance.

Banks disclose their CSR information and activities to stakeholders via CSR reports, and then their CSR behavior images are constructed and transmitted via CSR activities. A text's keywords represent the unique keyword features of one text compared to others. CSR Keyword analysis of CSR reports can identify companies' unique CSR behaviors, the content of CSR, and banks' CSR behavior image, from the linguistic level. The co-constructive mechanism between CSR behavior image and CSR keywords in CSR reports is illustrated in Fig. 3.8.

Then, based on CSR hub's classification of commercial bank' CSR performance and Zhu's (2009) framework of commercial bank CSR performance, keywords in banks' CSR reports can be divided into CSR keywords pertaining to "communities and society", "employees", "environment" and "corporate governance". This reflects banks' CSR behavior about communities and society, employees, the environment, and corporate governance, respectively, at the content level.

3.2.2.3 Visual Identity

A company's visual identity system (VI) refers a visually recognizable symbol with a high degree of recognition that is designed and displayed based on the business ideas and strategic goals from MI and the feedback of specific market information. VI enhances the sense of image of the target audience by displaying the characteristics of the company's personality and distinctive features visually. The current information society demands that VI should be designed with precision. It is a key part of determining the success or failure of a business. VI is divided into two components: a basic element system and an application element system. The basic element system includes enterprise name, enterprise logo, standard wording, standard color,

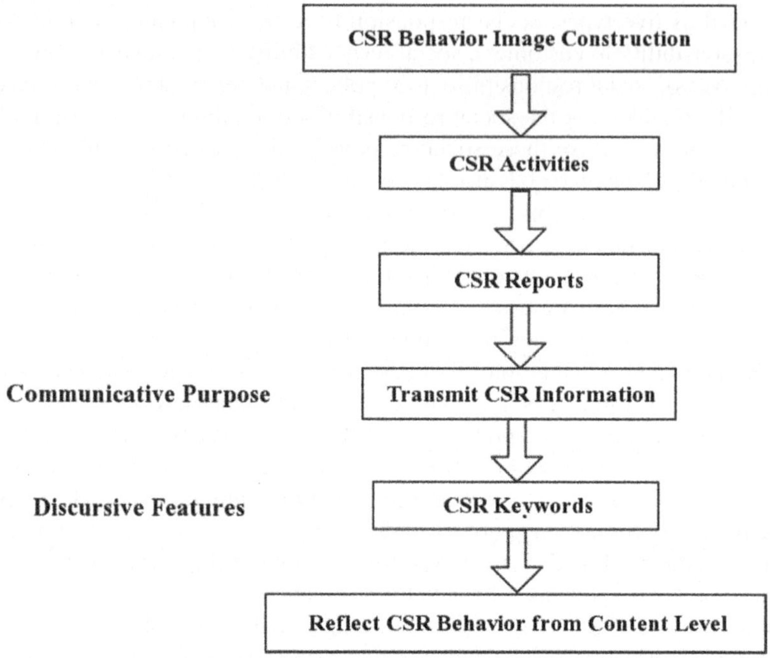

Fig. 3.8 Co-constructive mechanism between CSR behavior image and CSR keywords in CSR reports

symbol pattern, a propaganda slogan, and a marketing report. The application system of VI includes production equipment, construction environment, product packaging, advertising media, transportation, uniforms, flags, signboards, office supplies, identification cards, window displays and exhibitions (Liu, 2008). In addition, VI must be combined with MI and BI. Companies need unified planning and consistent design in order to communicate a visual identity system that satisfies the public.

A CSR report is a company's public narrative and its main target readers are its stakeholders. Since CSR reports transmit corporate image directly to their stakeholders, stakeholders' first impressions of the company are based on the visual attributes of CSR reports. Kress and Van Leeuwen's (1996) *Reading Images* points out the semiotic elements and images' function in communicate meanings. With the development of technology and new media, a successful CSR report should be a fine representation of the combination of verbal and visual semiotic modes in order to establish a good CSR visual image and achieve smoother communication with stakeholders.

The visual design of a CSR report can present a company's CSR concept and CSR behavior. The visualization of CSR disclosure, including the employment of pictures and type settings of pictures and words in CSR reports enhances stakeholders' impressions and perceptions of a company's CSR concept and activities,

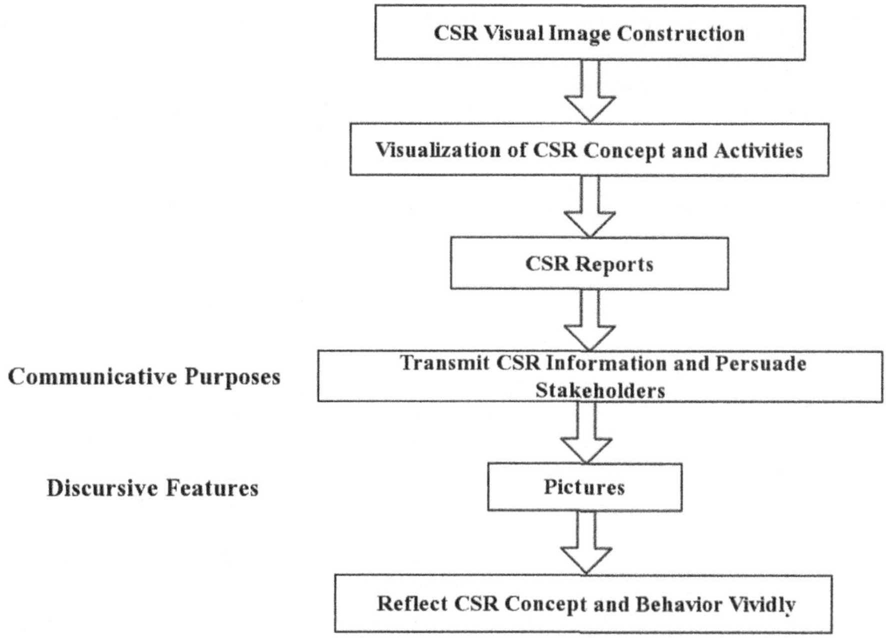

Fig. 3.9 Co-constructive mechanism between CSR visual image and visualization in CSR reports

and also the company's CSR image. The co-constructive mechanism between CSR visual image and visualization in CSR reports is illustrated in Fig. 3.9.

Three major strategic CIS systems constitute an organic whole. Among them, the MI is the theoretical guidance and direction of corporate image creation, and it determines the formulation of companies' value, vision and target decision strategy, the market positioning of product precision. If the CI strategy is regarded as a person metaphorically, then MI is the "brain", BI is the "hand", and VI is the "face." In other words, mind image plays a dominant role. It determines the behavior image and visual image, and ultimately forms a complete corporate identity system.

3.2.3 Previous Multi-dimensional Business Discourse Evaluation Frameworks

The selection of discursive indicators for this study's multi-dimensional discourse evaluation framework of banks' CSR reports in banks' image construction is also enlightened by previous evaluation frameworks on CSR report and financial reports.

Merkl-Davies and Brennan (2007) propose seven strategies in corporate narratives for impression management. Two of these obfuscate bad news by manipulating verbal information, and four strategies emphasize good news by manipulating verbal

Table 3.1 From Merkl-Davies and Brennan (2007) framework in corporate narratives strategies for impression management

Obfuscate bad news by manipulating verbal information	Reading ease manipulation (i.e. making text more difficult to read)
	Rhetorical manipulation (i.e. using persuasive language)
Emphasize good news by manipulating verbal and/or numerical information	**Thematic manipulation** emphasizes positive words and themes, or emphasizes positive financial performance
	Visual and structural manipulation involves the way in which information is presented (i.e. visual emphasis or ordering of verbal/numerical information)
	Performance comparisons involve choosing benchmarks that portray current financial performance in the best possible light
	Choice of **earnings number** involves selecting one of a number of earnings amounts for disclosure to favorably portray current financial performance
Attribution	**Attribution of organizational performance**

and/or numerical information. Additionally, performance attribution is regarded as the disclosure strategy and managers usually attribute the positive organizational outcomes to internal factors and negative ones to the external factors (Merkl-Davies & Brennan, ibid). Sentimental words and persuasive language are means for rhetorical manipulation and impression management, and readability is the reading ease manipulation for impression management. All of them influence stakeholders' attitudes and perceptive efficiency of corporate narratives and corporate image. Thematic and visual manipulation can emphasize stakeholders' perceptions of corporate narratives, corporate behavior image, and visual image (Table 3.1).

Muslu et al. (2019) have developed a disclosure score to measure the credibility of CSR reports. They find a positive relationship between CSR disclosure scores and analyst forecasts. Investors' investment decisions are, to a significant degree, influenced by analyst forecasts. The tone, readability, numerical content and horizon content of CSR reports are the crucial factors in evaluating a CSR report's credibility. Thus, these discursive features also influence analysts' perceptions of corporate image and corporate investment value. In turn they also influence investors' investment choices, and finally capital market performance (Table 3.2).

Li and Wang (2017) establish a three dimensional discourse appraisal framework (appraisal resources, metaphors, semantic prosody) to measure UK and US companies' CEO's risk perceptions, conveyed via risk discourse in corporate annual reports. They point out discursive features' predicative functions in corporate financial performance via the CEO's risk perceptions, both theoretically and empirically. The present study is enlightened by Li and Wang's (ibid) framework, and tries to

Table 3.2 From Muslu et al. (2019) framework in CSR report disclosure score

Credibility of CSR report	Tone
	Readability
	Length
	Numerical content of CSR report
	Horizon content of CSR report

analyze the function of CSR reports' discursive features in companies' CSR image construction and capital market performance.

Li and Wang's (ibid) framework highlights that discursive features reflect corporate managerial groups' implicit conceptions, and have a predicative function in corporate financial performance.

Also, based on the theory of impression management, information asymmetry, signaling theory, discourse and institutional identity, previous research on sentiment, readability and keywords has indicated that these three textual characteristics in corporate non-financial information disclosure reflect corporate attitudes, communicative styles, and managerial groups' governing cognition. They reflect corporate governance, culture and strategy in discourse level, then influence stakeholder's attitudes and perceptions towards corporate governance, culture and strategy and performance.

Sentiment, readability, keywords of various thematic contents, and visual and structural manipulation are the commonly-used indicators in research of Merkl-Davies and Brennan (2007) and Muslu et al. (2019).

Then, based on the research objective of this study—banks' CSR image construction and the theory of institutional identity, the corporate identity system (CIS) and the functions of various textual features in corporate concept transmission and corporate performance promotion verified by previous research both theoretically and empirically, this study integrates previous studies' narrative and discursive indicators. Doing so, the multi-dimensional discourse evaluation framework of banks' CSR reports for banks' international image construction (sentiment, readability, CSR keywords and visualization, which cover the lexical, syntactic, semantic and textual levels of discourse) is established.

Banks' CSR mind image construction in CSR reports can be realized by implicit discursive indicators of sentiment and readability. This is because these indicators reflect banks' managerial groups' attitudes towards stakeholders, CSR concepts and communication styles. These are the embodiments of banks' CSR concepts of governance, culture value, and development strategy. Banks' CSR behavior image construction in CSR reports can be realized by explicit discursive indicator CSR keywords, since CSR keyword lists from one corpus of a group of banks' CSR reports can reflect the unique features of that group banks' CSR activities at the content level. Banks' CSR visual image construction in CSR reports can be realized by the explicit discursive indicator—visualization. This is because the pictures contained in CSR reports are selected and arranged by management groups in order to shape and enhance the reader's impression of banks' CSR concept, behavior, image. Those four kinds of evaluation indicators indeed are discursive strategies by which banks construct their CSR mind image, CSR behavior image, and CSR visual image, respectively, in their CSR reports, and then build a comprehensive CSR image among their stakeholders. Also, the theoretical foundations behind these 4 kinds of discursive evaluation indicators for CSR image construction are explored below.

3.2.4 Discourse Appraisal Theory

Sentiment analysis is a branch of content analysis, which aims at "automatic detection of sentiment, often negative or positive sentiment, in natural language text." (Tang, 2015). Tang(ibid) claims that it is widely used in polarity analysis of massive media and business texts, such as the emotive orientation of comments on Twitter towards an election, or customers' feedback on a product on e-commerce.

Textual sentiment examines the degree of emotional tendencies in a text. Emotion is usually used to indicate subjective feelings towards various cognitive and evaluative behaviors. What's more, another term, "affect", has the same connotation as "emotion" (ibid). Affect is also one part of the subsystem of Appraisal Theory. Appraisal Theory (2005) is an extension and development on interpersonal meaning within Systemic Functional Linguistics in 3 axes: attitude, graduation and engagement. Attitude is related to feelings or emotions, which is sub-divided into "affect", "judgment" and "appreciation"; engagement is concerned with sourcing attitude and the play of voices around opinions in discourse; graduation attends to grade phenomena and adjusts the degree of feelings (Martin & White, 2005) (Fig. 3.10).

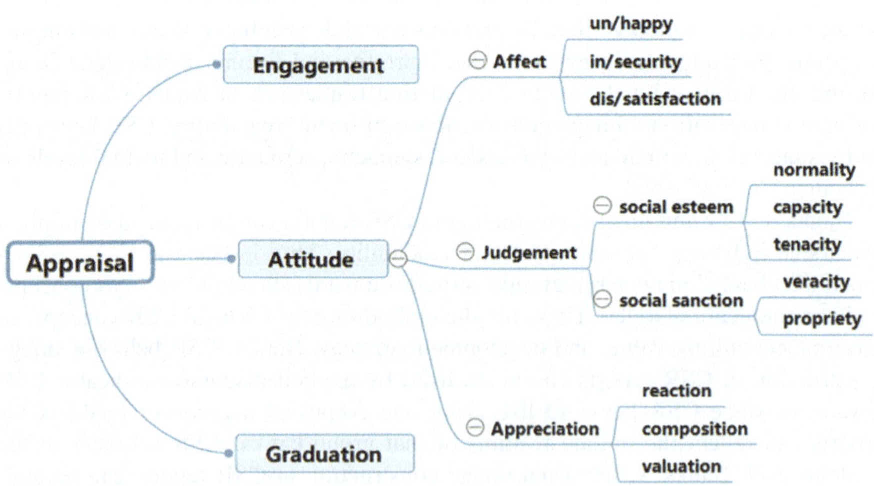

Fig. 3.10 Overview of appraisal systems (Martin & White, 2005)

Table 3.3 Choices of lexical items under each categories of affect (Martin & White, 2005: 51)

Affect	Positive	Negative
(Un)happiness	Cheerful, buoyant, jubilant, liked, loved, adored	Sad, melancholy, despondent, cut-up, heart-broken…broken-hearted, sorrowful…dejected…joyless, dreary, cheerless, unhappy, sad, gloomy, downcast, low, down, depressed, weepy, tearful, wet-eyed…
(In)security	Together, confident, assured; comfortable, confident, trusting	Uneasy, anxious, freaked out; startled, astonished
(Dis)satisfaction	Involved, absorbed, engrossed, satisfied, pleased, chuffed, impressed, thrilled	Flat, stable, jaded, cross, furious; bored with, sick of, fed up with
(Dis)inclination	Miss, yearn for, long for	Wary, fearful, terrorized

Appraisal theory is used to explore, describe and explain how language is used to evaluate and construct textual personas, and to manage interpersonal positioning and relationships (ibid). Affect, in the sub-system of attitude, is the core subsystem in the framework of appraisal theory and is designed to illustrate emotive talk. There are various degrees of positive and negative tendencies, embodied in a series of evaluation terminology expressing happiness, sadness, anger, hatred, and satisfaction (Tang, 2015).

Martin and White (2005) also provide choices of lexical items under each category of affect and emphasize "it is by no means exhaustive, but simply to give the gist of the range of meanings involved." (Table 3.3).

Appraisal theory, and especially the Affect subsystem, provides an insightful perspective to identify and evaluate the lexicalization of emotion (Tang, 2015), which enlightens sentimental evaluation of banks' CSR report and sheds light on the choices of lexicalization of emotion on a micro level. Munday (2012) defines these lexis "value-rich" terms and suggests the possibility that they will affect the reception of text in a "sensitive" or "critical" way. These value-rich terms in CSR reports can be analyzed to value managerial manipulation. This offers the possibility to uncover firms' motives and communicative intentions for stakeholder engagement and CSR image construction.

3.2.5 Readability

As an important textual feature in content analysis, readability has been the research focus of various disciplines such as linguistics, management and accounting. Readability, also known as reading ease, refers to the degree to which English text is easy to read and understand. According to Betts (1949), readability is a two-way proposition. The first consideration is the reader—his experience, interests, feelings, motivation, language facilities, needs, and reading and studying conditions. Any means of predicting readability is valid to the degree that the reader is taken into account. The second consideration is the interest level—the language, mental constructions, and mechanical features of reading material. Each of these factors are inter-related (Betts, ibid).

English readability depends on a variety of factors, including: (1) word length; (2) the proportion of different words; (3) the level of abstraction of the vocabulary (conceptual load); (4) the number of pronouns (5) the number of prepositions; (6) the number of affixes; (7) the number of difficult words identified by vocabulary; (8) sentence length; (9) factual density and frequentness; (10) number of illustrations; (11) interest and authorship purpose of writing; (12) organizational structure and printing layout of materials; (13) interrelationships among content; (14) cultural load of texts; (15) and background knowledge of readers and their motives for reading motivations (Betts, ibid; Smith & Dechant, 1977). Since the 1920s, the quantitative analysis of the linguistic features of texts through corpora and computer-assisted tools has made readability formula mainstream in readability studies. Scholars of linguistics, management, accounting and nature language processing have studied hundreds of equations for determining readability. Commonly used formulas include Dale-Chall, Fry, Flesch Reading Ease, FOG Index, SMOG, Coh-Metrix, FORCAST, Powers-Somner-Kearl and Spache (Kearney & Liu, 2014). Linguists have used readability formulas to measure the syntactic and textual complexity of different genres of discourse, and have made some breakthroughs in fields such as second language acquisition and textbook compilation.

Scholars in management and accounting have used readability formulas to measure the readability of corporate narratives, and have connected them with corporate performance, capital market reaction based on theories of impression management, and signaling theory. The readability of the information will directly affect the reader's understanding of the content of the report, which in turn will affect his or her evaluation of the company.

3.2.6 Keyword Analysis in Corpus Linguistics

Corpus linguistics and discourse analysis can work together in tandem. This has become the consensus of both the Chinese and international linguistics academic community. Corpus linguistics can make up for the inadequacies of traditional qualitative discourse analysis based on small amounts of text. The former can make large-scale discourse analysis possible and ensure the accuracy and repeatability of the analytical process, avoiding "over-interpretation" or "insufficient interpretation" of specific linguistic phenomena (Baker, 2006). Keyword analysis is one of the most commonly used methods in corpus linguistics. Scott defines keywords are words whose frequency is unusually high in comparison with some norm (Scott, 1996).

Through the corpus tool WordSmith or Antconc's keyword function, a researcher can compare one frequency wordlist with another, in order to obtain a keyword list showing those words occurring significantly more often than expected in a corpus (Baker, 2006). Without statistical examination, it would be impossible to state whether a difference is real or coincidental. Thus, the program conducts statistical tests on all words, attributing each one a "p" or probability value, a number ranging between 0 and 1 (in this case the threshold is set at 0.000001). The "p" represents the amount of confidence that a word is a keyword only by chance. A smaller p-value indicates a lower risk of error in claiming a relationship, and thus a higher probability that the repeated use of a word is indeed due to authorial choices (ibid). Since most linguistic data are asymmetrically distributed or 'skewed', non-parametric statistical tests are preferred (i.e. tests that make no assumption on whether the data analyzed have normal or non-normal distributions). The program offers the possibility to choose between two tests—chi-square test of significance and log-likelihood. The latter is considered to provide a better estimate of "keyness", allowing the user to compare the significance of the occurrences of both rare, and common, phenomena (Meyer, 2002; Baker, 2006).

Keyness does not simply mean high frequency, but unusual frequency by comparison with a reference corpus (Baker, ibid). Keywords will not reveal discourses, but can help to spot traces of discourses within language, directing the researcher to important concepts in a text that may contribute to highlighting the existence of (embedded) discourses or ideologies (Burman & Parker, 1993; Baker, 2006). It is, although, necessary to remember that keyword analysis will only focus on lexical differences, not on lexical similarities. For example, comparing the CSR keyword list of corpus of Chinese banks' CSR reports with that of general English corpus can indicate the thematic features of Chinese banks' CSR reports. This can be regarded as Chinese banks' CSR reports typical CSR activities, and also its behavior image.

3.2.7 A Multi-dimensional Discourse Evaluation Framework of Banks' CSR Reports

Under the theoretical background of Fairclough's three-dimensional model and Biber's register analysis, and based on Chen's (2017) framework on the discursive construction of institutional identity, CIS, discourse appraisal theory, readability, and corpus linguistics' keyword analysis, a cross-disciplinary, multi-dimensional discourse evaluation framework of Chinese and American banks' CSR reports for banks' CSR image construction is constructed, as shown in Fig. 3.11. This inter-disciplinary evaluation framework examines the multi-dimensional discursive features in Chinese and American banks' CSR reports for their CSR image construction, in order to improve the Chinese banks' CSR disclosure system and international CSR image.

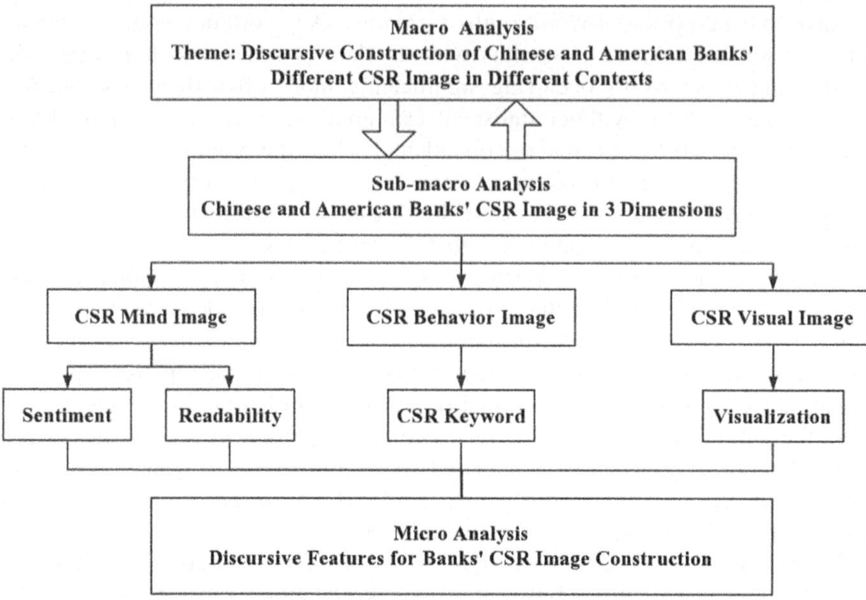

Fig. 3.11 Multi-dimensional discourse evaluation framework of banks' CSR reports

This study is enlightened by Chen's (ibid) framework of discursive construction of institutional identity. The multi-dimensional discourse evaluation framework of Chinese and American banks' CSR reports for banks' CSR image construction in this study are integrated along three levels: macro, sub-macro and micro.

Macro level analysis is the theme of this study—discursive construction of Chinese and American banks' varying CSR images in different contexts.

Sub-macro level analysis is the discursive analysis of Chinese and American banks' CSR image construction on three dimensions: CSR mind image, CSR behavior image, and CSR visual image based on CIS.

Micro level analysis refers to the discursive features along 4 dimensions: sentiment, readability, CSR keywords, and visualization. These construct and reflect banks' 3 levels of CSR image, as well as comprehensive CSR image.

The co-constructive mechanisms between 3 levels' CSR images and various discursive features based on information asymmetry, the CIS system, and linguistic theories or functions behind the discursive features have been explained and illustrated in the above session. Discursive features in sentiment and readability used in CSR reports can influence stakeholders' attitudes and the perceptive efficiency of banks' CSR images. These are employed to rhetorically persuade stakeholders. They can implicitly reflect banks' CSR strategies, CSR value, or corporate culture—the constituents of banks' CSR mind image. CSR keyword features in CSR reports are used to examine and evaluate banks' CSR behaviors that compose banks' CSR behavior image. Visualization of CSR information used in CSR reports is banks' visual presentation of their CSR concepts and behavior. This is part of banks' CSR visual image.

3.3 The Theoretical Foundation Behind Banks' CSR Image Construction Via CSR Reports

Since the present research is an interdisciplinary study with a linguistic, management and economic approach, this section will focus on management theories concerning banks' discursive CSR image construction. The corporate identity system is the fundamental framework for banks' image construction. Since it has been discussed in above section, this section will report on information asymmetry theory which enables banks to construct their image discursively from management perspective. It will also address stakeholder theory and legitimacy theory which can explain causes for different discursively constructed CSR images between the Chinese and American banks under their own political, social, economic, cultural and regulatory contexts.

3.3.1 Information Asymmetry Theory

Information asymmetry refers to the asymmetry of information held by parties in a market transaction when one of the parties is unable to observe and supervise the other's behavior. It also refers to situations in which one party is unable to obtain complete information about the other's actions, or when the costs of observation and supervision are high (Akerlof, 1970). Company shareholders, managers, creditors, potential investors, accounting firms, securities underwriters, and securities regulatory authorities are all participants in capital markets. They each need to understand the accounting information and market transaction information provided by the company. Powerful groups always want to determine levels of information disclosure according to their own interests.

Good corporate governance includes multiple levels and forms of expression, including adequate disclosure of information. Enterprises with good governance will inevitably provide more information to the small and medium shareholders in the market and reduce information asymmetry. It is generally believed that companies that voluntarily disclose their earnings forecasting information perform better than those that don't. On the contrary, companies with poor profitability, or even losses, often do not disclose this. The management of high-quality companies is incentivized to reduce the information asymmetry that exists among stakeholders. If this problem of asymmetric information cannot be solved, the costs of external financing to the company will increase. Therefore, the management of the company conducting capital market transactions tends to actively disclose this information to reduce information asymmetry, thereby reducing the company's external financing costs (Han, 1994).

Based on the information asymmetry between company and stakeholder, it is possible for companies to conduct impression management via public corporate narratives.

Impression management is an important component of corporate statements (Kress, 1993). According to the theory of impression management, impression management is the use of language information by a company's management. It consciously manipulates the content and form of language information disclosure and tries to control the main stakeholders' (investors, creditors, government agencies, suppliers) perceptions of corporate image. The ultimate goal is influencing their investment decisions. The degree of flexibility of the language information determines the size of the manipulation space for the impression management behavior. Corporate information disclosure systems are based on mandatory and voluntary disclosure. Since mandatory disclosure of information is based on data information, and the detailed disclosure content and format are regulated, the space for the impression management of mandatory disclosure is small. Meanwhile, the voluntary disclosure of information is based on language information, and the content and format of its disclosure are loosely regulated, so that the space for the manipulation of impression management is large.

Thus, it can be inferred that the existence of corporate impression management is primarily in the disclosure of voluntary information. CSR reports are a form of voluntary disclosure. They are presented to stakeholders, so that companies can leave readers with the impression that they are responsible and reliable corporate citizens that will achieve sustainable development in their business operations. CSR reports are non-financial information disclosures. Thus, they may contain the management group's impression management of discursive features due to the information asymmetry between company and stakeholder. The company's concept, culture, strategy, and intention may be conveyed through those "manipulated" discursive features in CSR reports. Correspondingly, those discursive features influence stakeholders' attitude and the perceptive efficiency of a company's concept, culture, strategy, intention, and ultimately company's CSR image.

3.3.2 Legitimacy Theory

Within social and political theory studies (Gray et al., 1995), social disclosures including CSR reports have been explored from the perspectives of political economy (Adams & Harte, 1998; Tinker et al., 1991), stakeholder (Roberts, 1992; Ullmann, 1985) and legitimacy (Fuoli, 2012). While there remains no universally acknowledged theory of social reporting, legitimacy theory has already been used as the prominent analyzing framework of organizations' social disclosure practices (Deegan et al., 2000; Bebbington et al., 2008; Campbell et al., 2003; Deegan, 2002; Gray et al., 1995; Fuoli, 2012).

On the basis legitimacy theory, organizations' social reporting behavior is facilitated by the need to justify their activities and obtain legitimization from the public (Fuoli, ibid). The existence of a social contract governing the relationship between business and society are pointed out by Legitimacy theory (Shocker & Sethi, 1973). Organizations are expected and required to behave within the broader social system in order to be considered legitimate, and thus to continue to exist and develop (ibid). A violation of the social contract might lead the negative consequences to a business, including customers' reduced demand for its products, restricted access to labor supply, less financial capital, increased pressure from lobbies, and stricter government regulation (Brown & Deegan, 1998; Fuoli, 2012). Organization's failure to observe the principles of social contract may threaten its legitimacy, and bring the withdrawal of its license to operate in the end (Tilling & Tilt, 2010).

Since expectations from the public and society change over time, an organization will need to respond to social expectations and voluntarily take actions to social changes in order to maintain its legitimacy (Suchman, 1995). Communicating with a variety of stakeholders via disclosing CSR information according to the changing social norms and values plays a crucial role in maintaining organizations' legitimacy (Fuoli, 2012). Thus legitimacy theory valid the necessity of companies' CSR reporting and the adoption of suitable discursive features in CSR reports in order to maintain its legitimacy as well as the research objectives of this study. Different communicative purposes and motives behind Chinese and American banks' CSR information reporting and accounts for Chinese and American banks' different discursively constructed CSR images via the multi-dimensional discursive features in CSR report can be analyzed and explained on the basis of legitimacy theory.

3.3.3 Stakeholder Theory

Stakeholder theory advocates and defines a series of CSR fulfillment objects. Its aim is to explore the issue of CSR management. Both Stakeholder theory and legitimacy theory regard companies' CSR disclosure as the responses to the demands and expectations of multiple stakeholders, such as shareholders, employees, customers, suppliers, government and communities.

The arguments about stakeholders can be traced back to the 1960s. However, academics generally regard Freeman's (1984) *Strategic Management: A Stakeholder Approach* as a sign of the proposal of stakeholder theory. Freeman believes that stakeholders are all individuals and groups that can influence the achievement of organizational goals, or the impact of organizational goals (Freeman, ibid).

Freeman proposes 3 dimensions of stakeholder classification: ownership, economic dependence, and social benefits, and divides stakeholders into 3 categories accordingly: stakeholders who have ownership of the enterprise, stakeholders who are the economic dependents of the enterprise, and stakeholders who are related with the enterprise's social interests. The first category includes shareholders outside the company and internal shareholding directors and managers; the second category includes managers, creditors, internal service agencies, employees, consumers, suppliers, competitors, local communities and regulatory agencies; The third category includes special groups, governments, and the media (Freeman, ibid).

Corporations are assumed to engage in impression management to manipulate a particular stakeholder group's perceptions of corporate image via narrative disclosure and communication (Leung et al., 2015). Hooghiemstra (2000) shows how Shell, after abandoning its plans to sink the Brent Spar in the Atlantic, engaged in a dialogue with its key stakeholder groups to change their perceptions. Since Chinese and American banks have different key stakeholder groups under their different social, political, economic, cultural and regulatory contexts, the employment of discursive features in their CSR reports and their CSR images are different. This is so as to cater to the varying demands of their stakeholder groups.

3.4 Theoretical Foundation Behind Banks' Discursive Construction of CSR Image's Effects on Capital Markets

This session will illustrate signaling theory and behavioral finance—the theoretical foundation of CSR reports' multi-dimensional discursive features' influence as well as discursively constructed CSR images' effects on capital markets. Banks' discursively constructed CSR image's are realized by the multi-dimensional discursive features in CSR reports in this study.

Discursive feature in banks' CSR reports can influence stakeholders', and especially investors', perceptions and attitudes towards a bank's image and corporate value. Thus discursive feature may have the function of signaling. This may influence capital markets according to signaling theory. Also, the discursive features in banks' CSR reports have the persuasive function. This also can influence the emotions of stakeholders, especially investors. This, in turn, can influence investors' decision-making process, according to behavioral finance.

The actual effect of the discursive construction of banks' CSR image is measured by bank stocks' cumulative abnormal return (CAR) within 30 days after CSR report disclosure. This is assessed via event study, and supported by signaling theory and behavioral finance. Then this study analyzes the ranking of correlation degrees between different discursive features of banks' CSR reports and CAR of banks' stock price in capital markets through gray relational entropy analysis.

3.4.1 Signaling Theory

Signaling theory theoretically support banks' CSR report's discursive features' influence and effect on banks' CSR image construction. It also supports their influence on changes in banks' stock price (CAR) in capital markets.

Signal transmission theory is an important part of information economics. In 1973, A· Michael Spence (1973) first proposed a theory of signal transmission in the article *Job Market Signaling*. In this article, Spence uses the employees' education level as an indicator to measure their employability. The manager of the enterprise can identify employees with different abilities according to this indicator. Subsequently, signaling theory is applied to the research field of company. A company's capital structure can reflect the value of the company and its profitability. For companies with high performance, they can fully disclose information related to their capital structures. This is helpful in gaining investors' favor. The role of signal transmission is reflected in the following aspects: investors in capital markets will give positive feedback on favorable signals disclosed by a company. By analyzing these favorable signals and making relevant investment decisions, the company's stock price will change. Thus, signal transmission can reduce, and even solve, information asymmetry in capital markets.

Information asymmetry theory holds that in capital markets, market information held by both parties is unbalanced; the seller has more information than the buyer (Spence, ibid). In this case, the buyer will try to obtain information from the seller, and the information asymmetry will increase the cost of corporate finance. As costs increase, the more private information a business manager has, the higher the investor's expected return on the investment. Establishing the signal transmission mechanism and an incentive mechanism for the enterprise will reduce the information asymmetry, adverse selection cost and moral hazard. That is to say, signaling theory can solve the risk problem caused by information asymmetry.

The information dissemination of listed companies in their annual reports is also the performance of signal transmission. For companies with good performance, they will actively disclose information to stakeholders to avoid adverse selection problems caused by information asymmetry. The management groups fully disclose the financial information in the annual report, so that investors can comprehend the company's financial situation in a timely manner, make judgments on the company's value, and make investment decisions. Listed companies can therefore obtain ideal financing opportunities. Thus, companies with good performance disclose more financial information. On the contrary, the management obfuscation hypothesis argues that managers have incentives to obfuscate information in order to transmit less information when firm performance is poor (Bloomfield, 2002).

Information is the root cause of investors' stock trading. Investors only trade stocks based on the expected difference in information pricing. Information disclosure is an important means to eliminate information asymmetry between listed companies and investors, and to reduce the information risk to investors. In most countries, CSR reports are considered voluntary disclosure. Since CSR performance is connected with corporate financial performance and corporate value, companies need to transmit more signal to their stakeholders via CSR reports in order to induce information asymmetry and improve stakeholders' perception towards corporate CSR image and investors' expectation of corporate value.

Discursive features in CSR reports serve as signals that can transmit information as well as influence information transmission about corporate CSR concepts, strategies, corporate governance and CSR behaviors to their stakeholders. This information can be either implicit or explicit. Stakeholder's attitudes and evaluation towards corporate image and corporate value, as well as investors' investment decisions, will be influenced. Thus, signaling theory validates CSR reports' discursive features' influential function in banks' CSR image construction, investors' expectations of corporate value and capital market performance.

3.4.2 Behavioral Finance

Behavioral finance is a theory that discusses the decision-making behavior of investors based on the psychological activities of investors (Shiller, 2003). Behavioral finance provides this study with theoretical basis for the relation between banks' CSR reports' discursive features and investors' decision-making behavior, as well as discursive features' influence on capital markets.

Modern finance began with Markowitz's portfolio selection theory in the early 1950s. Over the next 30 years, there have been important original theories, including the Modigliani-Miller theory on corporate finance, Efficient Market Theory, Option Pricing Theory, and Arbitrage Pricing Theory. These theories are developed on the basis of the hypothesis of the rational economic man. Finance that uses these theories is called classic finance. Classic finance in-depth discloses the operating rules of the financial markets. This has influenced the development of financial markets, as well as corporations' financial management practices (Xiao et al., 2016).

With the deeper academic exploration among financial research, an increasing number of empirical phenomena, being inconsistent with the classic financial theory, have been pointed out and have become the financial market's anomalies or unsolved mysteries. The further consideration of classical financial theory is driven by those empirical phenomena. Since decision-making behavior in reality is different from the rational economic person hypothesis, the rational economic man hypothesis is broadened based on the research results of psychology (Shiller, 2003). Further financial problems are studied on the basis of psychology. This leads to a new research direction in finance—behavioral finance.

The theoretical study of behavioral finance has found that investors' irrational trading behaviors and investors' psychological emotions often are correlated. Furthermore, irrational trading behaviors have a significant impact on market effectiveness. Behavioral finance uses psychological research to describe the irrationality of actors and to explain various phenomena in financial markets. The famous behavioral finance scholar Robert J. Shiller defines behavioral finance as follows: (1)

Behavioral finance is a discipline that combines psychology and decision theory with classical economics and finance; (2) behavioral finance attempts to explain the anomalies that are actually observed in the financial markets or that are contrary to the standard financial theory discussed in the financial literature; (3) behavioral finance studies how investors generate systemic deviations when making decisions (ibid).

Investigating investor behavior under realistic market conditions is the most basic and important topic in behavioral finance. Academic research in this field focuses on two main issues: First, do investors exhibit irrational behaviors that cannot be explained by classical finance theory in their investment decisions and trading behaviors? Second, can these so-called irrational investment behaviors be explained by investors' psychological biases?

All activities in human society, especially economic activities, are ultimately psychological games (ibid). The growth environment, experience, mentality, personality, ability to control emotions, judgment, and other psychological factors vary from person to person. According to behavioral finance, in the face of a complex external environment, cognitions will affect individuals' decisions regarding economic activities. The decision-making rationality of participants in economic behavior is relative, and irrationality is absolute. Taking stock investment for example, when people decide to buy stock in a company, they will not only be influenced by the company's basic financial information, such as existing and future earnings and P/E ratio. They are also influenced by perceived non-financial information, such as the content, the sentimental tendency and readability of CSR reports.

According to cognitive linguistics, language activates a wide range of cognitive processes. These processes are similar with other general human cognitive processes. Language can direct us to different understandings of the same situation (Langacker, 1987, 2001; Croft & Cruse, 2004). Thus, language will influence and shape one's cognitions, and influence one's investment decisions in economic activities. CSR reports' discursive features will shape investors' perceptions of corporate image, thus influencing their investment decisions after they read the CSR reports.

Since the investors of financial markets cannot obtain complete information, it is impossible to for them to analyze all the information and process complex judgments. Therefore, psychology believes that a heuristic method may be adopted during the actual decision-making process (Tversky & Kahneman, 1974). The way of knowing is to use simple methods for complicated problems. In the case of uncertainty, people will infer a result by grasping on to a certain feature a problem, irrespective of the true probability of this feature and other characteristics related to it. This approach is an effective way to help grasp the nature of a problem in many cases, but sometimes it may cause serious deviations (ibid).

The discursive features of CSR reports, which reflect CSR concepts, strategic development and the managerial group's attitudes towards corporate future development may influence investors' cognition, emotional attitudes towards corporate image, and valuation during their decision-making process. Thus, in certain degree, discursive features influence investors' expectations of corporate value and return on investment, from the perspective of behavioral finance.

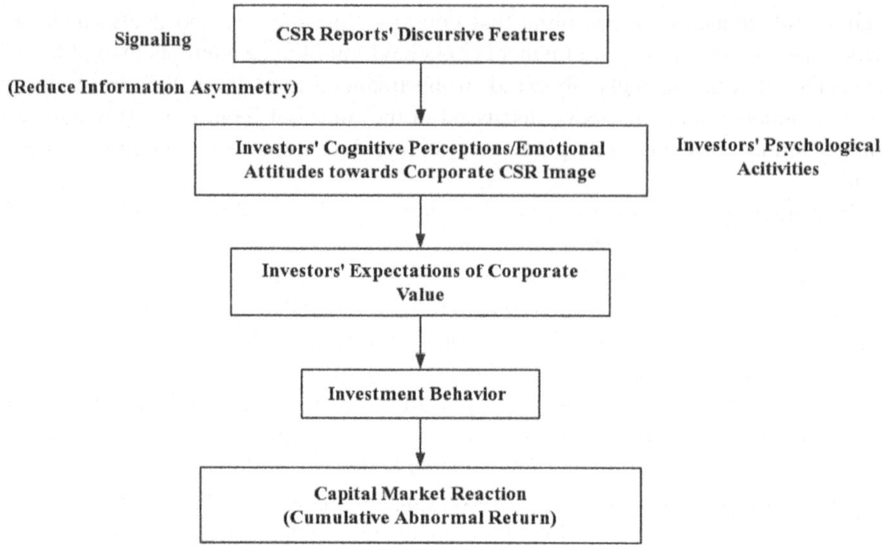

Fig. 3.12 The Influencing Mechanism of CSR Reports' Discursive Features on Capital Market Reaction

Based on signaling theory and behavioral finance, Fig. 3.12 illustrates the influencing mechanism of CSR reports' discursive features on capital market reaction (banks' stock price trend) in this study. Discursive features in CSR reports serve as signals that can transmit and influence the transmission of incremental information concerning companies' CSR values and performances and reduce the information asymmetry between stakeholders and companies. Thus it may influence investors' psychological activities (attitudes towards banks' CSR images and corporate value) during their decision-making process and bring effects on capital market reaction. This mechanism further analyzes and verifies language's function in economic practice as well as provides more suggestions for Chinese banks to achieve internationalization and corporate value enhancement. It also promotes the cross-disciplinary research in business discourse and sheds light on the research of capital market and behavioral finance.

3.5 A Proposed Analytical Model of This Study

This study's analytical model of the multi-dimensional discursive features in banks' CSR report for their CSR disclosure system refinement, CSR image construction and corporate value enhancement is integrated based on the multi-dimensional discourse evaluation framework of banks' CSR report for discursive CSR image construction, as shown in Fig. 3.11 and the influencing mechanism of CSR reports' discursive features on capital market reaction, as shown in Fig. 3.12.

The existing single-dimensional and single-perspective research into discourse evaluation analysis and corporate image construction via CSR reports in the fields of linguistics, management, and economics are unable to explain language's discursive functions in social and economic practice, such as corporate image construction, corporate financial performance and capital market performance. The integrated analytical model in this study is a further inter-disciplinary trial of the relations between CSR reports, CSR images construction and capital market performance under a "linguistic + management + economics" approach. It integrates theories from linguistics, management and economics, and promotes cross-disciplinary research in business discourse analysis. It also sheds light on research into organizational discourse, institutional identity construction, corporate governance, behavioral finance and capital market.

By establishing a multi-dimensional discourse evaluation framework of Chinese and American banks' CSR reports, the employment of various discursive features along the 4 dimensions of sentiment, readability, CSR keyword and visualization in Chinese and American banks' CSR reports are explored with the help of corpus and computer-assisted tools.

The discursive construction of Chinese and American banks' CSR image on 3 dimensions (CSR mind image, CSR behavior image and CSR visual image) are examined and compared in an inter-disciplinary approach based on linguistic theories of discourse and institutional identity, discourse appraisal theory, readability, corpus studies' keyword analysis as well as management theories of corporate identity system (CIS) and information asymmetry. CIS provides this study an "entry point" to integrate the multi-dimensional discursive features of banks' CSR report with the banks' discursive CSR image construction on 3 dimensions.

Additionally, legitimacy theory and stakeholder theory will be used to explain the differences of the discursively constructed CSR images between the Chinese and American banks under their unique political, social, economic, cultural and regulatory contexts.

Empirical research guided by signaling theory and behavioral finance will be conducted to investigate the effects of banks' image construction on capital markets. This will enable the examination and exploration of discursive features' influence on capital market performance. It will also provide cross-disciplinary corroboration of language's functions in economic practices: banks' CSR image construction and corporate value improvement (Fig. 3.13).

Enlightened by Biber's register analysis and MDA, a multi-dimensional discourse evaluation of various co-occurring discursive features in bank's CSR reports which exist in not only MDA's lexical and grammatical level but also syntactic, semantic, textual and discourse level is conducted. The multi-dimensional discourse evaluation framework in this study is a further application of Biber's register analysis and MDA. It expands Biber's MDA to other levels of language, but also applies Biber's register analysis and MDA to business discourse research.

The multi-dimensional discursive construction of Chinese and American banks' CSR image in this study is also enlightened by Chen's (2017) framework of Chinese and American universities' discursive construction of institutional identities. Chen's

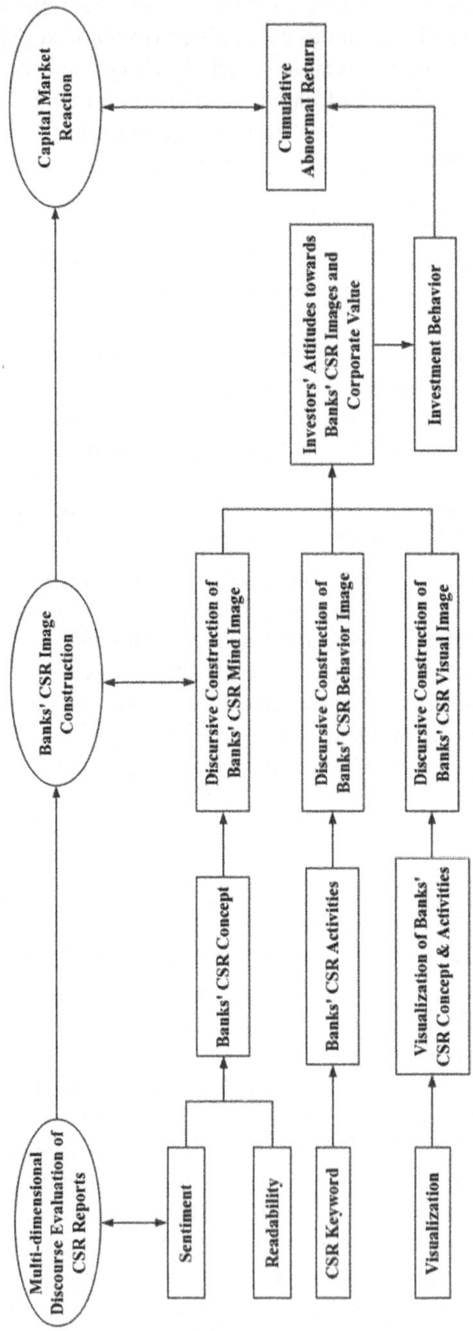

Fig. 3.13 Analytical model of this study

framework is expanded to the field of business discourse and corporate image construction in this study. The analytical model in this study also promotes the inter-disciplinary research in discourse and institutional identity.

Due to the similar generic features of the "report clan" concerning corporate disclosures given by Bhatia, the multi-dimensional discourse evaluation framework of banks' CSR reports for CSR image construction, the analytical model in this study can also be conducted for other industries' corporate image constructions through corporate narratives in various genres, such as annual reports, corporate culture brochures, mission statements, IPO prospectuses, earning-release conferences and calls.

Also, since the corporate identity system (CIS) has already been applied from corporate image to university image and national image, this study's multi-dimensional discourse evaluation framework can also be used to examine, for example, a university's image construction through its website or promotional brochure, China's national image construction through foreign publicity discourse in the new era.

Chapter 4
Research Methods

4.1 Corpus Data

The corpus in this study is made up of Chinese and American banks' CSR reports. Selection of banks in this study is according to the ranking of global banks for the year 2017 given by the magazine *The Banker* in the United Kingdom. Each year, *The Banker* ranks the world's top 1,000 banks according to banks' tier one capital, assets, capital/assets ratio, profitability, etc. It has become the most important and authoritative measure of the overall strength of global banks.

Based on the ranking from *The Banker* magazine and whether Chinese banks have published English versions CSR report for continuous 5 years (2013–2017), 5 years of CSR reports for 10 A-share listed Chinese banks and 10 American banks listed in New York Stock Exchange are selected as the research corpus (Since most Chinese banks have a short history in English version CSR report disclosure, only 5 years of English version CSR reports could be collected for this study.). Some American banks release Sustainability Reports or ESG Reports which have the same function as CSR reports. The selected corpus does not include the independent statements published by the accounting firms and the GRI index.

The 10 Chinese listed banks include, Industrial and Commercial Bank of China, China Construction Bank, Agricultural Bank of China, Bank of China, Bank of Communications, China Merchants Bank, China Industrial Bank, Shanghai Pudong Development Bank, China Minsheng Bank, China Citic Bank. 8 of the 10 selected Chinese banks are listed both in Hong Kong and Shanghai Stock Exchange. Thus most of the selected Chinese banks in this study are the international banks which are favored by the foreign investment since Hong Kong Stock Exchange is one of the most international investment markets, like American Stock Exchange. Thus the English version CSR reports of those listed Chinese banks will be followed with great interests by international investors.

M. Wan, *CSR Image Discursive Construction of Banks and the Effects on Capital Markets*,
https://doi.org/10.1007/978-981-19-6012-3_4

Also, in recent years, the two connecting schemes of Shanghai-Hong Kong Stock Connect and Shenzhen-Hong Kong Stock Connect provide foreign investment with almost full access to A-share market and booster the internalization of mainland capital market. As the crucial weighted stocks in A-share market, the 10 target Chinese banks will definitely embrace increasing international investment.

What's more, on May 15, 2018, MSCI, one of the largest and most authoritative index providers in the world, announced the inclusion of 234 stocks of A-share into the MSCI Emerging Markets Index. This will bring considerable foreign institutional investors' incremental funding to Chinese capital market. It is worth mentioning that 18 Chinese major commercial banks including the 10 target banks in this research are included in MSCI Emerging Markets Index and the market value of those 18 Chinese banks covers more than 70% of the market value of the 234 MSCI index stocks. All of these indicates that international investment is optimistic about development and return on investment of Chinese banks, thus Chinese banks will welcome a large number of foreign institutional investments. Additionally, MSCI mentioned that later on they will carry on a continuous ESG index evaluation (Environment, Social and Governance) of the chosen Chinese companies and the listed companies who fail in the ESG evaluation perhaps will be removed from MSCI index. Thus the English version CSR reports, the most important means for Chinese banks to disclose their ESG performance to international stakeholders, will become the vital reference and focus when foreign investors make their investment decisions.

The corpus of 50 English version CSR reports from 10 Chinese listed banks is referred as CSR-C and the corpus of 50 CSR reports from 10 American listed banks is regarded as CSR-A in Table 4.1. The time range is 2013–2017. CSR-C contains 1,936,471 tokens; CSR-A contains 1,267,392 tokens.

All the CSR reports in this study were obtained from banks' websites, the website of the Hong Kong Stock Exchange, American' Electronic Data Gathering or Analysis and Retrieval System (Edgar). In addition, the author also called or emailed banks' Investors Relation Departments and asked them for one or two years' of unreleased CSR reports after stating they would be used for academic research.

4.2 Research Tools

4.2.1 DICTION

DICTION 7.1.3 is used to measure the sentimental tendencies of Chinese and American banks' CSR reports.

Currently, there are more and more computer-assisted content analysis methods, and most programs are based on word frequency statistics. DICTION is a computer-assisted content analysis program based on linguistic theory. It was developed by Roderick Hart, an expert in politics and mass media. DICTION uses a series of dictionaries to search a passage for five semantic features—Activity, Optimism,

Table 4.1 The corpus source of Chinese and American Banks' CSR reports

Classification	List of banks
Chinese Banks (CSR-C)	1. Industrial and Commercial Bank of China (ICBC) 2. China Construction Bank (CCB) 3. Agricultural Bank of China (ABC) 4. Bank of China (BOC) 5. Bank of Communications (BOCOM) 6. China Merchants Bank (CMB) 7. China Industrial Bank (CIB) 8. Shanghai Pudong Development Bank (SPDB) 9. China Minsheng Bank (CMBC) 10. China Citic Bank (CNCB)
American Banks (CSR-A)	1. JPMorgan Chase & Co. 2. Bank of America 3. Citigroup 4. Wells Fargo & Co. 5. Goldman Sachs 6. Morgan Stanley 7. Bank of New York Melleon 8. American Express Company 9. PNC Financial Services Group 10. State Street Corp.

Certainty, Realism and Commonality—based on 31 wordlists with different characteristics embedded in DICTION. DICTION uses predefined dictionaries and can use up to 30 custom dictionaries built with user defined words, such as topical or negative words, for particular research needs. DICTION can be used to automatically analyze sentimental characteristics of the sample text.

4.2.2 Coh-Metrix

Coh-Metrix is used to measure some of the readability indicators of Chinese and American banks' CSR reports.

Coh-Metrix is a computational tool that produces indices of the linguistic and discourse representations of a text. Developed by Dr. Arthur C. Graesser and Danielle McNamara, distinguished linguists who specialize in discourse analysis, cognitive scientific, and syntax. Coh-Metrix can generate 106 linguistic indicators in 10 dimensions, mainly measuring text cohesion and readability: descriptive, reading ease, principle component, reference cohesion, LSA (latent semantic analysis space), lexical diversity, connectives, situation model, syntactic complexity, word formation, and readability. Coh-Metrix calculates the coherence of texts along many measures. Coh-Metrix analyzes texts based on over 200 indicators of cohesion, language, and readability. Its modules use lexicons, part-of-speech classifiers, syntactic parsers, templates, corpora, latent semantic analysis, and other components that are widely used in computational linguistics (Graesser & McNamara, 2011; Graesser et al., 2004). Standard text readability formulas scale texts by relying on word and sentence length, whereas Coh-Metrix is sensitive to cohesion relations, world knowledge, and language and discourse characteristics (ibid).

4.2.3 Antconc and WordSmith

Antconc's keyword function is used for CSR keyword evaluation in Chinese and American banks' CSR reports when compared to the general English corpus. Antconc is a freeware corpus analysis tool for concordance and text analysis developed by Dr. Laurence Anthony. It provides the 7 functions of concordance, concordance plot, file view, clusters/N-Gram, collocate, word list and keyword list which have been used widely in corpus linguistics for textual analysis. Antconc provides a list of all the negative keywords which did not occur in the target corpus, but less frequently than would have been expected by chance alone when compared to the reference corpus (Baker, 2006). As Baker says, "a keyword is only available to researchers in the form of language, in order to answer specific research questions, researchers must carry out in-depth explanations" (ibid). Therefore, after CSR keyword extraction, the keywords need to be placed in the context of the CSR report and combined with Antconc's concordance function to conduct a qualitative study of quantitative language patterns (Hu, 2015a). This can reveal Chinese and American banks' CSR behavior in specific contexts. Concordance tools are also used for the calculation of the frequency of CSR keywords.

Similar with Antconc, WordSmith is a comprehensive corpus analysis tool for textual analysis. It was developed by Mike Scott (Scott, 2004). WordSmith has three main functions: Concord, Wordlist and Keywords. WordSmith can also calculate some basic statistical information from a text, such as the mean word length, mean sentence length, type/token ratio, and standardized type/token ratio (STTR). In this study WordSmith is used for the statistical description of some readability indicators (lexical density, mean word length, mean sentence length) in Chinese and American banks' CSR reports.

4.2.4 Event Study

As a statistical method, event analysis is used to study whether a stock price will fluctuate after the occurrence of a market event, and whether it will generate abnormal returns and market value.

Economists are always trying to answer the question of how to measure the impact of economic events on corporate value, and the emergence of event analysis solves this problem. Because the event analysis method is objective and simple, it has been widely applied to companies and various market events in the fields of finance, economics, and management. Examples include applications to earnings announcements, non-financial announcements, mergers and acquisitions, and new shares issuance. The use of event analysis has also made important achievements in the practical exploration of effective financial markets. In addition, the event analysis method is widely used in the legal field to explore changes in the market value of enterprises when policy regulatory environments change. Therefore, by collecting financial market data in a short period of time, event analysis can measure the economic impact of certain events.

In the field of capital market research, the event study method focuses on the impact of events (such as mergers, acquisitions, earnings announcements, or refinancing activities) on capital markets, stock prices (or corporate value). The impact can be reflected in aspects such as average stock price effect, changes in market return variance, cumulative abnormal return, changes in stock trading volume, and changes in operating (accounting) performance (Zhang, 2013). In this study, event study is used to examine the effect of discursive features used to discursively construct banks' CSR image in their CSR report in capital markets This effect is measured by cumulative abnormal return (CAR).

The event analysis method typically includes the following steps: (1) definition of event and event windows; (2) determination of the research sample; (3) estimation of normal return; (4) measurement of abnormal returns. (5) significance test of abnormal return (ibid).

By using Chinese and American banks' CSR reports from 2013 to 2017 as the research sample, event study is used to test the cumulative abnormal return of banks' stock within 30 days after their CSR report disclosure. This is used to examine capital markets' reactions to CSR reports' discursive features or CSR reports' discursive features' influence on capital markets.

4.2.4.1 Selection of Event Window and Estimation Window

This research uses the event analysis method to study the impact of an event—banks' disclosure of CSR reports' effect on the cumulative abnormal return (CAR) rate of banks' stock. The public release date of banks' CSR reports is used as the event date, and the time of the day is defined as $t = 0$. The investigation period selected for the whole event is [−180, 30]. The estimation window is set as [−180, −1]—that is 180 days before the selected event date to 1 day before the event date. The event window is set from the selected event date to 30 days after the event date, that is, [0, 30].

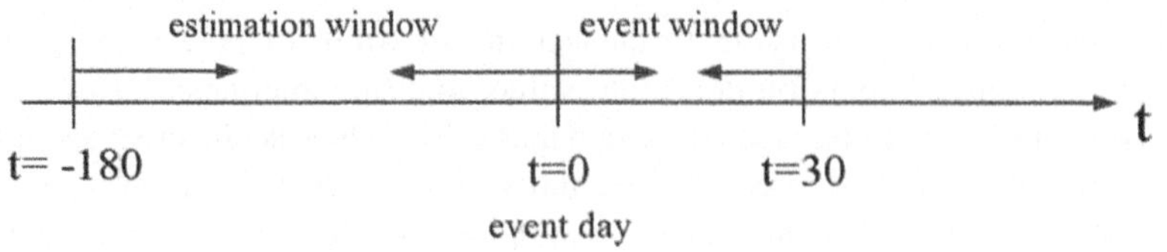

Fig. 4.1 Timeline diagram of event analysis

According to the market model, the abnormal return rate is obtained by using the stock's actual rate of return to subtract the normal rate of return estimated from the absence of the event. The abnormal rate of return is used to measure the bank's CSR reports' influences or effects on bank's stock price trend and capital market performance (Fig. 4.1).

4.2.4.2 Calculation of Normal and Abnormal Return

The abnormal rate of return is equal to the difference between the actual rate of return of the stock in the event window and the normal rate of return calculated using the estimation window. It is important to choose the appropriate model to calculate the normal rate of return for the unbiasedness of the outcome of cumulative abnormal return rates. In the event analysis method, the methods used to estimate the normal rate of return include the mean value adjustment method, the market adjustment method, and the capital market model method.

(1) Mean value adjustment method. This method assumes that the return rate of a certain security in the estimation window is equal to a constant and that the returns of different stocks are not equal. Also, a non-event window period that is not affected by the event is selected to calculate the return of each stock.
(2) Market adjustment method (Index Method). This model assumes that the ex-ante returns are equal and that the normal return of each stock equals the return of the Market Index. Although this method is simple, there are some problems. Due to the different development stages and operating efficiencies of different companies, the companies' stock price growth rates are also different. Some companies' returns exceed the Market Index return rate, which may be misjudged as an abnormal return of the stock.
(3) Capital market model method (CAPM Method). This method calculates the normal rate of return on the theoretical basis of the capital asset pricing model (CAPM). The stock's return is calculated using the stock price data in the estimated window. The return data of the estimation window is used, combined with the market model:

$$R_{it} = \alpha_i + \beta_i R_{mt} + \varepsilon_{it} \tag{4.1}$$

In formula 4.1, the least squares linear regression method is used to estimate the parameters and α_i and β_i are obtain, among which $E(\varepsilon_{\text{it}}) = 0$, $\text{Var}(\varepsilon_{\text{it}}) = \sigma^2$.

$R_{\text{it}}$and R_{mt} are the actual rate of return of the securities i and the market index m in the t period. ε_{it} is the disturbance term. Its mean is 0 and variance is σ^2. α_i and β_i are the parameters in the market model. The formula for calculating the normal rate of return for stocks in the event window is as follows:

$$E[R_{\text{it}}] = \alpha_i + \beta_i R_{\text{mt}} \tag{4.2}$$

The formula for calculating the abnormal return rate of individual stocks i in the event window on t day is as follows:

$$\text{AR}_{\text{it}} = R_{\text{it}} - E[R_{\text{it}}] \tag{4.3}$$

The formula for calculating the cumulative abnormal return (CAR) rate of the i-th stock during the window period is as follows:

$$\text{CAR}_i = \sum \text{AR}_{\text{it}} \tag{4.4}$$

The cumulative return of all sample stocks is calculated as follows (where N is the number of sample companies):

$$\text{CAR}_t = \sum_{1}^{N} \text{AR}_{\text{it}} \tag{4.5}$$

The cumulative average excess return for all sample stocks is calculated as follows:

$$\text{CAAR}_t = \sum_{n}^{t} \text{AAR}$$

$$\text{AAR}_t = 1/N \sum_{1}^{N} \text{AAR} \tag{4.6}$$

Most scholars, both in China and overseas, have chosen the CAPM model to estimate the normal rate of return. Therefore, the CAPM model is also used in this research, as the estimation model of normal rate of return.

The rate of return is calculated using the ratio between the closing price of the day and the closing price of the previous trading day.

In this study, stock price data of 10 Chinese banks listed on the Shanghai Stock Exchange and 10 American banks listed on the New York Stock Exchange before and after their release for the years 2013–2017 CSR reports are selected from the CSMAR and Wind databases. We collect the closing price of individual stocks i at the time point t P_{it} and Q_{it}, the closing price of the Market Index (the A-share market uses the Shanghai and Shenzhen 300 Index-CSI 300, and the US stock market uses the New York Stock Exchange US 100 Fund Index) and calculate the daily return of individual stocks i and Market Index m: R_{it} and R_{mt}. The calculation formulas used are:

$$R_{\text{it}} = \frac{P_{\text{it}}}{P_{\text{it}-1}} - 1 \tag{4.7}$$

$$R_{\text{mt}} = \frac{Q_{\text{it}}}{Q_{\text{it}-1}} - 1 \tag{4.8}$$

In Formula 4.7, P_{it} indicates the closing price of the i-th stock on t day; $P_{\text{it}-1}$ indicates the closing price of the i-th stock on $t - 1$; if the Ex-Dividend is encountered, the stock price after Restoration of Rights is used. The dividend-paying factor in the stock is removed, and the stock price without the dividend is used.

With the data of the estimation window, the CAPM model is used, that is, the parameters in the model are obtained by least squares estimation. Then, the market index return rate of the window period is input into the model to obtain the normal rate of return for the window period. The excess return rate AR_{it} of individual stocks i in the event window is calculated according to Formula 4.3. The cumulative excess return rate CAR_t is calculated for all sample stocks according to Formula 4.5, and the cumulative average excess return rate CAR_t is calculated according to Formula 4.6.

4.2.4.3 T-Test

A single-sample T-test was conducted on the annual average cumulative abnormal return rate for all selected sample banks from 2013 to 2017. The single-sample T-test was used to test whether the annual average cumulative abnormal return rate for each bank from 2013 to 2017 was significantly different from 0 or not. The test hypothesis is $H_0 : \text{CAR}_i = 0$and the test statistic is t_{CAR}. If the $t_{\text{CAR}} > 0$ test result did not equal zero, there were two possibilities. If $t_{\text{CAR}} > 0$, it shows that this event—CSR report had a positive impact on the stock CAR rate, which increases the stock's rate of return; If $t_{\text{CAR}} < 0$, it shows that this event—the disclosure of CSR reports, also the various discursive features in CSR report, may have a negative impact on the stock CAR rate, which reduces the stock's rate of return. If $t_{\text{CAR}} = 0$, the null hypothesis is accepted, and the disclosure of CSR reports has no effect on the stock's return. In the T-test, the constructed t statistic is:

$$t_{\mathrm{CAR}} = \frac{\mathrm{CAR}_i}{\frac{S(\mathrm{CAR}_i)}{\sqrt{n}}} \tag{4.9}$$

In the above formula, n is the number of event windows, $t = 0, 1, 2, 3, 4 \ldots 30$.

4.2.5 Gray Relational Entropy Analysis Model

Grey correlation analysis is used primarily in the multi-factor analysis of gray systems. A gray system is a concept which differs from the white system and the black system. A white system refers to a system with sufficient information. A black system represents a system in which the structure is unclear, and a gray system is somewhere in between: some information is clear, and some is not clear (Deng, 1990). Many information systems in the real world have the characteristics of distinct gray systems.

This dissertation examines the relationship between various discursive features of banks' CSR reports and their influence on capital markets after the release of the 10 Chinese and 10 American listed banks' CSR reports from 2013 to 2017. This is a typical small-sample-size problem which reflects inaccurate, incomplete, and gray information, thus adopting grey system theory to evaluate various discursive features' affecting or contributing to capital market (banks stocks' CAR) is suitable.

Gray relational analysis is an effective method, and is based on the microscopic or macroscopic geometric approximation of the behavioral factor sequence. This analyzes the degree of correlation between the factors and confirms the degree of contribution from the factor to the main behavior (ibid). Grey relation analysis can be used to evaluate the original data directly, and does not require additional interactions during the process. This method has been widely used in many applications concerning performance evaluations and multi-criteria decision-making. It has been used primarily for the optimization of location issues, online learning performance, companies' financial performance and product's design concept evaluation (Li, 2005; Chou & Tsai, 2009; Zhai et al., 2009).

The grey entropy method is an objective weighting technique without rigorous statistical requirements and assumptions. Gray relational entropy analysis (GREA) is a method developed on the basis of gray relational analysis. It can compensate the partial association tendencies, and the loss of personalized information, in gray relational analysis (Zhang et al., 1996). GREA is more scientific and reasonable than gray correlation analysis, in certain degree.

This study employs the grey relation entropy analysis of Wen et al. (1998), to evaluate CSR report' multi-dimensional discursive features' different affecting degrees on capital market performances (CAR). This study looks for different correlation degrees between banks' CSR reports' different discursive features and banks' stock price change (CAR) through gray relational entropy analysis. To be specific, grey relation entropy analysis is used to objectively evaluate which discursive features have more effects on capital market or contribute more to the CAR of banks' stocks. Thus, the CSR reports' discursive features with higher degrees of correlation need to be valued by banks in order to attract more investment, achieve more capital market return and improve banks' CSR images and corporate value discursively.

The mathematical model for GREA is as follows:

(1) Calculating the Gray Correlation Coefficient

$X_0{}^* = [X_0{}^*(1), X_0{}^*(2), ..., X_0{}^*(n)]$ is set as the reference sequence. In this study, the cumulative abnormal return is the reference sequence. $X_j{}^* = [X_j{}^*(1), X_j{}^*(2), ..., X_j{}^*(n)]$ is set as the corresponding comparison sequence. In this study, various discursive features along 4 dimensions of CSR reports are the comparison sequences. $j = 1, 2, ..., m$. To eliminate the different effects of the units, initialization is required by computing:

$$
\begin{aligned}
&X_i(k) = X_i^*(k)/X_i^*(1)\\
&k = 1, 2, \ldots, n\\
&i = 0, 1, 2 \ldots m
\end{aligned}
\tag{4.10}
$$

This outputs $\Delta_{\min} = \min_j \min_k |X_0(k) - X_j(k)|$ and $\Delta_{\max} = \max_j \max_k |X_0(k) - X_j(k)|$.

Conduct $\Delta_{\min} = \min_j \min_k |X_0(k) - X_j(k)|$, $\Delta_{\max} = \max_j \max_k |X_0(k) - X_j(k)|$. Then the gray correlation coefficient is obtained between each comparison sequence and reference sequence:

$$
\zeta_{jk} = \frac{\Delta_{\min} + \rho\Delta_{\max}}{|X_0(k) - X_j(k)| + \rho\Delta_{\min}}
\tag{4.11}
$$

In the above formula, ρ is the distinguishing coefficient, $\rho \in (0, 1)$. Generally $\rho = 0.5$ is adopted in the simplified calculations. In order to avoid the calculation of abnormalities, and to increase the ability to distinguish and reflect the integrity of the system, ρ is valued according to the following principles. Set Δ as the absolute value of all the difference, that is:

$$
\Delta = \left\{ \sum_{j=1}^{m} \sum_{k=1}^{n} |X_0(k) - X_j(k)| \right\} / (\mathrm{m} \times \mathrm{n})
\tag{4.12}
$$

And record $\varepsilon = \Delta/\Delta_{\max}$, When $\Delta_{\max} > 3\Delta$, $\varepsilon \le \rho < 1.5\varepsilon$; When $\Delta_{\max} \le 3\Delta$, $1.5\varepsilon \le \rho \le 2\varepsilon$.

(2) Calculating the Gray Correlation Entropy and Entropy Correlation Degree

The gray correlation coefficients of the comparison sequences and the reference sequences are mapped to obtain the gray correlation coefficient distribution map:

$$P_{jh} = \zeta_{jh} / \sum_{k=1}^{n} \zeta_{jk}, h = 1, 2, \ldots, n \tag{4.13}$$

Thus, the gray relational entropy for P_{jh} as the attribute information is obtained.

$$H_{jh} = -\sum_{h=1}^{n} P_{jh} \ln P_{jh} \tag{4.14}$$

The gray entropy and the Shannon information entropy have the same structure and properties. When the attributes of P_{jh} are equal, the gray correlation coefficient distribution is the most normal and the gray entropy reaches the maximum value. This value is independent from the sequence attribute and is only related to the number of attribute elements. Conduct $H_m = \ln n$ and then the entropy correlation degree of each comparison sequences is obtained.

$$E_{jh} = H_{jh} / H_m \tag{4.15}$$

According to the above calculation, the ranking criterion which determines the gray correlation sequence is derived. When gray correlation entropy and the entropy degree of the comparison sequences are big, the gray relation coefficient mapping of the comparison sequences and the reference sequences is more balanced. The higher the degree of coincidence with the reference sequence, the greater the relevance between the comparison sequences and the reference sequences, and the more contribution that the comparison sequence (multi-dimensional discursive features) has made to the development of reference sequence (abnormal cumulative return of banks' stock).

4.3 Data Selection and Processing

Data selection and processing includes the selection and processing of discursive indicators, indicators of capital market reaction, and gray relational entropy model indicators.

4.3.1 Selection and Processing of Discursive Indicators

The selection and processing of discursive indicators refer to the selection and processing of various discursive features in the multi-dimensional discourse evaluation of banks' CSR reports for banks' CSR disclosure improvement, CSR image construction and corporate value enhancement.

4.3.1.1 Sentimental Evaluation Indicators

This study uses the automatic analysis software DICTION 7.1.3 for textual sentiment analysis. DICTION's embedded wordlist is used to measure the sentimental tendencies between the CSR reports of Chinese and American banks. DICTION can measure 5 sentimental indicators of the input texts based on the inputted sentimental wordlist or embedded sentimental wordlist. DICTION's 5 sentimental evaluation indicators are Certainty, Optimism, Activity, Realism, and Commonality. Thus, those above five sentimental tendencies in CSR reports are selected as the sentimental evaluation indicators to investigate banks' CSR mind image construction in this study. According to DICTION, 5 sentimental indicators refer to:

- **Certainty** = Language indicating resoluteness, inflexibility, and completeness and a tendency to speak ex cathedra.
- **Activity** = Language featuring movement, change, the implementation of ideas and the avoidance of inertia.
- **Optimism** = Language endorsing some person, group, concept or event, or highlighting their positive entailments.
- **Realism** = Language describing tangible, immediate, recognizable matters that affect people's everyday lives.
- **Commonality** = Language highlighting the agreed-upon values of a group and rejecting idiosyncratic modes of engagement.

4.3.1.2 Readability Evaluation Indicators

Discourse studies suggest that indicators of discursive features affect the effectiveness of discourse communication. Complexity is one of the factors that affect the communicative validity of the comprehensibility of discourse. The readability of CSR reports influence stakeholders' perceptive efficiency of CSR information. Thereupon, they influence stakeholders' attitudes towards corporate value and images. Lexical complexity and syntactic complexity refer to vocabulary and syntactic features that affect text comprehensibility, such as lexical length, sentence length, and syntactical structures (Smith & Taffler, 2000).

Cohesion is a characteristic of the text. Usually long and complex sentence contains comparatively more connectives. Cohesion of the discourse influences readers' understanding and perception of text content (Graesser & Mcnamara, 2011). Connectives provide clues about text organization, which is vital in the creation of cohesive links between ideas and clauses. Connectives are crucial indicators in the assessment of cohesion. Thus, the density of connectives as well as the various subcategories of connectives requires focused (Graesser et al., 2004). Graesser et al. (ibid) divide connectives into clarifying connectives, logical connectives, additive connectives, temporal connectives, causal connectives, adversative and contrastive connectives, expanded temporal connectives, positive and negative connectives. Coh-Metrix provides an incidence score (occurrence per 1,000 words) for all connectives (CNCAll) as well as the incidence score for different types of connectives. Indices

Table 4.2 Readability evaluation variables and indicators

Evaluation variables	Evaluation indicators	Statistical indicators
Lexical readability	Lexical density	Standardized type/token ratio
	Mean word length	Mean word length (counted by letter)
Syntactic readability	Mean sentence length	Mean sentence length (measured by word number)
	Cohesion	All connectives incidence
Textual readability	Flesch reading ease	Flesch reading ease indicator
	Flesch-Kincaid grade level	Flesch-Kincaid grade level indicator

are provided on five general classes of connectives (Halliday & Hasan, 1976): causal (because, so), logical (and, or), adversative/contrastive (although, whereas), temporal (first, until), and additive (and, moreover). In addition, there is a distinction between positive connectives (also, moreover) and negative connectives (however, but).

Based on Wang and Li's (2018) and Liu's (2017) selection of readability indicators, as well as Graesser et al.'s (2004) conceptions of cohesion and readability, CSR reports' readability evaluation is investigated along 3 dimensional variables: lexical, syntactic and textual readability. All readability indicators of CSR reports are processed by Coh-Metrix and WordSmith. Readability evaluation indicators for each dimension are shown in the following Table 4.2.

4.3.1.3 Keyword Evaluation Indicators

Keywords can reflect the unique thematic features of one corpus against another. the corpus used in this study as a reference corpus for banks' CSR reports is a general English corpus which contains two corpora: British English BE06 and American English AmE06. This is done in order to find the unique "aboutness" of banks' CSR reports. These corpuses have been developed by the famous scholar in the field of corpus linguistics, Professor Paul Baker from Lancaster University. AmE06 and BE06, published between the years 2003 and 2008 contain 2,059,753 words and 1,000 written text. Each text contains around 2,000 words. The BE06 Corpus is a one-million-word corpus of published material written in common British English. The AmE06 Corpus is a one-million-word corpus of published material written in common American English. Both consist of 500 files of 2,000 word samples taken from 15 genres of writing (Baker, 2006). AmE06 and BE06 have the same sampling frame as the LOB and FLOB corpora and include 15 sub-categories: news reports (A); Editorials (B); News comments (C); Religion (D); Technology, business and hobbies (E); Popular social life (F); Biography and essay (G); Others: government documents and industrial reports (H); Academic papers (J); General novels (K); Detective novels (L); Fiction novels (M); Adventure and Western novels (N); Love novels (P); And humor (R).

First, the general English corpus (AmE06 and BE06) was used as the reference corpus, and the two corpora of CSR reports from Chinese banks (CSR-C) and American banks (CSR-A) were used as the observing corpora. This generated the unique keyword lists (top 50 keywords) from Chinese and American banks' CSR reports based on Antconc's keyword function.

Next, based on CSR database CSRhub's classification of commercial banks' CSR performance and Zhu's (2009) framework of commercial banks' CSR performance, CSR keyword lists of CSR-C and CSR-A are selected and classified into 4 categories: CSR keywords pertaining to "community and society", "employees", "environment" and "corporate governance". These reflect banks' CSR behavior concerning communities, employees, the environment, and corporate governance, respectively, at the content level. Those 4 types of CSR keywords reflect Chinese and American banks' different CSR behaviors which convey banks' CSR behavior images. Thus, the CSR keywords in CSR-C and CSR-A help examine Chinese and American banks' different contents of CSR performance, at the linguistic level.

Keyword indicators in this study refer to the frequency rate of each kind of CSR keyword in Chinese and American banks' CSR reports, and the frequency rate of CSR keywords concerning "community and society", "employees"; "the environment"; and "corporate governance".

4.3.1.4 Visual Evaluation Indicators

The construction of meaning in CSR reports is realized by the integration of two semiotic resources, visual and verbal modes. CSR reports are accompanied by many pictures which visually present banks' CSR value and performance, which not only enrich the textual content, but also make the report colorful and convincing. At the same time, it also express banks' CSR visual image to the stakeholders. The visual evaluation indicator of CSR reports is measured by the number of pictures illustrated on the cover and content of CSR reports. The number of pictures is processed according to Ji et al.'s (2016) standardized processing method. CSR visual score = number of pictures in one CSR report/ (the maximum number of pictures in the CSR report − the minimum number of pictures in the CSR report). The visual scores in each Chinese and American banks' CSR reports (100 reports) are calculated. Then, the mean score of Chinese banks' CSR reports (50 reports) and American banks' CSR reports (50 reports) are collected as visual indicators of Chinese and American banks' CSR reports.

4.3.2 Selection and Processing of Indicators of Capital Market Reaction

Indicators of capital market reaction are used to measure the actual effect of CSR reports and discursive construction of banks' CSR image on capital market performance. In this study, this refers to banks' stock price change after CSR disclosure. Stock price data of 10 A-share listed Chinese banks and 10 American banks listed in New York Stock Exchange before and after their release for the years 2013–2017 CSR reports are obtained from the CSMAR and Wind databases. An event study is conducted to analyze the influences CSR disclosure; also discursive construction of banks' CSR images brings to capital market. This actual effect refers to capital market reaction after banks' CSR disclosure as measured by cumulative abnormal return. We set the day when banks release CSR report as the event day, 30 days after CSR disclosure as the event window, and 180 days before CSR disclosure as the estimation window. The annual average cumulative abnormal return within 30 days after the release of CSR reports of Chinese banks and American banks during the years 2013–2017 as calculated by event study are the indicators of capital market reaction in this study.

Usually, Chinese banks will release their CSR reports together with their annual reports. The China Securities Regulatory Commission (CSRC) requests that each listed company release its annual reports by the end of April every year. As for American banks, there is no compulsory deadline for the disclosure of annual reports or CSR reports from the U.S. Securities and Exchange Commission (SEC). Thus, the dates of American banks' CSR disclosure are flexible.

4.3.3 Selection and Processing of the Gray Relational Entropy Model's Indicators

This study tries to find different correlation degrees between CSR reports' multi-dimensional discursive features and stocks' price trends (cumulative abnormal return) of Chinese and American banks through gray relational entropy analysis in order to examine various discursive features' contribution degree or influential degree to capital market performance.

16 multi-dimensional discursive indicators on 4 dimensions in banks' CSR reports are used: sentimental tendencies of Activity, Optimism, Certainty, Realism, Commonality in sentiment evaluation; lexical density, mean word length, mean sentence length, cohesion, Flesch Reading Ease, Flesch-Kincaid Grade Level in readability evaluation; CSR keyword categories of "communities and society", "employee", "environment", "corporate governance" in CSR keywords evaluation, visualization in visual evaluation of CSR report as comparison sequences. Banks' stock' cumulative abnormal return within 30 days after CSR disclosure is used as the reference sequence. Empirical research of different correlation degrees between

comparison sequences and reference sequence is conducted by gray relational entropy analysis in order to compare and examine banks' CSR reports' discursive features' affecting degree on capital market performance.

4.4 Research Procedures

Since discourse is a carrier of corporate image transmission, an interdisciplinary research is conducted to resolve banks' image construction issues discursively by exploring the multi-dimensional discursive features in banks' CSR reports. A pilot study, related literature and the theory reviewed above show that various discursive features along the dimensions of sentiment, readability, CSR keyword and visualization, in banks' CSR report may shape and reflect banks' CSR mind image, CSR behavior image and CSR visual image. They then influence stakeholders' conceptions of bank image and valuation. First, the multi-dimensional discourse evaluation framework of Chinese and American banks' CSR reports is integrated. This interdisciplinary framework can help banks improve their CSR disclosure system and CSR images discursively.

Then the study conducts a quantitative analysis to investigate, describe and contrast various discursive features in Chinese and American banks' CSR reports. The corpus and computer-assisted tools (DICTION, Coh-Metrix, Antconc, WordSmith) are used to investigate and evaluate Chinese and American banks' CSR reports' multi-dimensional discursive features along the dimensions of sentiment, readability, CSR keywords and visual evaluation. (1) The computer program DICTION is used to measure Chinese and American banks' sentimental tendencies. DICTION's 5 sentimental indicators: Certainty, Optimism, Activity, Realism and Commonality are adopted. (2) Coh-Metrix, which integrates the technologies of computational linguistics and corpus linguistics, is used to measure the part of readability indicators of cohesion, Flesch Reading Ease, Flesch-Kincaid Grade Level in Chinese and American banks' CSR reports. WordSmith is used to calculate the readability indicators of STTR, mean word length and mean sentence length. (3) The combination of AmE06 and BE06 is used as the referential corpus to examine 4 categories of keyword features ("community and society", "employees", "environment" and "corporate governance") of the two observed corpuses: CSR-C and the CSR-A based on Antconc's keyword function, in order to uncover banks' unique CSR behaviors and CSR content. (4) The visual values of Chinese and American banks' CSR reports are calculated by the number of pictures and processed according to standard formula in Ji et al. (2016). Independent Sample T-test is used to measure whether there are significant differences of multi-dimensional discursive features between Chinese and American banks' CSR reports.

Additionally, based on the outcomes of quantitative analysis, this study conducts a qualitative examination to explain how multi-dimensional discursive features construct and transmit Chinese and American banks' CSR images discursively by investigating the specific discursive contexts in which those linguistic features situated with a "linguistic + management" approach. Without such close qualitative analysis, corpus and computer-assisted automatic analysis may miss important information. The corporate identity system (CIS), the theory of institutional identity, linguistic theories behind discursive features are used to explain how Chinese and American banks discursively construct their CSR mind images, CSR behavior images and CSR visual images. Through the discursive features that realizes sentiment and readability, CSR reports can implicitly and explicitly reflect and construct banks' CSR concepts, development strategies, and corporate philosophy. These are the major components of banks' CSR mind image. CSR keywords in CSR reports can reflect banks' CSR activities which present banks' CSR behavior images. Visual resource used in CSR reports can reflect and evaluate the visual presentation of banks' CSR, which is part of their CSR visual image. At the same time, information asymmetry theory will be used to explain and corroborate the discursive construction of Chinese and American banks' CSR image from perspective of management.

Legitimacy theory and stakeholder theory will be used to explain reasons behind the different discursively constructed images of Chinese and American banks, via CSR disclosure under their different social, cultural, economic, political and regulatory contexts.

Moreover, event study in the field of economics is conducted to measure the actual effect that CSR reports' discursive features, also the discursive construction of CSR images bring to market guided by signaling theory and behavioral finance. This actual effect is calculated by cumulative abnormal return (CAR) of banks' stock price within 30 days after the release of their CSR report, regarding discursive features in CSR report as the signal/event which influences investors' perceptions of banks' image and expectations of corporate value. Event study further explains and corroborates discursive features' functions in banks' CSR image construction and influences on capital markets from an interdisciplinary perspective.

Finally, an empirical study is conducted on the ranking of affecting degrees between various discursive features and capital market performance based on gray relational entropy analysis. The empirical study provides more advices for banks' improvement of CSR disclosure systems and international CSR image construction, as well as corporate value enhancement.

The research procedures in this study, as shown in Fig. 4.2, also follows Fariclough's three-dimensional model: description, interpretation and explanation.

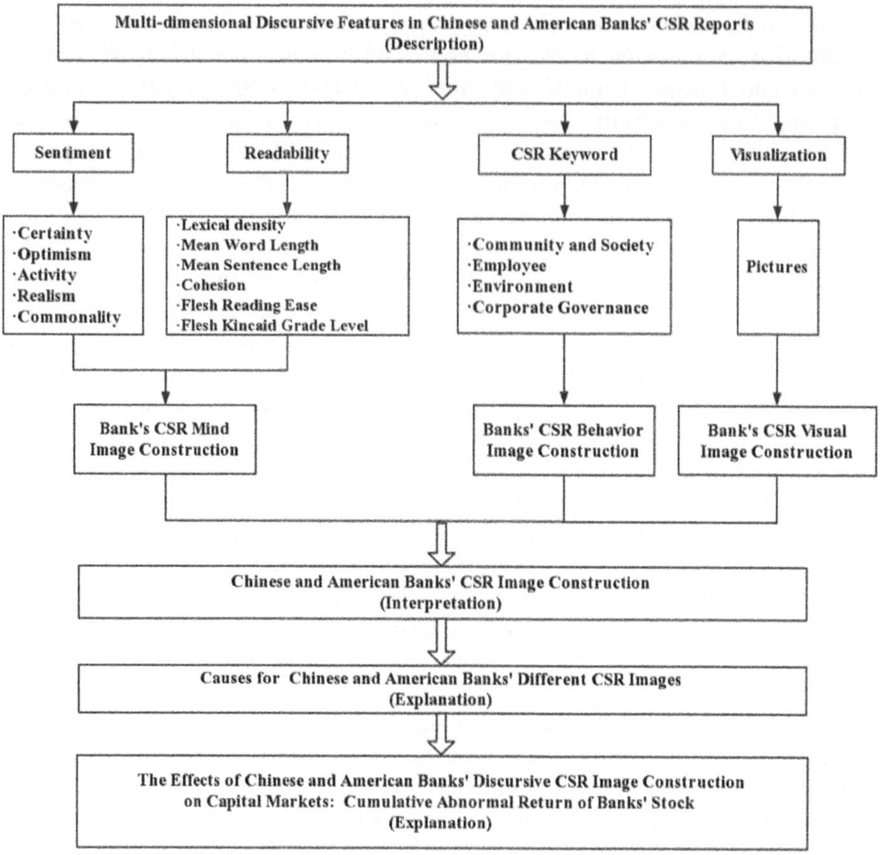

Fig. 4.2 Research procedures of this study

Chapter 5
A Descriptive Study of Multi-dimensional Discursive Features in Chinese and American Banks' CSR Reports

This chapter will answer the first research question in this study: What are the differences of the multi-dimensional discursive features between Chinese and American banks' CSR reports? This question will be addressed by examining, describing the multi-dimensional discursive features in Chinese and American banks' CSR reports respectively in the first place, and comparing their different discursive features in the second place.

Due to the different social, cultural, political and economic contexts in which Chinese and American banks are located, they have different organizational practices. This includes practices such as ownership structure, corporate structure, corporate culture, and corporate stakeholder groups. According to Fairclough (1995), "text" is used for both written texts and transcripts of spoken interaction, and a text is regarded as a form of social practice. Thus, when Chinese and American banks use "text" to interact with their stakeholders, they will employ different discursive features, both consciously and unconsciously, in their CSR reports which are the major media for communication with stakeholders. In order to analyze Chinese and American banks' different CSR images constructed via CSR reports, and to help Chinese banks establish international CSR images, the multi-dimensional discursive features that Chinese and American banks employ in their CSR reports warrant analysis.

In this chapter, quantitative methods are used to describe and contrast various discursive features of Chinese and American banks' CSR reports on 4 dimensions: sentiment, readability, CSR keywords and visualization, based on the following corpus and computational linguistic tools: Antconc, WordSmith, DICTION, Coh-Metrix. Next, an Independent Sample T-test measures whether there are significant differences of discursive features on 4 dimensions between Chinese banks' CSR reports and those of American banks' CSR reports. Finally, possible reasons for the different discursive features in Chinese and American banks' CSR reports will be explained.

M. Wan, *CSR Image Discursive Construction of Banks and the Effects on Capital Markets*,
https://doi.org/10.1007/978-981-19-6012-3_5

5.1 Sentiment in Chinese and American Banks' CSR Reports

DICTION 7.1.3 is used to measure sentimental tendencies of Chinese and American banks' CSR reports on 5 dimensions: Certainty, Optimism, Activity, Realism, and Commonality. Figure 5.1 is a copy of DICTION operation interface.

DICTION measures these 5 sentimental indicators of the CSR reports, based on the embedded 31sub-feature sentimental wordlists. The sentimental value of each group wordlist is calculated from their contained sentimental words. Each wordlist contains 10 to 745 sentimental words (Table 5.1).

The measurement equations of thc 5 sentimental indicators are:

Certainty = (Tenacity + Leveling + Collectiveness + Insistence)/ (Numerical Terms + Ambivalence + Self Reference + Variety)

Optimism = (Praise + Satisfaction + Inspiration)/ (Blame + Hardship + Denial)

Activity = (Aggression + Accomplishment + Communication + Motion)/ (Cognitive Terms + Passivity + Embellishment)

Realism = (Familiarity + Spatial Awareness + Temporal Awareness + Present Concern + Human Interest + Concreteness)/ (Past Concern + Complexity)

Commonality = (Centrality + Cooperation + Rapport)/ (Diversity + Exclusion + Liberation)

A constant of 50 will be added to the above calculated value to eliminate any negative numbers (Wang and Bu 2018).

Before the overall sentimental tendencies of the Chinese and American banks will be measured, Bank of China's CSR report 2017 is randomly selected among the CSR reports of 50 Chinese banks and 50 American banks using Excel's random selection

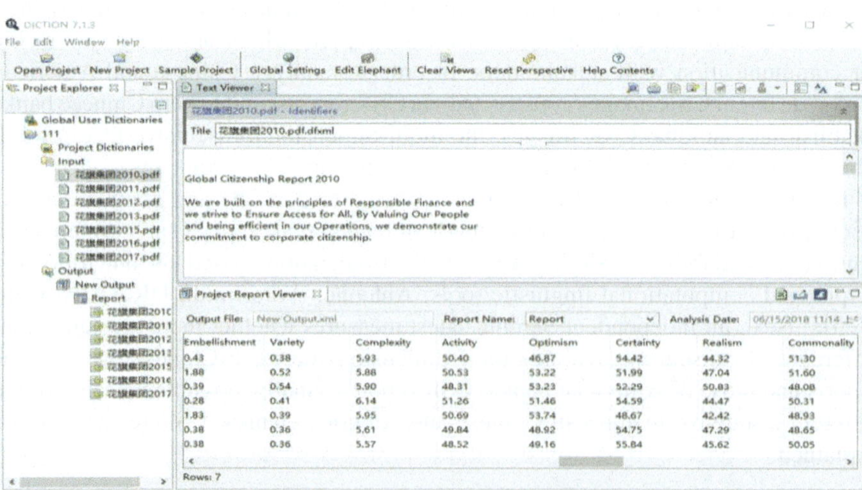

Fig. 5.1 DICTION operation interface

Table 5.1 S 31 Sub-feature wordlists of DICTION

	Wordlist		Wordlist
1	Numerical terms	17	Cognitive terms
2	Ambivalence	18	Passivity
3	Self-reference	19	Spatial terms
4	Tenacity	20	Familiarity
5	Leveling terms	21	Temporal awareness
6	Collectiveness	22	Present concern
7	Praise	23	Human Interest
8	Motion	24	Denial
9	Satisfaction	25	Past concern
10	Inspiration	26	Centrality
11	Blame	27	Cooperation
12	Hardship	28	Rapport
13	Aggression	29	Diversity
14	Accomplishment	30	Exclusion
15	Communication	31	Liberation
16	Concreteness		

function. Bank of China's CSR report 2017 is selected as the representative in order to find common sentimental tendency of the genre of CSR report. We input Bank of China's CSR report 2017 into DICTION and get the following outcome (Fig. 5.2).

The 4 dimensions of sentimental indicators (Optimism, Certainty, Realism and Commonality) in Bank of China's 2017 CSR report are higher than the normal range low sentimental tendency in DICTION's standard corpus which includes the comprehensive genre with contents such as financial reports, news report, academic articles and legal documents. Of note is sentimental tendency of optimism, which at 62.47 is much higher than the normal range high sentimental tendency of DICTION's standard corpus. This outcome, processed by DICTION, shows that the sentimental

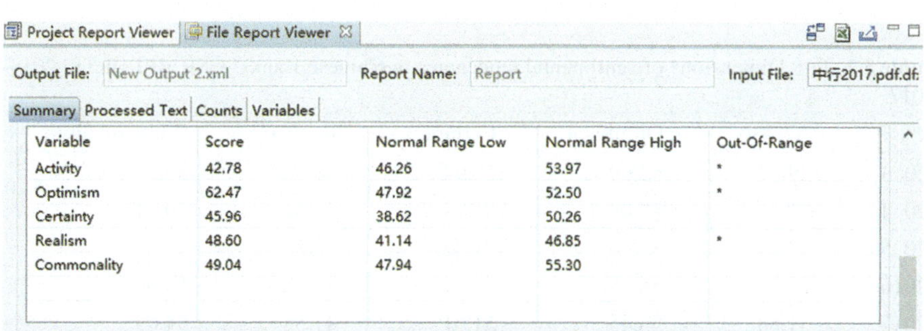

Variable	Score	Normal Range Low	Normal Range High	Out-Of-Range
Activity	42.78	46.26	53.97	*
Optimism	62.47	47.92	52.50	*
Certainty	45.96	38.62	50.26	
Realism	48.60	41.14	46.85	*
Commonality	49.04	47.94	55.30	

Fig. 5.2 Sentimental tendencies of Bank of China's CSR report 2017

resources are abundant in CSR reports. This finding indicates CSR reports' hybrid genre of information and promotion, as put forward by Bhatia. It also shows that managerial groups persuade stakeholders into accepting their CSR concepts and performances using sentimental resources in CSR reports. Additionally, it reveals CSR reports' function of incremental information transmission. These have all been discussed in previous literature.

5.1.1 Sentiment in Chinese Banks' CSR Reports

After inputting 10 Chinese banks' CSR reports from 2013 to 2017 into DICTION, the 5 dimensions of sentimental tendencies for each bank from 2013 to 2017: 50 groups of sentimental tendencies are got. Average calculations were conducted for the outcomes according to year by Excel, and this returned the 5 cumulative dimensions of sentimental tendencies of Chinese the banks from 2013 to 2017.

In order to find the variation trend among 5 dimensions of sentimental tendencies of Chinese banks' CSR reports, a line chart was drawn based on the data from Table 5.2.

Figure 5.3 shows that the 5 sentimental indicators in the Chinese banks' CSR reports are rather consistent. In general, growth has been gradual.

5.1.2 Sentiment in American Banks' CSR Reports

After inputting 10 American banks' CSR reports from 2013 to 2017, DICTION returned the 5 dimensions of sentimental tendency for each bank, for every year from 2013 to 2017: 50 group of sentimental tendencies in total. Average calculations were conducted for the outcomes according to year by Excel. This returned the cumulative 5 dimensions of sentimental tendencies of the American banks' CSR reports from 2013 to 2017.

Table 5.2 D 5 Dimensions of sentimental tendencies in Chinese Banks' CSR REPORTS, 2013–2017

	Activity	Optimism	Certainty	Realism	Commonality
2013	49.52	52.69	50.09	38.56	50.14
2014	51.55	55.08	51.14	40.66	50.71
2015	50.14	53.78	51.32	40.36	53.66
2016	51.74	56.18	49.91	40.62	53.60
2017	51.88	56.45	51.61	41.58	54.09

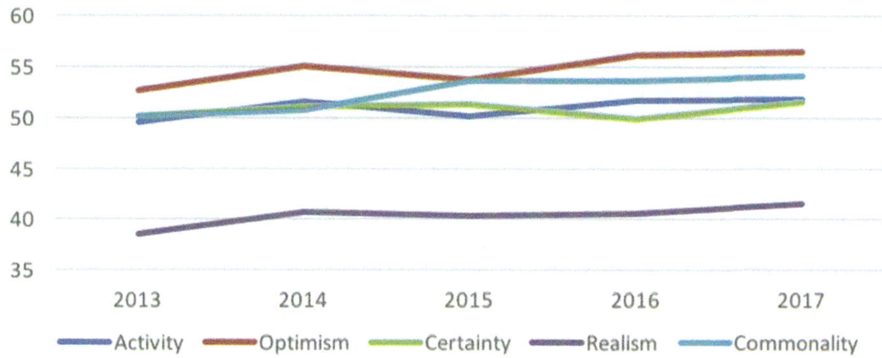

Fig. 5.3 Variation trend of sentimental tendencies in Chinese Banks' CSR reports, 2013–2017

Table 5.3 5 dimensions of sentimental tendencies in Americans' CSR reports, 2013–2017

	Activity	Optimism	Certainty	Realism	Commonality
2013	49.76	50.21	50.05	40.56	49.85
2014	48.58	50.82	48.86	41.76	51.18
2015	49.60	50.67	47.59	42.06	51.38
2016	49.75	50.80	49.33	42.26	49.65
2017	50.00	51.44	50.73	42.09	50.73

In order to identify the variation trend among the 5 dimensions of sentimental tendencies of American banks' CSR reports, a line chart was drawn based on the data from Table 5.3.

Figure 5.4 shows that the 5 sentimental indicators of the American bank's CSR reports experienced a trend of stable variation from 2013 to 2017.

5.1.3 Comparison of Sentimental Tendencies in Chinese and American Banks' CSR Reports

The mean values of the 5 dimensions of sentimental indicators in Chinese and American banks' CSR reports from 2013 to 2017 constitute the overall sentimental tendencies of the Chinese and American banks' CSR reports. They are listed in Table 5.4 and compared in Fig. 5.5.

Figure 5.5 shows that the mean values of the 4 dimensions of sentimental indicators (Activity, Optimism, Certainty and Commonality) in Chinese banks' CSR reports from 2013 to 2017 are higher than those of American banks. Chinese banks' CSR reports have a lower sentimental tendency of realism than do American banks' CSR reports.

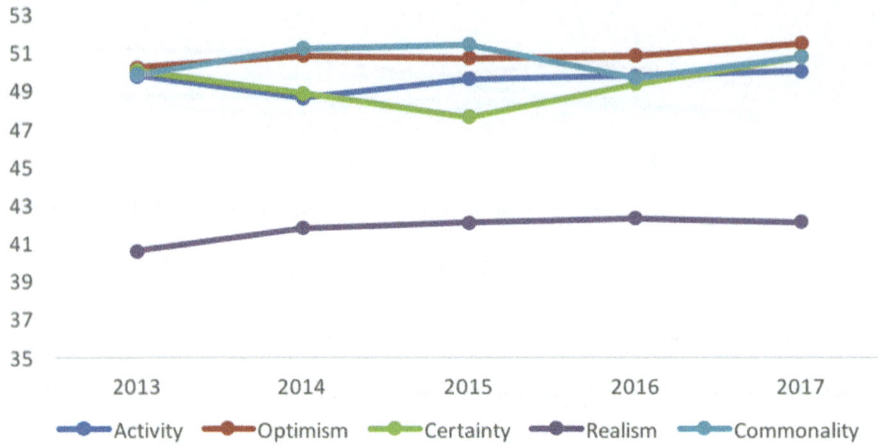

Fig. 5.4 Variation trend of sentimental tendencies in American Banks' CSR reports, 2013–2017

Table 5.4 Sentimental tendencies in Chinese and American Banks' CSR reports

	Activity	Optimism	Certainty	Realism	Commonality
Chinese banks	50.97	54.84	50.81	40.35	52.44
American banks	49.54	50.79	49.31	41.75	50.56

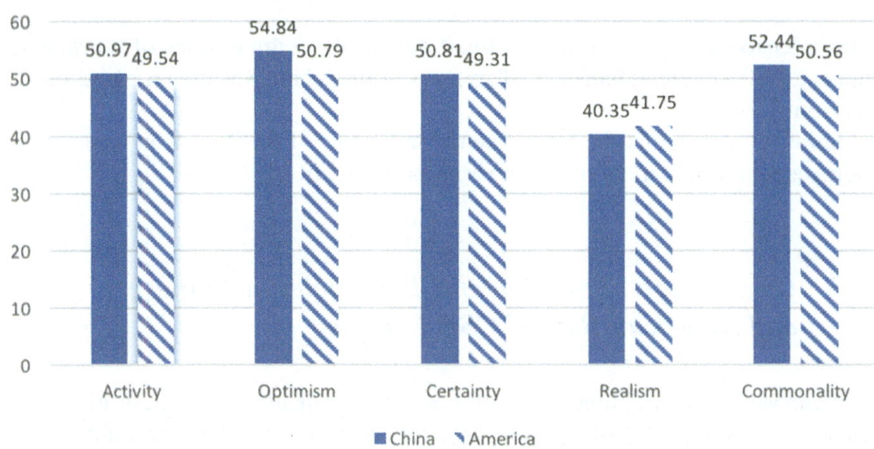

Fig. 5.5 Comparison of sentimental tendencies in Chinese and American Banks' CSR reports

Next, an Independent Sample T-test was used to examine whether there is a significant difference between Chinese and American banks' CSR reports' 5 dimensions of sentimental values (Table 5.5).

Table 5.5 Differences of sentimental tendencies between Chinese and American Banks' CSR reports

Group: Chinese banks' CSR reports (n = 50) and American banks' CSR report (n = 50)			
Indicators	T Stat	P-value (two-tailed)	Mean difference
Activity	2.657	0.038	1.428
Optimism	5.467	0.003	4.048
Certainty	2.366	0.049	1.502
Realism	−2.388	0.048	−1.39
Commonality	2.556	0.038	1.882

The outcome of the Independent Sample T-test shows that the Activity of Chinese banks' CSR reports is significantly higher than that of American banks' (mean difference: 1.428); the sentimental feature of Optimism of Chinese banks' CSR reports is significantly higher than that of American banks' (mean difference: 4.048); the sentimental feature of Certainty among Chinese banks' CSR reports is significantly higher than that of American banks' (mean difference: 1.502); the sentimental feature of Commonality of Chinese banks' CSR reports is significantly higher than that of American banks' (mean difference: 1.882); the sentimental feature of Realism of Chinese banks' CSR reports is significantly lower than that of American banks' (mean difference: −1.39).

The results show that the sentimental tendencies of Chinese banks' CSR reports are significantly higher than those of American banks' along 4 dimensions (Activity, Optimism, Certainty and Commonality). Also, the sentimental tendencies of Realism of Chinese banks' CSR reports are significantly lower than those of American banks'. Furthermore, Chinese banks' CSR reports contain more sentimental words and show an overall higher sentimental tendency than do American banks' CSR reports. This finding is contrary to Wang and Bu's (2017) research and several other studies of corporate narratives from the perspective of SFL and appraisal theory. These researches usually insist that American corporations are more positive and active than Chinese corporations, due to their culture differences.

The higher sentimental tendencies of Chinese banks' CSR reports than those of American banks can be explained from the two perspectives:

The first perspective is that the research objects in this study are Chinese banks and American banks, which are different from previous research. It must be pointed out that Chinese banks have experienced rapid, even crazy, development and growth, relative to American banks from 2013 to 2017. The total value of their assets and their number of sub-branches are both expanding rapidly. Furthermore, the future of Chinese banks is promising, due to positive growth trends, both in China and internationally. At the end of 2017, according to the statistics of the China Banking and Insurance Regulatory Commission (CBIRC), the total asset value of the Chinese banking industry was 252.40 trillion RMB ($38.79 trillion USD). The total asset value of the American banking industry was $16.82 trillion USD at the end of 2017. Thus, the total asset value of the Chinese banking industry is more than twice as

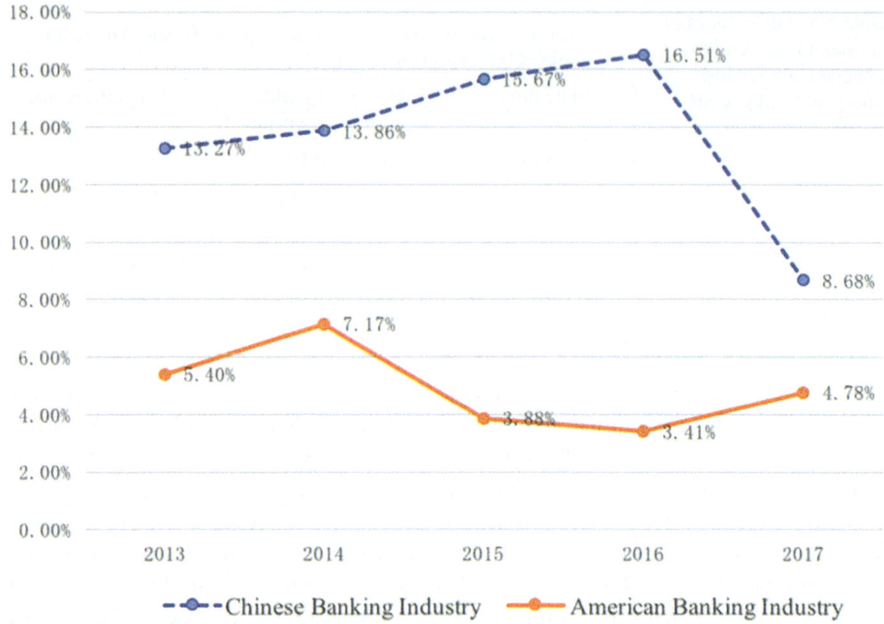

Fig. 5.6 Asset growth rate of the Chinese and American Banking industries, 2013 to 2017 (*Data Source* Wind Database)

much as that of the American banking industry. In addition, the asset growth rate of Chinese banking industry was higher than that of the American banking industry from 2013 to 2017. Details are illustrated in Fig. 5.6. Thus, the Chinese banking industry has experienced rapid and sound growth, and has achieved more than the American banking industry. Chinese banks are confident about their future development, and hold positive development strategies, as well as active concepts of governance. These are conveyed by numerous sentimental words in their CSR reports such as:

(1) *Through its continuous endeavor and stable development, the Bank has developed into the leading bank in the world, possessing an excellent customer base, a diversified business structure, strong innovation capabilities and market competitiveness. (Industrial and Commercial Bank of China, 2016)*

(2) *As China' s most globalized and integrated bank, Bank of China has a well-established global service network with institutions set up in the Chinese mainland as well as 54 countries and regions. (Bank of China, 2017)*

(3) *As the most internationalized Chinese bank, BOC actively responded to the Belt and Road Initiative by continuously improving the institutional network layout in the countries along the Belt and Road... It gave full support to the construction of major Belt and Road projects, helped enterprises to "go global" and "attract foreign investment", provided assistance for the development of local enterprises, and deepened the communication and cooperation with the countries along the Belt and Road, aiming to render a full range of services for the economic construction and industrial development in these countries. (Bank of China, 2017)*

Additionally, China has experienced faster and steadier growth than the United States from 2013 to 2017, and is now the world's second largest economy. As the most important financial resource allocators in China, Chinese banks have implemented and expanded numerous financial businesses, both domestically and internationally. They have also benefited from China's economic reforms. Chinese banks have experienced explosive and sustained high growth rates, mainly due to continuous growth in the Chinese economy. This has come along with series of economic reforms and the liberalization of regulatory policies by the China Banking and Insurance Regulatory Commission (CBIRC). There is also no denying that China's economy and comprehensive national strength will embrace steady and healthy growth in the future. Thus, as the leading power in China's economic development, Chinese banks will also embrace promising future prospects. These factors each shape Chinese banks' active, optimistic and expansive development strategies which are embedded in the sentimental words of their CSR reports. Chinese banks' CSR reports' higher sentimental tendencies indicate their optimistic, positive, and active attitudes towards their current operations, future prospects, and the contributions they will make for their stakeholders.

Furthermore, the higher sentimental tendencies in Chinese banks' CSR reports may also be influenced by the common values of Chinese people, and the characteristics of Chinese style reporting (i.e. reporting only the positive while concealing the unpleasant).

Overall, Chinese banks' achievements, current development status and future growth prospects determine their corporate concepts of governance and strategy. At the same time, corporate mind concepts also influence and guide their future development. These positive, active, optimistic concepts will be expressed in banks' public reports such as CSR reports in the form of various sentimental words. Banks will then use them to communicate with/persuade their stakeholders, express the contribution they have made for stakeholders and influence their stakeholders' perceptions and attitudes towards banks' values and images. The CSR concepts Chinese and American banks transmit to their stakeholders and the CSR images they convey via sentimental words in their CSR reports will be explained in Chap. 6.

5.2 Readability of Chinese and American Banks' CSR Reports

The readability of CSR report influences the efficiency and validity of CSR information signaling between a company and its stakeholders. Readability will influence readers'/stakeholders' understanding and perceptions of a company's CSR value, behavior, and thus stakeholders' attitudes toward the company's CSR image. However, companies with different corporate culture, values, strategies and different governance concepts within the management group will have different writing styles and communicating characteristics when they compose CSR reports intended for public eyes.

The readability of Chinese and American banks' CSR reports is measured from 3 levels: lexical, syntactic, and textual level based on the illustration of selection and the processing of readability indicators. Evaluation indicators on the lexical level are lexical density and mean word length. Lexical diversity refers to the variety of unique words (types) that occur in a text relative to the total number of words (tokens). Standardized type/token ratio (STTR) is used by Word Smith's statistics function to calculate the lexical density of CSR reports. STTR refers to the percentage of unrepeated words per 1,000 words in texts. STTR is high when lexical density is high and the text has more unrepeated words, making it difficult to read. Another evaluation indicator on lexical level is mean word length, also measured by Word Smith's statistics function. When value of a text's mean word length is high, it has more long words and is difficult to understand.

Evaluation indicators in the syntactic level are mean sentence length and cohesion. The former is calculated by Word Smith and the latter is calculated by Coh-Mertix. When the value of a text's mean sentence length is high, the text is difficult to read because it has many long sentences.

Usually long and complex sentence contains comparatively more connectives. Coh-Mertix is used to analyze the density of connectives in syntactic level: the all connectives incidence (CNCAll)—incidence score (occurrence per 1,000 words). The higher the "all connectives incidence" is, the more connectives the text contains (Graesser et al. 2004). Then the text may have more long sentences and complex sentence structures, making it difficult to read.

This is part of Coh-Metrix operation interface (Fig. 5.7).

These are the presentations of two dimensions of Coh-Metrix used in this study: connectives and readability (Fig. 5.8).

Coh-Mertix is also used to measure textual readability by Flesch Reading Ease indicator and Flesch-Kincaid Grade Level indicator. When the Flesch Reading Ease score is high, the text is easy to read; lower score indicates that text that is difficult to read. Table 5.6 shows the connotation of scores in Flesch Reading Ease.

The Flesch–Kincaid Grade Level indicator instead presents scores as U.S. grade levels, and its result is a number that corresponds with a U.S. grade level. For instance,

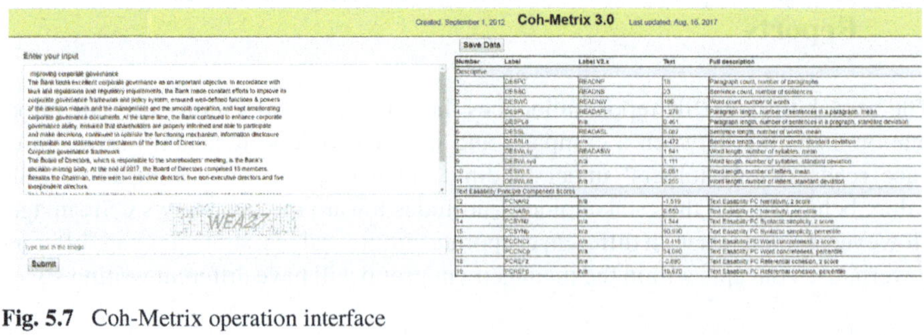

Fig. 5.7 Coh-Metrix operation interface

Connectives				
50	CNCAll	CONi	112.903	All connectives incidence
51	CNCCaus	CONCAUSi	16.129	Causal connectives incidence
52	CNCLogic	CONLOGi	5.376	Logical connectives incidence
53	CNCADC	CONADVCONi	10.753	Adversative and contrastive connectives incidence
54	CNCTemp	CONTEMPi	10.753	Temporal connectives incidence
55	CNCTempx	CONTEMPEXi	0	Expanded temporal connectives incidence
56	CNCAdd	CONADDi	86.022	Additive connectives incidence
57	CNCPos	n/a	0	Positive connectives incidence
58	CNCNeg	n/a	0	Negative connectives incidence

Readbility				
104	RDFRE	READFRE	28.570	Flesch Reading Ease
105	RDFKGL	READFKGL	13.294	Flesch-Kincaid Grade level
106	RDL2	L2	3.181	Coh-Metrix L2 Readability

Fig. 5.8 Dimensions of connectives and readability in Coh-Metrix

Table 5.6 Interpretation of Flesch Reading Ease score

Score	School level	Notes
100.00–90.00	5th grade	Very easy to read. Easily understood by an average 11-year-old student
90.0–80.0	6th grade	Easy to read. Conversational English for consumers
80.0–70.0	7th grade	Fairly easy to read
70.0–60.0	8th and 9th grade	Plain English. Easily understood by 13- to 15-year-old students
60.0–50.0	10th to 12th grade	Fairly difficult to read
50.0–30.0	College	Difficult to read
30.0–0.0	College graduate	Very difficult to read. Best understood by university graduates

if a text's Flesch–Kincaid Grade Level is 9, this text can be understood by 9th grade high school students.

5.2.1 Readability of Chinese Banks' CSR Reports

Based on the outcomes of readability calculations of the Chinese banks' CSR reports (CSR-C) via Coh-Metrix and WordSmith, the readability values of the Chinese banks CSR reports are shown in the following 3 levels (Table 5.7).

Table 5.7 Readability of Chinese Banks' CSR reports

Group: Chinese banks' CSR reports (n = 50)			
Evaluation variables	Evaluation indicators	Statistical indicators	Value
Lexical readability	Lexical density	Standardized type/token ratio	43.99
	Mean word length	Mean word length	5.46
Syntactic readability	Mean sentence length	Mean sentence length	30.91
	Cohesion	All connectives incidence	105.67
Textual readability	Flesch Reading Ease	Flesch Reading Ease score	32.593
	Flesch-Kincaid Grade Level	Flesch-Kincaid Grade Level	12.885

5.2.2 *Readability of American Banks' CSR Reports*

Based on the outcomes of readability calculations for the American banks' CSR reports (CSR-A) via Coh-Metrix and WordSmith, the readability values for the American banks' CSR reports are presented in the following 3 levels (Table 5.8).

Table 5.8 Readability of American Banks' CSR reports

Group: American banks' CSR reports (n = 50)			
Evaluation variables	Evaluation indicators	Statistical indicators	Value
Lexical readability	Lexical density	Standardized type/token ratio	40.49
	Mean word length	Mean word length	4.96
Syntactic readability	Mean sentence length	Mean sentence length	27.41
	Cohesion	All connectives incidence	88.16
Textual readability	Flesch Reading Ease	Flesch Reading Ease	45.416
	Flesch-Kincaid Grade Level	Flesch-Kincaid Grade Level	10.172

5.2.3 Comparison of Readability of Chinese and American Banks' CSR Reports

The histogram in Fig. 5.9 compares the readability of Chinese and American banks' CSR reports. It is based on the readability values of 6 readability evaluation indicators calculated by Coh-Metrix and WordSmith.

According to Fig. 5.9, all readability indicators (except Flesch Reading Ease indicator) of Chinese banks' CSR reports, on the lexical, syntactic and textual levels, are higher than those of American banks. Flesch Reading Ease indicator in CSR-C is lower than CSR-A which also shows that American banks' CSR reports are easier to comprehend than those of Chinese banks. The other readability indicators all indicate that Chinese banks' CSR reports are more complex and difficult to understand than those of American banks.

An Independent Sample T-test was then used to measure whether there was a significant difference of these 6 readability indicators between Chinese and American banks' CSR reports. Results of the T-test are illustrated in Table 5.9.

The standardized type/token ratio (STTR) in Chinese banks' CSR reports is 43.99, significantly higher than the 40.49 in American banks' CSR reports. This indicates that Chinese banks' CSR reports have a higher lexical density than do American banks'. Chinese banks use a wider variety of words to express a larger quantity of information than do American banks. This makes Chinese banks' CSR reports more different to comprehend than American banks'. The mean word lengths for Chinese and American banks' CSR reports are 5.46 and 4.96 respectively. The mean word length for Chinese banks' CSR reports is significantly higher than that of American banks' (mean difference: 0.494). Thus, Chinese banks tend to use longer words than American banks in their CSR reports. Generally speaking, longer words are difficult

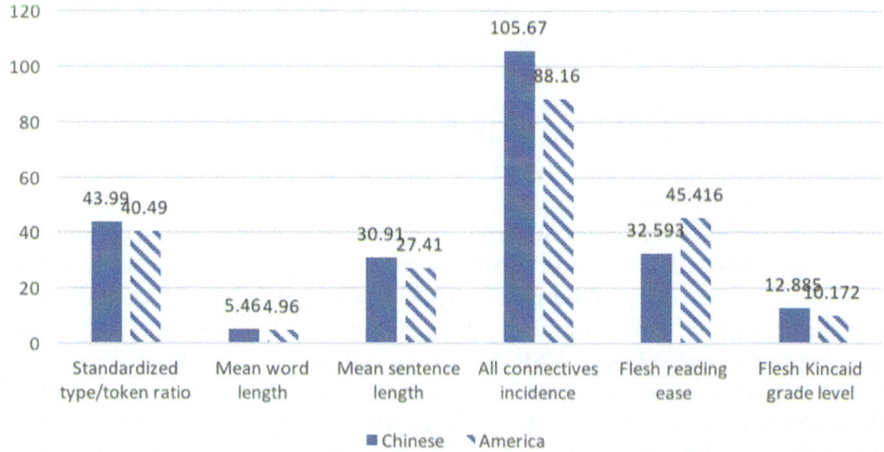

Fig. 5.9 Comparison of readability in Chinese and American Banks' CSR reports

Table 5.9 Differences of readability between Chinese and American Banks' CSR reports

Group: Chinese banks' CSR reports (n = 50) and American banks' CSR reports (n = 50)			
Indicators	T Stat	P-value(two-tailed)	Mean difference
Standardized type/token ratio	8.516	0.000	3.398
Mean word length	7.962	0.000	0.494
Mean sentence length	2.919	0.022	3.506
All connectives incidence	2.698	0.036	17.51
Flesch Reading Ease	−3.495	0.01	−12.823
Flesch-Kincaid Grade Level	3.125	0.014	3.713

to comprehend. The values of two indicators, STTR and mean word length, both indicate that Chinese banks' CSR reports convey more information, and use longer words, than do those of American banks. Chinese banks' CSR reports are also more difficult to comprehend than those of American banks' at the lexical level.

The value of mean sentence length of Chinese banks' CSR reports is significantly higher than that of American banks (mean difference: 3.506). Generally speaking, long sentences contain more information and more complex logical relations which are difficult for readers to comprehend. Thus, readers' perceptive efficiency of CSR reports' information and their attitudes towards banks' images will be influenced. The value of cohesion of Chinese banks' CSR reports is significantly higher than that of American banks (mean difference: 17.51). Chinese banks also tend to use more connectives in their CSR reports than do American banks. Usually, long sentences contain more connectives and express more complex logical relations and sentence structures than short sentences. The value of two indicators: mean sentence length and all connective incidence indicate that Chinese banks' CSR reports convey more information and complex sentence structures, via longer sentences and more connectives than do those of American banks. Thus, Chinese banks' CSR reports are comparatively more difficult to comprehend than American banks on the syntactic level.

The value of Flesch Reading Ease in Chinese banks' CSR reports is 32.593. For that of American banks, it is 45.416. This means that both Chinese banks' and American banks' CSR reports are in the "difficult to read" category according to their Flesch Reading Ease score. This may be a result of the business genre of CSR reports, or the generic features of corporate narratives and information conveyed in them. Regardless, Chinese banks' CSR reports are more difficult to read than those of American banks (mean difference: −12.823 in Flesch Reading Ease indicator). The Flesch-Kincaid Grade Level of Chinese banks' CSR reports is 12.885. This indicates that Chinese banks' CSR reports are difficult to read for American 12th graders. The Flesch-Kincaid Grade Level of American banks' CSR reports is 10.172. This indicates that American banks' CSR reports are difficult to read for American 10th graders, and thus easier to read than Chinese banks' CSR reports. The values of the two indicators—Flesch Reading Ease and Flesch-Kincaid Grade Level—both indicate that Chinese banks' CSR reports are more difficult to read and comprehend than those of American banks on the cumulative textual level.

Readability evaluation of Chinese and American banks' CSR reports via Word-Smith and Coh-Metrix and T-test outcomes all indicate that Chinese banks' CSR reports are significantly more difficult to read than those of American banks.

The two explanations below can illuminate some of the reasons for the differences of readability between Chinese and American banks' CSR reports:

First, most English versions of Chinese banks' CSR reports are translated from the Chinese versions by the companies' employees. Thus, this likely reduces the readability of their CSR reports. The author of this study investigated the English versions of 10 target banks' CSR reports by calling their investor relations departments, or contacting bank employee directly. It was found that 8 banks had chosen to translate the Chinese version their CSR reports into English themselves, rather than hire a specialist to either translate them or compose them in English directly. Only 2 banks mentioned that they had made adjustments to their recent English versions during the translation. Also, many Chinese banks mentioned that they had disclosed English versions of their CSR reports only because that they had been listed on the Hang Seng Index. The author's investigation reveals that the lower readability of Chinese banks' English versions of their CSR reports is due to their unprofessional and direct translation of the Chinese version CSR reports, as well as the transfer of Chinese language and culture during translation.

However, a different explanation is that when comparing Chinese banks' English versions of their CSR reports with the Chinese versions, the author finds that the Chinese versions also convey various information via long and official sentence. Since CSR report can be considered part of the business discourse genre, they are generally more difficult to read than other genres of discourse, due to their own generic features. More importantly, the complex words and sentences in Chinese banks' Chinese versions CSR reports that decrease the reading ease are a result of Chinese banks' unique writing and communicating styles, and the content of their CSR disclosure aiming at both the public and their preferred stakeholder groups. After examining several Chinese CSR reports, the author finds that Chinese banks frequently use long words, especially adjectives and nouns, as well as compound sentences to express their CSR information towards Party principles, government and superior administrative units. They also use similar language to highlight their internal business transformations and improvements, under the background of China's comprehensive reforms in the modern era. Examples include:

(4) *The year 2017 is ground-breaking. In this year, the 19th CPC National Congress drew a grand blueprint for socialism with Chinese characteristics in the new era, and started a new chapter of securing a decisive victory in building a moderately prosperous society in all respects and embarking on a journey to fully build a modern socialist China. The Party Committee of BOC led all the staff to uphold the leadership of the CPC Central Committee with Xi Jinping as the core, actively serve the real economy, practically prevent and control financial risks, deepen reform and innovation, earnestly participate in social welfare undertakings and wholeheartedly create values for customers, shareholders and the society. (Bank of China 2017)*

(5) *2017 saw the 19th National Congress of the Communist Party of China (the 19th CPC National Congress), a critical period during which the ABC met tough challenges in reform and forged ahead. Adhering to the fundamental principle of serving "Sannong" and the real economy, focusing on the general requirements for promoting development of the economy, and firmly upholding the underlying principle of pursuing progress while ensuring stability, ABC remains true to our original aspiration and keeps our mission firmly in mind, and applies the guiding principles of the 19th CPC National Congress into all operations and reforms. (Agricultural Bank of China 2017)*

Furthermore, Chinese banks, especially the big ones, are initiated by the Chinese government, and most of their stock equity is controlled by either the government or central enterprise controlled by the government. Table 5.10 illustrates Chinese Banks' equity structures, and only their major shareholders are displayed. Major shareholders refer to those who hold more than 5% of a company's total shares.

Table 5.10 shows that Chinese banks' equity structure is concentrated among the central enterprises owned by the state, and 9 of the 10 Chinese banks (China Minsheng Bank is the lone exception) are state-owned enterprises. Thus, as the most vital state-owned financial enterprises in China, the government is Chinese banks' most important stakeholder. Chinese banks have the responsibility to coordinate with and support the country's financial development strategies. Therefore, Chinese banks devote much text to disclosing their contributions to the government and their performance of national strategy. This may include numerous special terms, policies, and strategies that are not germane to other stakeholders. Thus, some international stakeholders may feel the unreadability in Chinese banks' CSR reports, when they read Chinese banks' society and government focused CSR information.

However, most American banks are initiated and controlled by personal financial groups, such as Vanguard Group Inc., Blackrock Inc., and Berkshire Hathaway Inc., owned by Warren Buffet. American banks' equity structures are more dispersed and privately owned than those of Chinese banks. Table 5.11 illustrates the equity structure of American Banks, displaying only their major shareholders. Major shareholders refer to those shareholder groups who control over 5% of a company's total shares.

Most of the American banks regard their shareholders and customers as the most important stakeholders. Thus, they need be profitable for their shareholders, as well as provide excellent service to their clients and customers. In their CSR reports, American banks focus on the concerns of their shareholders and customers directly—this kind of CSR information is easy for their stakeholders to comprehend. In order to persuade their shareholders to invest in them, and to convince their customers to trust them and use their financial services, American banks usually convey their corporate culture, corporate governance to shareholders and customers in a straightforward and plain way. Examples include the following:

(6) *Our strategy and programs in place to ensure best-in-class customer service, strong results from customer satisfaction surveys, and/or outreach mechanisms, and recognition* via *customer service awards. (American Express 2017)*

(7) *We interact and communicate with shareholders through several forums, including our annual investor Days, quarterly earnings call, Securities and Exchange Commission*

Table 5.10 Equity structure of Chinese Banks

Chinese banks	Major shareholders holding more than 5% of shares	Shareholding ratio (%)
Industrial and Commercial Bank of China	Central Huijin Investment Co., Ltd.	34.71
	Ministry of Finance	34.6
China Construction Bank	Central Huijin Investment Co., Ltd.	57.11
Agricultural Bank of China	Central Huijin Investment Co., Ltd.	40.03
	Ministry of Finance	39.21
Bank of China	Central Huijin Investment Co., Ltd.	64.02
Bank of Communications	Ministry of Finance	26.53
	Hongkong and Shanghai Banking Corporation Limited	18.7
China Minsheng Bank	Anbang Life Insurance Co., Ltd.—Robust portfolio	6.49
China Citic Bank	China CITIC Limited	65.37
China Industrial Bank	Fujian Provincial Department of Finance	18.78
	China National Tobacco Corporation	5.34
Shanghai Pudong Development Bank	Shanghai International Group Co., Ltd.	21.57
	China Mobile Communications Group Guangdong Co., Ltd.	18.18
	Funde Sino Life Insurance Co., Ltd.—Traditional Products	9.47
	Funde Sino Life Insurance Co., Ltd.—Capital	6.01
China Merchants Bank	China Merchants Steamship Co., Ltd.	13.04
	Anbang Property Insurance Co., Ltd.—Traditional Products	10.72
	China Ocean Shipping Co., Ltd.	6.24

Table 5.11 Equity Structure of American Banks

American Banks	Major shareholders holding more than 5% of shares	Shareholding ratio (%)
JP Morgan Chase & Co.	Vanguard Group Inc.	7.35
	Blackrock Inc.	6.61
Bank of America	Berkshire Hathaway Inc.	6.60
	Vanguard Group Inc.	6.51
	Blackrock Inc.	6.49
Citigroup	Blackrock Inc.	7.30
	Vanguard Group Inc.	7.06
Wells Fargo & Co.	Berkshire Hathaway Inc.	9.37
	Vanguard Group Inc.	6.53
	Blackrock Inc.	5.86
Goldman Sachs	Blackrock Inc.	6.33
	Vanguard Group Inc.	6.32
	State Street Corp.	6.16
Morgan Stanley	Mitsubishi Ufj Financial Group Inc.	24.16
	State Street Corp.	8.47
	Price T Rowe Associates Inc. /MD/	6.23
	Blackrock Inc.	5.90
	Vanguard Group Inc.	5.24
Bank of New York Melleon	Vanguard Group Inc.	6.74
	Berkshire Hathaway Inc.	6.00
	Blackrock Inc.	5.79
American Express Company	Berkshire Hathaway Inc.	17.65
	Vanguard Group Inc.	5.66
	Blackrock Inc.	5.02
PNC Financial Services Group	Wellington Management Group LLP.	7.28
	Vanguard Group Inc.	6.95
	Blackrock Inc.	5.96
State Street Corp.	Price T Rowe Associates Inc. /MD/	7.45
	Massachusetts Financial Services Co. /MA/	7.43
	Vanguard Group Inc.	6.82
	Blackrock Inc.	5.87
	State Street Corp.	5.12

Data Source Wind Database

Filings, Annual report and Proxy Statement, annual meeting, investor conferences and web communications...In all these meetings we solicit shareholders' perspectives and share information about our management of a range of matters, including ESG topics. (JPMorgan Chase & Co. 2017)

The linguistic features of the high lexical density, long words, and long compound sentences in Chinese banks' CSR reports based on corpus and computer-assisted tools indicate that Chinese banks' CSR reports contain the generic feature of administrative documents. This is because most of them regard country as their primary stakeholder to which they must contribute. This finding also corroborates Bhatia's definition of the hybrid CSR report genre: informational and promotional (Bhatia 2012).

Moreover, Chinese banks' CSR reports show higher connective incidence and higher percentages of connectives than those of American banks. This also decreases the reading ease of Chinese banks' CSR reports. This can be explained because in the Chinese context, the eye-catching part of a text will always come at the end, after the body. However, in English, important information comes at the beginning (Wu and Li 2017).

More importantly, however, the high percentage of connectives is also due to writing style. The hybrid genre of the administrative document in Chinese banks' CSR reports is influenced by their managerial groups' corporate concept of governance. Since some Chinese banks' leadership teams may use CSR reports to report their performance to their higher-level units during their office sessions, they may utilize connectives for bedding effect and foreshadowing. This is done in order to explain the perseverance, the pay-offs behind those achievements.

Previous literature on the readability of non-financial information disclosure shows that readability can reflect corporate communication styles as well as managerial groups' preferences and intentions (Li 2008; Bakar and Ameer 2011; Ji et al. 2016). Banks' managerial groups' public-oriented corporate concept of governance, and their equity structures, influence their public writing and communicative styles. They also influence their preferred contents of CSR disclosure. At the same time, stakeholders' perceptions of banks' CSR images are also shaped by this communicative style, as well as the contents of CSR reports. The CSR images that Chinese and American banks construct based on the discursive features of their CSR reports on readability dimension will be explained in Chap. 6.

5.3 CSR Keywords in Chinese and American Banks' CSR Reports

Corpus linguistics keyword analysis can help uncover the salient features of a text, relative to another one. Keywords do not reveal discourses, but they can help spot traces of discourse within language, directing the researcher to important concepts in a text that may contribute to highlighting the existence of (embedded) discourses or ideologies (Burman and Parker 1993; Baker 2006).

To begin, general English corpus (AmE06 and BE06) is used as the reference corpus, and CSR reports of Chinese banks (CSR-C) and American banks (CSR-A) are used as the observing corpus. With these corpora, a unique top 50 keyword list is generated from Chinese and American banks' CSR reports compared to general English, based on Antconc's keyword function. That is, the top 50 keywords from CSR-C against AmE06 and BE06; and the top 50 keywords from CSR-A against AmE06 and BE06. Keyness is calculated by selecting statistical indicators of Log-likelihood in Antconc (we select a p-value of 0.05 as the cut-off point for determining whether a word is a keyword). Keywords are then ranked according to keyness, from highest to lowest. Proper nouns, such as "Bank", "China", and the names of banks, were removed.

Next, those top CSR keywords in each corpus are selected and classified into 4 categories: CSR keywords concerning "community and society", CSR keywords concerning "employees", CSR keywords concerning "environment" and CSR keywords concerning "corporate governance". These each reflect the content of banks' CSR behavior concerning their communities and society, employees, the environment, and corporate governance, respectively.

Then the frequency rate of each CSR keyword in Chinese and American banks' CSR reports are counted to generate the total frequency rate of CSR keywords concerning "communities and society", "employees", "environment" and "corporate governance" in both Chinese and American banks' CSR reports. The classification of 4 categories of CSR keywords is based on the connotation and classification of CSR in Carroll Construct (1991) and the classification of commercial banks' 4 areas of CSR concerns provided by the authoritative CSR information database CSRhub, based on stakeholder theory in Table 5.12.

These 4 categories of CSR keywords reflect Chinese and American banks' different CSR behaviors. These convey banks' CSR behavior images. Thus, the different frequencies of the 4 categories of CSR keywords, and also the keywords' function, exhibit the different contents of Chinese and American banks' CSR performance, from the level of linguistics.

5.3.1 CSR Keywords in Chinese Banks' CSR Reports

The top 50 keyword list of in Chinese banks' CSR reports, relative to the general English corpus (AmE06 and BE06), are calculated by Antconc's keyword function. After deleting proper nouns such as "China", "Chinese", "CSR", "Financial", and banks' names, the following 42 CSR keywords emerge from Chinese banks' CSR reports (Table 5.13).

Next, those CSR keywords in Chinese banks' CSR reports are divided into 4 categories: "communities and society", "employees", "the environment" and "corporate governance", based on the CSRhub's classification of CSR concern in Table 5.12. These are illustrated in Table 5.14. The altogether frequency rate of 4 categories'

Table 5.12 4 Areas of CSR Concern for Commercial Banks

	Communities and society	Employees	The environment	Corporate governance
Areas of concern	Charitable donations	Healthy and safety issues	Renewable energy	Corporate policies and procedures
	Educational supporting	Labor union relations	Pollution prevention	Independence and diversity of the Board of Directors
	Innovation supporting	Retirement welfare	Recycling	investors, customers, communities regulatory measures
	Housing support	Employee engagement	Sustainable management systems	Leadership system values
	Volunteer projects	Cash paid by employees	Sustainable products and services	Corporate culture
	Negative economic impact	Training	Resource management	Principal agent
	Product quality	Labor relationships	Energy efficient operations	Bank equity structure
	Product safety issues	Labor rights	Environmental policy	External market environment
	Consumer interest	Diversity	Environmental disclosure	Investor protection measures
	Monopoly problem	Long-term incentives for employees	Regulatory issues	Information disclosure
	Other aspects	Other aspects	Other aspects	Risk management

Information Source CSRhub

CSR keywords: "community and society", "employees", "environment" and "corporate governance" in Chinese banks' CSR reports, relative to the general English corpus (AmE06 and BE06) are counted.

Table 5.13 CSR keywords in Chinese Banks' CSR reports

Rank	Freq	%	Keyness	Effect (P-value)	Keywords
1	28,588	1.48	24,308.8	0.0195	Loans
2	25,636	1.32	16,236.96	0.0175	Poverty
3	10,415	0.54	9,550.66	0.0071	Projects
4	10,726	0.55	8,694.98	0.0074	Economy
5	11,489	0.59	8,694.01	0.0079	Responsibilities
6	10,408	0.54	8,621.71	0.0071	Branch
7	9,228	0.48	8,491.37	0.0063	Development
8	8,795	0.45	8,092.27	0.006	Employees
9	11,016	0.57	8,062.41	0.0076	Service
10	9,274	0.48	7,447.21	0.0064	Alleviation
11	7,790	0.40	7,167.09	0.0053	Innovation
12	10,609	0.55	6,643.85	0.0073	Customers
13	7,069	0.37	6,470.63	0.0049	Green
14	6,987	0.36	6,427.11	0.0048	Environmental
15	7,909	0.41	6,104.66	0.0054	Rural
16	6,634	0.34	6,102.2	0.0046	Agricultural
17	10,927	0.56	5,984.23	0.0075	Micro
18	6,323	0.33	5,815.92	0.0043	Energy
19	6,229	0.32	5,729.08	0.0043	Training
20	9,117	0.47	5,679.12	0.0063	Supporting
21	6,070	0.31	5,582.73	0.0042	Governance
22	8,788	0.45	5,376.8	0.006	Risk
23	5,654	0.29	4,756.02	0.0039	Promote
24	5,467	0.28	4,716.34	0.0038	Provided
25	7,832	0.40	4,603.14	0.0054	Farmers
26	4,925	0.25	4,529.53	0.0034	Payment
27	5,736	0.30	4,475.49	0.0039	Sustainable
28	4,854	0.25	4,463.61	0.0033	Welfare
29	5,891	0.30	4,440.05	0.004	Online
30	4,731	0.24	4,351.08	0.0033	Strategic
31	4,536	0.23	4,171.02	0.0031	Carbon
32	4,359	0.23	4,008.66	0.003	Stakeholders
33	7,514	0.39	3,954	0.0052	Regulations
34	4,357	0.23	3,850.48	0.003	Donated
35	5,040	0.26	3,770	0.0035	Implementation

(continued)

Table 5.13 (continued)

Rank	Freq	%	Keyness	Effect (P-value)	Keywords
36	3,842	0.20	3,532.87	0.0026	Supervisors
37	3,788	0.20	3,483.04	0.0026	Charity
38	5,853	0.30	3,482.18	0.004	National
39	4,343	0.22	3,405.85	0.003	Technology
40	3,678	0.19	3,381.79	0.0025	Housing
41	4,689	0.24	3,212.28	0.0032	Infrastructure
42	3,447	0.18	3,169.63	0.0024	Urbanization

Table 5.14 4 categories of CSR keywords in Chinese Banks' CSR reports

CSR keyword categories (total frequency rate)	CSR keywords
Community and Society (6.7%)	Poverty, micro, projects, alleviation, supporting, rural, farmers, agricultural, national, promote, provided, implementation, infrastructure, donated, charity, housing, urbanization
Employee (1.03%)	Employees, training, welfare
Environment (1.29%)	Green, environmental, energy, carbon
Corporate governance (8.06%)	Loans, responsibilities, service, economy, customers, branch, development, risk, innovation, regulations, governance, online, sustainable, payment, strategic, stakeholders, technology, supervisors

5.3.2 CSR Keywords in American Banks' CSR Reports

The top 50 keyword list of American banks' CSR reports relative to the general English corpus (AmE06 and BE06) was calculated by Antconc's keyword function. After deleting proper nouns, such as "US", "American", "CSR", "financial", and the names of banks, the following 40 CSR keywords from Chinese banks' CSR reports were generated (Table 5.15).

These 40 CSR keywords from American banks' CSR reports are then divided into 4 categories: "community and society", "employees", "the environment" and "corporate governance". This is based on CSRhub's classification of CSR concerns in Table 5.12, and they are illustrated in Table 5.16. The cumulative frequency rate of the 4 categories of CSR keywords in American banks' CSR reports, relative to general English corpus (AmE06 and BE06) are then counted.

Table 5.15 CSR keywords in American Banks' CSR reports

Rank	Freq	%	Keyness	Effect (P-value)	Keyword
1	38,408	3.03	27,326.12	0.0388	Our
2	25,821	2.04	8,649.71	0.0261	We
3	7,624	0.60	6,873.03	0.0078	Environmental
4	9,076	0.72	6,524.24	0.0093	Customers
5	7,290	0.58	6,130.81	0.0075	Employees
6	5,636	0.44	6,005.88	0.0058	Global
7	7,898	0.62	5,860.27	0.0081	Risk
8	6,533	0.52	5,857.98	0.0067	Communities
9	6,294	0.50	4,978.27	0.0065	Governance
10	4,292	0.34	4,507.07	0.0044	Clients
11	5,739	0.45	4,430.57	0.0059	Energy
12	6,194	0.49	4,094.9	0.0064	Services
13	4,491	0.35	4,040.78	0.0046	Shareholders
14	6,817	0.54	3,912.98	0.007	Training
15	4,330	0.34	3,535.66	0.0045	Diversity
16	3,639	0.29	3,410.09	0.0038	Development
17	3,737	0.29	3,192.53	0.0039	Carbon
18	4,145	0.33	3,191.86	0.0043	Sustainable
19	3,498	0.28	3,169.52	0.0036	Emissions
20	3,131	0.25	3,124.63	0.0032	Solutions
21	2,934	0.23	3,096.79	0.003	Engagement
22	5,269	0.42	2,932.93	0.0054	Capital
23	4,128	0.33	2,874.23	0.0043	Opportunities
24	2,644	0.21	2,815.8	0.0027	Stakeholders
25	4,580	0.36	2,773.9	0.0047	Investing
26	4,124	0.33	2,716.11	0.0042	Wellbeing
27	2,515	0.20	2,678.58	0.0026	Volunteer
28	4,501	0.36	2,664.19	0.0046	Commitment
29	2,796	0.22	2,633.72	0.0029	Climate
30	2,805	0.22	2,535.59	0.0029	Suppliers
31	2,304	0.18	2,454.04	0.0024	Talent
32	2,419	0.19	2,453.35	0.0025	Culture
33	3,754	0.30	2,452.3	0.0039	Waste
34	4,346	0.34	2,426.96	0.0045	Education
35	4,011	0.32	2,363.19	0.0041	Veterans
36	2,026	0.16	2,157.17	0.0021	Renewable

(continued)

Table 5.15 (continued)

Rank	Freq	%	Keyness	Effect (P-value)	Keyword
37	2,398	0.19	2,156.52	0.0025	Ethics
38	2,637	0.21	2,120.08	0.0027	Philanthropic
39	2,691	0.21	2,105.22	0.0028	Gender
40	2,449	0.19	2,104.25	0.0025	Housing

Table 5.16 C 4 Categories of CSR Keywords in American Banks' CSR reports

CSR keyword categories (total frequency rate)	CSR keywords
Community and Society (1.43%)	Communities, volunteer, veterans, philanthropic, housing
Corporate governance (11.91%)	Our, we, customers, global, risk, governance, clients, services, shareholders, diversity, development, sustainable, solutions, engagement, capital, stakeholders, investing, commitment, suppliers, culture, ethics
Employee (2.5%)	Employees, training, opportunities, wellbeing, talent, education, gender
Environment (2.3%)	Environmental, energy, carbon, emissions, climate, waste, renewable

5.3.3 Comparison of Keyword Features in Chinese and American Banks' CSR Reports

Banks disclose their CSR information and activities to stakeholders via CSR reports. Then, their CSR behavior images are constructed and transmitted via CSR activities. A text's keywords represent the unique keyword features of one text relative to another. Keyword analysis of CSR reports can identify banks' unique CSR behaviors and the content of their CSR, from a linguistic level. Chinese and American banks' CSR behaviors differ because CSR behaviors are the implementation of CSR concepts (corporate culture and strategy and CSR values) and Chinese and American banks have different CSR concepts. Thus, they will have different CSR keywords in their CSR reports. These keywords transmit their different CSR behaviors and CSR content from the language level.

Based on the outcome of keyword analysis for Chinese and American banks' CSR reports via Antconc, CSR keywords from Chinese and American banks' CSR reports have been classified into 4 categories. The total frequency rate of each CSR keyword category for Chinese and American banks' CSR reports is listed in Table 5.17, and compared in the histogram in Fig. 5.10.

According to Fig. 5.10, Chinese banks' CSR reports contain a higher percentage of CSR keywords about "community and society" (6.7%) than do those of American banks (1.43%). Meanwhile, American banks' CSR reports contain a higher

Table 5.17 Comparison of CSR Keywords in Chinese and American Banks' CSR Reports

CSR keyword categories	Freq (%)	
	Chinese Banks' CSR Reports	American Banks' CSR Reports
Community and Society	6.7	1.43
Employee	1.03	2.5
Environment	1.29	2.3
Corporate governance	8.06	11.91

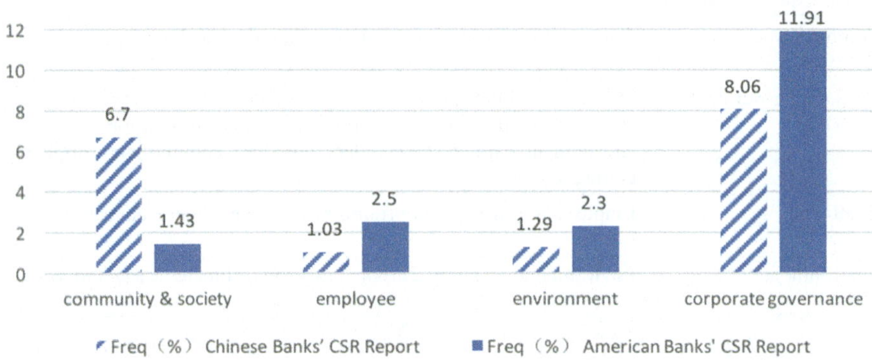

Fig. 5.10 Comparison of CSR keywords in Chinese and American Banks' CSR reports

percentage of CSR keywords about "employees" (2.5%), the "environment" (2.3%) and "corporate governance" (11.91%) than do those of Chinese banks (1.03%, 1.29%, 8.06% respectively). That is to say, Chinese banks tend to disclose more CSR information about their CSR activities concerning community and society than do American banks. On the contrary, American banks choose to disclose more CSR information about their CSR activities concerning employee relationships, environmental problems and corporate governance.

An Independent Sample T-test was then used to measure whether there was a significant difference between the 4 categories of CSR keyword indicators. The results of T-test are illustrated in Table 5.18.

Based on the results of the T-test, the percentage of the 4 categories of CSR keywords from Chinese banks' CSR reports is significantly different from that of American banks. Also, the percentage of CSR keywords about "community and society" in Chinese banks' CSR reports is significantly higher than that of American banks. In general, Chinese banks' CSR reports disclose more CSR information about our contribution to public and society than do those of American banks. See below for examples:

(8) *The Bank set up a leading group for financial poverty alleviation, and formulated the Work Plan of China CITIC Bank for Financial Poverty Alleviation in the "13th*

Table 5.18 Differences of CSR Keywords between Chinese and American Banks' CSR Reports

Group: Chinese banks' CSR reports (n = 50) and American banks' CSR reports (n = 50)			
Indicators	T Stat	P-value (two-tailed)	Mean difference
CSR keywords about community and society	6.65	0.002	5.27
CSR keywords about employees	−23.48	0.000	−1.47
CSR keyword about the environment	−9.51	0.000	−1.01
CSR keywords about corporate governance	−12.65	0.000	−3.85

Five-Year Plan" Period and the 2017 Financial Poverty Alleviation Work Plan of China CITIC Bank, supporting poor regions' infrastructure projects in the areas of transportation, water conservancy, power, energy and ecological environment, and basic public service projects in the areas of culture, healthcare and hygiene through its credit policy... (China Citic Bank, 2017)

(9) *As a large state-owned commercial bank serving Sannong, ABC has shown to be a champion of national macro-economic policies, focuses on the social responsibility to serve Sannong, and regards creating value for shareholders as its core goal. (Agricultural Bank of China 2017)*

The percentages of CSR keywords about "employees", "environment", and "corporate governance" in American banks' CSR reports are significantly higher than those of Chinese banks. In general, American banks' CSR reports disclose more CSR content about employees, environmental protection, CSR strategy and corporate governance to show their responsibility to their employees, customers and shareholders. See below for examples:

(10) *At Morgan Stanley, we believe a strong culture starts with our 55,000 employees. The firm's core values drive a shared set of behaviors and attributes that help employees make decisions consistent with the expectations of our clients, shareholders, regulators, Board of Directors and the public. (Morgan Stanley 2016)*

(11) *As one of the largest global financial institutions, Bank of America is in a unique position to help society transition to a low-carbon economy and support sustainable business activities. (Bank of American, 2017)*

(12) *Good governance is a fundamental principle at Citi, and we work to ensure that we are at the leading edge of best practices. We strive to maintain the highest standards of ethical conduct: reporting results with accuracy and transparency and maintaining full compliance with the laws, rules and regulations.... (Citi 2017)*

The different percentages for the 4 types of CSR keywords in Chinese and American banks' CSR reports reflect the different CSR concerns and preferred CSR behaviors of Chinese and American banks, respectively. CSR reports summarize CSR information about a company's concept, strategy, and methods of implementing social responsibility. They also disclose their impact on the economy, and the environmental and social fields. The information is geared towards their stakeholders. A CSR report is an important carrier for non-financial information disclosure, and an important bridge for companies to communicate with stakeholders. Thus, the varying percentages of CSR information disclosures in Chinese and American banks' CSR reports reflect their different concepts, strategies, and methods of implementing social responsibility. These different CSR concepts, strategies, and methods are decided and expressed by their different stakeholder engagements. To be specific, the different CSR keywords in Chinese and American banks' CSR reports are the result of their different stakeholder rankings. The stakeholder rankings decide to which group of stakeholders they need to be most responsible and contribute the most. Chinese and American banks have different stakeholder rankings. Thus, they will place different emphasis on their CSR information disclosures. Due to the different corporate nature, corporate and national culture, and different corporate values and strategies in implementing CSR, Chinese and American banks have different stakeholder rankings. This is illustrated Tables 5.19 and 5.20. The information of stakeholder rankings is obtained from the CSR report of each bank.

According to Table 5.19, most Chinese banks favor government and governmental regulatory authorities over employees, shareholders, and customers, as their primary stakeholders. Thus, Chinese banks disclose CSR information about society and public by using CSR keywords, such as "poverty" (the national poverty alleviation strategy), "micro" (supporting the development of small and micro enterprise), "projects", and "supporting".

Table 5.19 Stakeholder Rankings in Chinese Banks

Chinese Banks	Stakeholder Ranking
Industrial and Commercial Bank of China	Country; Shareholders; Customers; Employees; Communities; the Environment
China Construction Bank	Public; Customers; Shareholders; Employees; the Environment
Agricultural Bank of China	Government; Regulatory authorities; Shareholders and investors; Customers; Employees; Suppliers and Partners; Communities; the Environment
Bank of China	Country; Shareholders; Customers; Employees; Communities; the Environment
Bank of Communications	Customers; Shareholders; Government; Employees; the Environment; Communities; Partners; Social organizations
China Merchants Bank	Government; Regulatory authorities; Shareholders and investors; Customers; Employees; Partners; the Environment; Community
China Industrial Bank	Regulatory authorities; Shareholders; Clients; Partners; the Environment and resources; Employees; Communities
Shanghai Pudong Development Bank	Customers; Partners; Directors; Employees; Government; the Environment; Community; Charity Organization; Media
China Minsheng Bank	Governmental regulatory authorities; Shareholders and investors; Customers; Employees; Community; Suppliers
China Citic Bank	Government; Shareholders; Customers; Suppliers; Staff; Community

Table 5.20 Stakeholder rankings in American Banks

American Banks	Stakeholder Ranking
JP Morgan Chase & Co	Shareholders; Employees; Regulators and Policymakers; Customers; Research Analysts; Communities; NGOs
Bank of America	Employees; Investors; Customers and Clients; Community advocates;
Citigroup	Investors; Government and Regulators; Suppliers; Community Leaders and NGOs; Employees; Clients and Customers; Other Financial Institutions
Wells Fargo & Co	Employees; Customers; Shareholders; Communities; the Environment
Goldman Sachs	the Environment; Employees; Customers; Government and Regulators
Morgan Stanley	Shareholders; Clients and Customers; Government and Regulators; Employees; Communities
Bank of New York Melleon	Shareholders; Communities; Clients; Employees
American Express Company	Shareholders and socially responsible investors; Colleagues; Customers; Government and Regulators; Suppliers; Community and NGOs; Sustainability research firms; Other Financial Institutions
PNC Financial Services Group	Customers; Shareholders; Regulators; Employees; Communities; Suppliers; NGOs
State Street Corp	Clients; Shareholders; Employees; Suppliers; Communities; the Environment

According to Table 5.20, most American banks prioritize shareholders, employees, and customers as their stakeholders. Thus, in their CSR reports, they will disclose more CSR information about the profits they have made in the past and will achieve in the future for their shareholders in order to attract more investment. They also disclose more information about employees and customers in order to establish a responsible image to their customers and to achieve sustainable development.

In general, the different percentages of CSR information disclosure in CSR reports reflect that Chinese and American banks' different CSR concepts and strategies are decided by their different stakeholder rankings. Different stakeholder rankings thus influence their different CSR information disclosure. These differences are conveyed by the varying percentages for the 4 categories of CSR keywords in their CSR reports. CSR keywords reflect banks' CSR behaviors and CSR concern from a linguistic level. Chapter 6 will explore what kind of CSR behavior images Chinese and American banks construct and transmit via different and preferred CSR keywords in their CSR reports.

5.4 Visualization in Chinese and American Banks' CSR Reports

In linguistics, visual representation refers to non-linguistic symbols that convey and construct discourse along with linguistic symbols. Kress and Van Leeuwen (1996) point out the semiotic elements and images' function in communicate meaning in *Reading Images.*

Since CSR reports transmit companies' CSR images directly to stakeholders, stakeholders' first impression of a company is based on the visual design of its CSR report. With the development of technologies and new media, the world has transformed from a language-dominated culture to the one in which multimodal discourse is increasingly crucial.

Thus, a successful CSR report should be a fine and ingenious representation of the combination of verbal and visual semiotic modes in order to better interact with the stakeholders and establish a good corporate image. The visual and structural design of a CSR report can paint a picture of a company's CSR concepts and CSR behaviors.

CSRs' visual evaluation indicators are measured by the number of pictures illustrated on the cover and in the content of CSR reports. Since the length of each CSR report varies, direct comparison of number of pictures in each CSR report will lead to biased visual evaluation. To avoid this biased calculation, the number of pictures in each CSR report is processed according to Ji et al.'s (2016) standardized processing of corporate narrative pictures. CSR visual score = the number of pictures in one CSR report/(the maximize number of pictures in one CSR report—the minimum number of pictures in one CSR report). The visual scores in each Chinese and American banks' CSR reports (100 reports) are calculated, respectively, and the mean score of Chinese banks' CSR reports (50 reports) and American banks' CSR reports (50 reports) are output as visual indicators of Chinese and American banks' CSR reports.

5.4.1 Visualization in Chinese Banks' CSR Reports

The manual calculation of numbers of pictures contained in the covers and contents of 50 Chinese banks' CSR reports revealed that the Industrial and Commercial Bank had 159 pictures in their 2014 CSR report. This was the maximum number of pictures among the 50 CSR reports of Chinese banks. China Citic Bank had no pictures in their 2017 CSR report. This was the minimum. We can infer that Chinese banks show a wide variance in picture employment in their CSR reports. The CSR visual score/value of each Chinese banks' CSR report = the number of pictures in one CSR report/(159–0). Averaging the scores reveals the mean score of Chinese banks' CSR reports (50 reports) from 2013 to 2017, as shown in Table 5.21.

Table 5.21 Visual value of Chinese Banks' CSR reports

	2013	2014	2015	2016	2017	Average
Visual value	0.28	0.43	0.36	0.26	0.29	0.32

Table 5.22 Visual value of American Banks' CSR reports

	2013	2014	2015	2016	2017	Average
Visual value	0.41	0.57	0.62	0.58	0.53	0.54

5.4.2 *Visualization in American Banks' CSR Reports*

Manual calculation of the number of pictures on the covers and in the contents of 50 American banks' CSR reports showed that JP Morgan Chase & Co. had 73 pictures in their 2016 CSR report. This was the maximum number of pictures among the 50 CSR reports of American banks. Morgan Stanley had only 1 picture in their 2016 CSR report. This was the minimum. The use of pictures American banks' CSR reports varies less than in those of Chinese banks. The CSR visual value for each American banks' CSR report = the number of pictures in one CSR report/(73–1). After averaging them, the mean score of American banks' CSR reports (50 reports) from 2013 to 2017 were generated. See Table 5.22 for the results.

5.4.3 *Comparison of Visual Features in Chinese and American Banks' CSR Reports*

The histogram in Fig. 5.11 was used to compare the visual indicators in Chinese and American Banks' CSR Reports.

According to Fig. 5.11, visual indicators in Chinese Banks' CSR reports are lower than that of American banks from 2013 to 2017.

An Independent Sample T-test was then used to examine whether there was a significant difference between the visual indicators in Chinese and American banks' CSR reports. The results of the T-test are shown in Table 5.23.

The T-test results indicate that the visual value indicator of Chinese banks' CSR reports is lower than that of American banks (mean difference: −0.22).

Generally speaking, American banks are more skilled at employing pictures in their CSR information disclosure than Chinese banks. The number of visualizations in American banks' CSR reports was also more regular than Chinese banks. Also, some Chinese banks lack the awareness to use pictures to express their CSR information to stakeholders.

American banks tend to use pictures concerning CSR information on the cover designs of their CSR reports in order to attract the attention of stakeholder and express their CSR concept and behavior with their stakeholders in the beginning.

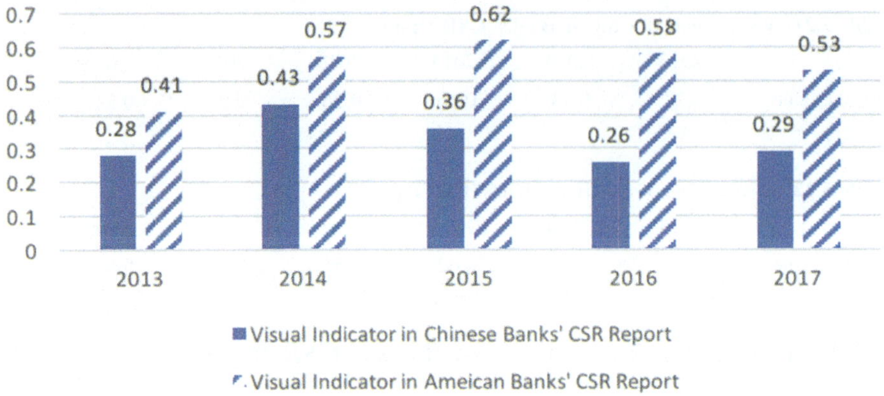

Fig. 5.11 Comparison of visual indicators in Chinese and American Banks' CSR reports

Table 5.23 Difference of visual values between Chinese and American Banks' CSR reports

Group: Chinese banks' CSR reports (n = 50) and American banks' CSR reports (n = 50)			
Indicator	T Stat	P-value(two-tailed)	Mean difference
Visual Values	−4.581	0.002	−0.22

Most Chinese banks, whereas, illustrate the title of their CSR reports or the banks' logos on the cover of their CSR reports. Thus, American banks have a strong sense of consciousness in the visual presentation of CSR information. Evidence can be seen in the covers from Chinese and American banks' CSR reports in Fig. 5.12.

Chinese banks tend to use pictures to reflect their CSR behaviors directly, and the pictures reaffirm their textual expression of CSR information visually. American banks use pictures to clarify the layout of their CSR reports and make them reader-friendly. The pictures in these reports convey incremental CSR information which supplements the verbal CSR information. American banks' CSR concepts and values are expressed via pictures in their CSR reports. American banks achieve additional visual effects by using more pictures in their CSR reports than Chinese banks. Evidence can be seen in Fig. 5.13.

Chinese and American banks' varying degrees of visual presentation of CSR information are the result from their different CSR behaviors and CSR concepts. Most Chinese banks' CSR behaviors are responsive CSR behaviors (Liu, 2008) since their CSR activities are the reaction to calls from the government and the public. Meanwhile, most American banks' CSR behaviors are strategic; they combine CSR activities and concepts with their corporate strategies and business operations.

In general, the visualization of CSR disclosure, including the employment of pictures, type setting of pictures and words, and layout of pictures and words in CSR reports function interactively. They enhance stakeholders' impressions of banks' CSR concepts and activities, and also their CSR images. Chapter 6 will address the

Fig. 5.12 Covers in Chinese and American Banks' CSR reports

Fig. 5.13 Pictures in Chinese and American Banks' CSR reports

visual CSR images that Chinese and American banks construct and express via the employment of pictures in their CSR reports.

5.5 Summary

In this chapter, the various discursive features along the dimensions of sentiment, readability, CSR keyword and visualization in Chinese and American banks' CSR reports for banks' CSR image construction are measured by corpus and computational linguistic tools. They are also compared by Independent Sample T-test.

The quantitative and descriptive analysis showed that Chinese and American banks' CSR reports contain different discursive features:

Sentimental evaluation indicators: Activity, Optimism, Certainty and Commonality in Chinese banks' CSR reports are significantly higher than those of American banks. Sentimental indicator of Realism in Chinese banks' CSR reports is significantly lower than those of American banks. In general, Chinese banks' CSR reports contain more positive, active and optimistic sentimental words, and show a higher sentimental tendency than American banks' CSR reports.

The higher sentimental value of Chinese banks' CSR reports may be the result of the Chinese banking industry's rapid grow the and expansive and optimistic development strategy from 2013 to 2017, relative to that of the American banking industry.

Readability evaluation indicators: STTR and mean word length on lexical level, mean sentence length and all connectives incidence on syntactic level, and Flesch-Kincaid Grade Level on textual level in Chinese banks' CSR reports are significantly higher than those of American banks. Flesch Reading Ease in Chinese banks' CSR reports is significantly lower than that of American banks. All of the above readability indicators show that Chinese banks' CSR reports contain more information, longer sentences and more complex logical relations than those of American banks.

The comparatively lower ease of reading for Chinese banks' English version CSR reports may the result of the Chinese language and also culture transfer during the translation. It also could be the result of different writing and communicative styles, and preferred CSR information disclosure between Chinese and American banks. These differences are the outcomes of the different equity structures and management groups' preferred governance values between Chinese and American banks.

CSR keyword evaluation indicators: The percentage of CSR keywords in the "community and society" category in Chinese banks' CSR reports is significantly higher than that of American banks. The percentage of CSR keywords in "employees", "environment" and "corporate governance" categories in Chinese banks' CSR reports are significantly lower than those of American banks. CSR keyword analysis helps analyze Chinese and American banks' varying CSR content and behaviors from the level of language. Chinese banks tend to disclose more CSR information about their contributions to society, whereas American banks prefer to disclose more CSR concerns for employees, customers, shareholders, the environment and corporate governance. These different percentages of CSR keywords in CSR reports may be the result of different stakeholder rankings among Chinese and American banks.

Visual evaluation indicator: The standardized processing of numbers of pictures illustrated on the covers and in the content of CSR reports in Chinese banks' CSR reports is significantly lower than that of American banks. American banks have more sense in visual presentation of CSR information than Chinese banks. Most of the pictures in Chinese banks' CSR reports consist of the repetitions of their verbal CSR information, whereas American banks employ pictures to express incremental and interactive information pertaining to their CSR values. These different CSR visual effects may be the result of Chinese and American banks' varying CSR concepts.

In general, Chinese banks' CSR reports show a higher sentimental tendency than American banks' CSR reports; American banks' CSR reports are comparatively easier to read than Chinese banks' CSR reports; Chinese banks disclose more CSR contribution to society and public, whereas American banks disclose more CSR concern for employees, the environment and corporate governance; American banks prefer to employ pictures in CSR reports to persuade and interact with their stakeholders than Chinese banks.

Different multi-dimensional discursive features in banks' CSR reports may influence stakeholders' perception of banks' CSR concepts and behaviors. They may also influence their attitudes towards banks' CSR mind image, behavior image and visual image. Multi-dimensional discursive features in banks' CSR reports construct and convey banks' CSR images to stakeholders. Different discursive features contained in Chinese and American banks' CSR reports may reflect and construct their different CSR images. Thus, Chap. 6 will focus on what kinds of CSR mind image, behavior image and visual image Chinese and American banks establish via different discursive features of sentiment, readability, CSR keywords and visualization in their CSR reports. It will also examine the causes for their different discursive construction of CSR images under the different social, cultural, economic, political and regulatory contexts in which Chinese and American banks are located.

Chapter 6
A Contrastive Study of Chinese and American Banks' Discursively Constructed CSR Images

This chapter will answer the second research question: How do Chinese and American banks construct their CSR images via the multi-dimensional discursive features in CSR reports and what are the differences between their discursively constructed images? To answer the second research question, Chinese and American banks' different discursive construction of CSR images based on the multi-dimensional discourse evaluation framework will be interpreted and compared under the interdisciplinary approach of linguistics and management. Additionally, reasons for their different CSR images will be explained. The above question will also be addressed based on the descriptive analysis and comparison of multi-dimensional discursive features in Chinese and American banks' CSR report in Chap. 5.

The theoretical chapter illustrated the co-constructed mechanisms between Chinese and American banks' CSR reports' discursive features and banks' CSR images along 3 dimensions. Discursive features contained in sentiment and readability evaluation can influence stakeholders' attitudes towards banks' CSR mind image. This is because they can reflect and transmit banks' CSR concept, development strategy and corporate philosophy—the major components of banks' CSR mind image. CSR keywords in CSR reports can be used to examine banks' CSR performances, which compose banks' CSR behavior image. Visual resources used in CSR reports can reflect and evaluate visual presentation of banks' CSR concepts and behaviors which transmit banks' CSR visual image.

This chapter focuses on how CSR reports' discursive features of sentiment, readability, CSR keyword and visualization reflect and construct Chinese and American banks' CSR images along 3 dimensions: mind image, behavior image and visual image. This is based on the corporate identity system (CIS), the theory of discourse and institutional identity and linguistic theory behind discursive features. The theory of information asymmetry will be used to consolidate discursive features' function in banks' CSR image construction from the perspective of management. Then, Chinese and American banks' discursively constructed CSR mind images, behavior images and visual images will be compared.

M. Wan, *CSR Image Discursive Construction of Banks and the Effects on Capital Markets*,
https://doi.org/10.1007/978-981-19-6012-3_6

Next, based on legitimacy theory and stakeholder theory, causes for Chinese and American banks' different discursively constructed CSR images are explained under Chinese and American banks' different political, economic, cultural, social, and regulatory contexts.

6.1 The Discursive Construction of Chinese and American Banks' CSR Mind Images

Based on the corporate identity system, banks' mind image refers to banks' corporate concept and value in performing CSR. Bank's CSR mind image is transmitted by banks' CSR concept. The CSR mind concept is formulated on banks' managerial group and employee's understanding of corporate nature and the relationship between bank and society. This includes especially their understanding of stakeholder relationships, including CSR philosophy, CSR declaration, CSR goals and the other conceptual guidelines of CSR behavior (Liu, 2008). According to Zhu's (2009) standard mechanism of commercial banks' CSR, commercial banks need to prioritize CSR value in order to improve their CSR contribution. Also, the CSR mind concept is realized and constructed via banks' corporate strategies and corporate culture.

Indeed, corporate strategy is an important part of corporate governance which is a component of economic CSR (Carroll, 1991). CSR is a comprehensive connotation which includes corporate conduct in economic aspects and is closely connected, achieved by company's economic conducts. Thus, the corporate governance, corporate strategy and corporate development that connect with a company's economic development are important components of banks' CSR. Banks' concepts of corporate governance, corporate strategy, and development are important components of their CSR values and CSR concepts.

Based on Liu's (2008) definition of CSR mind image and Zhu's (2009) framework of commercial banks' CSR, banks' corporate strategies and corporate values are vital components to the realization of banks' CSR value. This study focuses on banks' CSR mind image construction in terms of banks' CSR concepts including corporate governance, corporate strategy, corporate development concept, corporate culture, and corporate vision.

According to the theory of discourse and institutional identity, discourse can reflect an institution's values, concepts, and operations. At the same time, it constructs institutional identity. A CSR report is a valuable means of corporate discourse through which banks can dynamically construct, negotiate, manage and transmit their multidimensional identities to their stakeholders. According to functional linguistic theory, language is functional and persuasive in addition to its function of information transmission (Martin & White, 2005). Banks' CSR mind concept, including their corporate strategy and culture, attitudes towards different types of stakeholders and other CSR information are contained in banks' CSR reports, both implicitly and explicitly.

This section analyzes how the discursive features—sentiment and readability in banks' CSR reports—reflect banks' CSR concepts. This constructs and transmits Chinese and American banks' CSR mind image to their stakeholders, as well as the different discursively constructed CSR mind images of Chinese and American banks.

6.1.1 Chinese and American Banks' CSR Mind Image Construction Via Sentiment

Sentimental analysis is the study of emotions, opinions, appraisals and attitudes regarding "services, products, individuals, organizations, issues, topics and their attributes" (D' Andrea et al., 2015). Sentimental words in banks' CSR reports are used to express banks' CSR concepts, as well as to persuade stakeholders to accept banks' CSR concepts.

This section is based on the outcome of DICTION's sentimental analysis of Chinese and American banks' CSR reports in Chap. 5 and the co-constructive mechanism between sentimental tendencies and banks' CSR mind image. It analyzes the different sentimental tendencies (Certainty, Optimism, Activity, Realism, and Commonality) contained in Chinese and American banks' CSR reports. It explores how Chinese and American banks' CSR mind images are constructed and transmitted by sentimental words in their CSR reports and how Chinese and American banks persuade their stakeholders to accept their CSR concepts and images via sentimental words in CSR reports.

The measurement and comparison of sentimental tendencies of Chinese and American banks' CSR reports by DICTION and Independent Sample T-test reveals that 4 sentimental tendencies (Activity, Optimism, Certainty and Commonality) in Chinese banks' CSR reports are significantly higher than those of American banks. Sentimental tendencies of Realism in Chinese banks' CSR reports are significantly lower than those of American banks. Basically speaking, Chinese banks' CSR reports contain more certain, positive, active and optimistic sentimental words and show a higher sentimental tendency than American banks' CSR reports.

Assessing how banks use sentimental resources to express their CSR mind concept and construct their CSR mind image, and what mind image they construct requires the examination specific linguistic devices: sentimental words which realize the 5 sentimental tendencies. According to DICTION, the 5 sentimental tendencies of text are calculated based on the value of 31 sub-feature word groups. The value of each group is calculated by its sentimental words in DICTION's embedded wordlist. For example, the Satisfaction sentimental sub-wordlist contains the words: "triumph", "attraction", "encouraging", "pride", "cheerful", "favorable", "affection", and "simulated", to name a few. The Accomplishment sentimental sub-wordlist contains the words: "advances", "creates", "managing", "finished", "duties", "achieving", "effects", etc. Calculations of the value of the 5 sentimental tendencies are listed below.

- **Certainty** = (Tenacity + Leveling + Collectives + Insistence/ (Numerical Terms + Ambivalence + Self Reference + Variety)
- **Optimism** = (Praise + Satisfaction + Inspiration)/ (Blame + Hardship + Denial)
- **Activity** = (Aggression + Accomplishment + Communication + Motion)/ (Cognitive Terms + Passivity + Embellishment)
- **Realism** = (Familiarity + Spatial Awareness + Temporal Awareness + Present Concern + Human Interest + Concreteness)/ (Past Concern + Complexity)
- **Commonality** = (Centrality + Cooperation + Rapport)/ (Diversity + Exclusion + Liberation)

In each sentimental dimension, if a text contains more sentimental words in the numerator's word groups and the less in denominator's word groups, the text will have a higher sentimental tendency, and vice versa. For instance, since sentimental tendency of Certainty in Chinese banks' CSR reports is significantly higher than that of American banks, Chinese banks' CSR reports, on average, contain more sentimental words in Tenacity and Leveling word list and less sentimental words in e.g. Ambivalence and Self-reference sentimental wordlist than American banks' CSR reports.

In order to analyze Chinese and American banks' CSR mind image construction via discursive features of sentiment, Antconc's concordance function is used to find the discursive contexts in which various sentimental words are located in Chinese and American banks' CSR reports and to explain how various sentimental words construct banks' CSR mind image in specific contexts. The analysis of the discursive construction of Chinese and American banks' CSR mind image via sentiment will be explained in the 5 dimensions of sentimental tendencies: Certainty, Optimism, Activity, Realism, and Commonality.

6.1.1.1 Chinese and American Banks' CSR Mind Image Construction in Certainty

Based on the descriptive analysis in Chap. 5, sentimental tendency of Certainty in Chinese banks' CSR reports is significantly higher than that of American banks' CSR reports.

According to DICTION's explanation, Certainty means language indicating resoluteness, inflexibility, and completeness, and a tendency to speak ex cathedra. Chinese banks' CSR reports present a high Certainty value since they use many sentimental words that can be classified as Tenacity, Leveling, Collectiveness and Insistence and less sentimental words included in Numerical Terms, Ambiance, Self-reference and Variety. They use these words to express their corporate strategy, CSR value and corporate culture, and to construct CSR mind image.

Chinese banks use more Leveling words such as "most", "full", "always", "constantly", and "certain", and less Self-referential words such as "we" and "our", to express their development concept of establishing authority among stakeholders and prestige in the banking industry. American banks, on the other hand, use more Self-referential words and less Leveling words to express their solicitude for stakeholders and the considerate service concept.

Reference is a discourse analysis strategy according to Reisigl and Wodak's (2014) discourse-historical approach to critical discourse analysis. Reference is a discursive strategy that refers to the substitute of certain social actors, objects, phenomenon, events, process and actions in order to achieve the discursive construction of in-group and out-group identities (Reisigl & Wodak, ibid). The DICTION output shows a lower value for Self-reference in Chinese banks' CSR reports than in those of American banks. Chinese and American banks use different ways of locating themselves. American banks tend to use "we" or "our" to represent the company. However, Chinese banks tend to use the banks' name or "the bank" to represent themselves.

> *(1) As a leading global financial services provider, we advise, originate, trade, manage and distribute capital for governments, corporations, institutions and individuals. By putting clients first, leading with exceptional ideas, doing the right thing and giving back, we aim to deliver results today while advancing strategic goals for the future. (Morgan Stanley, 2017).*
>
> *(2) We tell our customers that the choices they make right now matter tomorrow. But these words would ring hollow if we didn't live by them ourselves. (PNC Financial Group, 2017).*
>
> *(3) As a Main Street bank, we take pride in how we relate to and serve our employees, customers and communities. (PNC Financial Group, 2017).*
>
> *(4) Corporate responsibility (CR) is a long-term commitment we've made to our clients, employees, shareholders and communities to conduct our business responsibly. (State Street, 2016).*

American banks use more first person pronouns (e.g. "we", "our") when they express CSR information to their stakeholders. "Our" and "we" are the top 2 keywords in American banks' CSR reports relative to the general English corpus based on CSR keyword analysis in Chap. 5. The word "our" appears 38,408 times in American banks' CSR reports for a percentage of 3.03%. The word "we" appears 25,821 times in American banks CSR reports for a percentage of 2.04%. The first person pronoun is a discursive strategy that personalizes the discourse used by the company to promote the proximity between the company and the reader (Degano, 2010). Banks referring to themselves from the first person perspective has the effect of affection and empathy. This aligns the two sides of the discourse, enhancing the persuasive power and appeal of the discourse (Xu, 2010; Fuoli, 2012). American banks' personalized communicative style eases the psychological relationship between banks and stakeholders, and forms an equal alliance between the two groups. Thus, American banks' customer, employee-centric and service-oriented CSR concepts are achieved and American banks construct an individual-oriented CSR mind image to identify themselves to their stakeholders.

However, the words "we" and "our" are not in the top 50 keywords for Chinese banks' CSR reports. Chinese banks usually use the third person perspective:

the company, company's, the bank or the banks' name when they express CSR information to their stakeholders.

> *(5) The Company is committed to establishing a high standard ESG management system to strengthen its core competitiveness and thus enhance its brand value. The Company had proactively carried out its ESG responsibilities and improved its ESG performance. (China Minsheng Bank, 2017).*

> *(6) ABC contributed wisdom to winning the battle of pollution prevention and control, striving to take a leading role in promoting the building of a more beautiful China. (Agricultural Bank of China, 2017).*

> *(7) As early as 2013, CMB took the lead in connecting credit card services with WeChat public accounts and created a smart WeChat customer service platform. (China Merchant Bank, 2016).*

> *(8) In response to regulatory requirements, prevailing CSR trends and stakeholders' concerns, BoCom regularly reforms its management of responsibility. The bank was the first listed company in China to establish a Social Responsibility Committee under the Board of Directors. During the reporting* period, *the bank improved its responsibility management structure … (Bank of Communication, 2016).*

This third person perspective self-reference mode in banks' CSR reports formulates Chinese banks' non-personal communicative style, or the authoritative communicative style (Wu & Zhang, 2019), by which Chinese banks' CSR concepts, behaviors and achievements are transmitted to their stakeholders, with few interaction or negotiation. With the third person self-reference mode in Chinese banks' CSR reports, distance is formulated between banks and stakeholders. Chinese banks' CSR concept of establishing and maintaining authority is achieved, and Chinese banks construct an authoritative, official corporate image via the third person perspective self-reference words in their CSR reports.

In addition to referring to themselves in the third person, Chinese banks use more Leveling words, such as "most", "full", "always", "constantly", and "certain" to transmit their pursuit of excellence and authority in the banking industry. Chinese banks use sentimental words to express their high-reaching and authority-pursuing development concept and to persuade their stakeholders to accepting their authoritative corporate image. They do so in their CSR reports by illustrating the CSR achievement they've gained and their status in the banking industry.

> *(9) As China's most globalized and integrated bank, Bank of China has a well-established global service network with institutions set up in the Chinese mainland as well as 54 countries and regions. (Bank of China, 2017)*

> *(10) As one of China's largest and most strategically positioned financial enterprises, Agricultural Bank of China is the leading practitioner of inclusive finance. (Agricultural Bank of China, 2017)*

> *(11) In 2016, BoCom ranked top among the Chinese retail banks in a customer satisfaction survey by J.D. Power. One hundred and forty of BoCom's outlets were placed on the Top 1,000 Model Outlets list, making us the bank with the most selected outlets and helping us break our record again. (Bank of Communication, 2016)*

Thus, Chinese banks use more Leveling words and less Self-reference words. Also, their high-reaching, authority-pursuing development concepts and official corporate images are constructed. However, American banks use more Self-reference words to express their employee-centric and service-oriented CSR concepts, and their individualistic CSR images are constructed to their stakeholder.

Additionally, Chinese banks use more sentimental words from the Tenacity and Insistence wordlists in Certainty, for example "will", "continue", "strive", "endeavor", "support", "commit", and "promote", to express their commitment, steadfast endeavors and resolute insistence in supporting national strategy and the CSR contributions they have made to the country. The word "will" has the semantic prosody of "intention" or "plan" which is in a commitment category speech act (Tang, 2008). Chinese banks tend to use "will" to express their CSR visions, commitment and promise of banks' future CSR performance to support national long-term projects.

(12) The Company is committed to establishing a high standard ESG management system to strengthen its core competitiveness and thus enhance its brand value. The Company had proactively carried out its ESG responsibilities and improved its ESG performance. (China Minsheng Bank, 2017).

(13) ABC contributed wisdom to winning the battle of pollution prevention and control, striving to take a leading role in promoting the building of a more beautiful China. (Agricultural Bank of China, 2017).

(14) As early as 2013, CMB took the lead in connecting credit card services with WeChat public accounts and created a smart WeChat customer service platform. (China Merchant Bank, 2016).

(15) In response to regulatory requirements, prevailing CSR trends and stakeholders' concerns, BoCom regularly reforms its management of responsibility. The bank was the first listed company in China to establish a Social Responsibility Committee under the Board of Directors. During the reporting period, the bank improved its responsibility management structure ... (Bank of Communication, 2016).

(16) In 2017, we continued to adhere to the strategic goal of becoming a "Light-operation Bank" and the strategic positioning of "One body with Two Wings" .... (China Merchants Bank, 2017)

Chinese banks' unwavering and insistent national-oriented, national-supporting CSR concepts are expressed via the above sentimental words. Most Chinese banks have integrated the national-supporting CSR concept and national project-orientation into their corporate governance, strategies and values. Thus, Chinese banks construct a country-responsible and national policy-supporting CSR image in their CSR reports.

As for American banks, they use less of the sentimental words from the Tenacity and Insistence wordlist such as "will", "strive", "endeavor", "support", "commit", and "promote". Instead of using "will" to express Certainty, American banks tend to employ "may", "can" or "could" to express their negotiation and communication with their customers, employees and stakeholders.

(17) By driving innovation at a faster pace, we believe that we may fundamentally change the way banking is done. (Morgan Stanley, 2017)

(18) Our goal is to engage deeply on how we can enhance our business approaches in this area, with leadership from senior management. (PNC Financial Group, 2017)

American banks also mention companies' commitment in their CSR reports. However, this is different from the way Chinese banks' express absolute and insistent commitment to national development strategy. American banks express their service commitments for their customers, employees and shareholders. American banks' CSR concepts are corporate value-oriented, unlike those of Chinese banks which tend to be oriented towards national strategy-oriented values. American banks have integrated CSR concepts into their business operations, and they perform CSR concepts throughout their service to customers, clients, employees and shareholders. As for Chinese banks, besides devotion to customers and employees, part of their CSR concepts and CSR activities are supporting national strategy, and are firstly driven by national projects and policies.

> *(19) Our people are our greatest asset — we say it often and with good reason. It is only with their determination and dedication that we can serve our clients, generate long-term value for our shareholders and make lasting contributions to our communities. (Goldman Sachs, 2014)*
>
> *(20) We remain committed to being vigilant to ensure that women and men who have the same roles and perform at the same level are paid equally. (Goldman Sachs, 2017)*
>
> *(21) As a Main Street bank, we take pride in how we relate to and serve our employees, customers and communities and are* committed to making business decisions that positively impact our stakeholders. *(PNC Financial Group, 2017)*

Thus, by using different sentimental words from the Tenacity and Insistence wordlist in Certainty, Chinese banks' unwavering national strategy-oriented and national project-supporting CSR concepts are expressed. Chinese banks construct their country-responsible CSR images as well as their CSR image of practitioners of national strategy in their CSR reports. Meanwhile, American banks convey individual-oriented CSR concepts and a CSR image of profit-creator for customers, employees, and shareholders. This, in turn, is transmitted to stakeholders.

6.1.1.2 Chinese and American Banks' CSR Mind Image Construction in Optimism

Based on the descriptive analysis in Chap. 5, the sentimental tendency of Optimism in Chinese banks' CSR reports is significantly higher than that of American banks.

According to DICTION's explanation, Optimism refers to language that endorses some person, group, concept or event or that highlights their positive entailments. Chinese banks' CSR reports present a high Optimism value since they use many sentimental words from the Praise, Satisfaction, Inspiration categories such as "positive", "successful", "honor", "great", "vigorous", "bright". They rarely use sentimental words from Blame, Hardship, and Denial, such as "suffer", "risk", "threat", "harder", "hadn't", "didn't", "no", "can't" to express their positive corporate strategies, positive CSR concepts and the numerous achievements, current successful undertakings and bright futures.

(22) In positive response to technological changes, we vigorously promoted the utilization of technologies such as big data, artificial intelligence and biometrics, to improve the efficiency of financial services by use of modern technologies. (Bank of China, 2017)

(23) It spends great efforts to promote inclusive finance, such as building the all-function WeChat Bank, initiating innovative mobile finance, and opening community banks. (Shanghai Pudong Development Bank, 2014)

(24) For a long time, the Company has been greatly improving the use efficiency of fixed assets in offices and reduced resource consumption by.... (China Minsheng Bank, 2016)

(25) The Bank was honored "Best Enterprise for Supply Chain Finance" by the organizing committee of the China Supply Chain Finance Annual Conference. (China Citic Bank, 2017)

Combined with the above contexts, high Optimism in Chinese banks' CSR reports indicates their optimistic attitude about their current operations, future prospect, and the contributions they will make for their stakeholders. To some degree, Chines banks experience a fast-growing and rapid development period, and they pay less attention to the potential risks of their business operations. Sentimental words of Optimism in banks' CSR reports indicate Chinese banks' risk preference and expansive strategy—how they continuously forge ahead with operating concepts and optimistic corporate values. There are several reasons why Chinese banks are experiencing explosive and sustained growth. These are mainly due to China's continuous economic growth, a series of economic reforms and comparatively loose regulatory policies. Additionally, there is no denying that China's economy and comprehensive national strength will embrace steady and healthy growth in the future. Thus, as the leading power in China's economic development, Chinese banks will also embrace bright and promising future prospects. Thus, each of these factors influence and shape Chinese banks' optimistic and positive development strategies, which are embedded in various positive sentimental words in their CSR reports.

The above sentimental words are indeed appraisal resources which are part of the Affect sub-system in Appraisal Theory's Attitude system. According to Appraisal Theory, language is used to evaluate, to adopt stances, to construct textual identity and to manage interpersonal relationships (Martin & White, 2005). The Affect sub-system is designated to illustrate emotion talk by examining the various degrees of positive and negative sentimental tendencies embedded in evaluation words that express concepts such as un/happy, in/security or dis/satisfaction (ibid). Appraisal Theory, especially the Affect sub-system, provides an insightful perspective to identify and evaluate the lexicalization of sentiment in a micro level. This sheds light on the sentimental evaluation of banks' CSR reports. Those positive sentimental words in banks' CSR reports affect the interpersonal relationship between the two parties, as well as stakeholders' perception and reception of banks' CSR values and images. Banks also use positive and optimistic words to better communicate with their stakeholders, as well as to construct and enhance their positive and promising CSR images. This enables them to convince stakeholders of the valuable returns that they can derive from the banks.

The higher Optimism of Chinese banks' CSR reports than American banks' CSR reports may indicate some subjectivity in Chinese banks' CSR reports and image construction in some degree.

(26) Our Tianjin branch strives to solve the financing problem faced by small and micro enterprises..., successfully fulfilling the regulatory requirements of "Three No Less Than". (Agricultural Bank of China, 2017).

Many positive sentimental words like "successfully" are examples of rhetorical manipulation (Merkl-Davies & Brennan, 2007). This is the result, to some degree, of banks' impression management. Managers are assumed to present companies' financial performance or themselves in more positive words or themes. However, Henry (2008) and Davis et al. (2015) propose that the use of sentimental words is a means of overcoming information asymmetries by providing stakeholders with more incremental information about a company's future performance. Previous literature and impression management theory show that the positive or negative words in banks' CSR reports can influence stakeholders' perceptions and attitudes of corporate values and corporate image. Thus, sentimental words in banks' CSR reports, like "successfully" and "great", may be subjective description and evaluation of banks' CSR performance in some degree, as given by the banks themselves in order to persuade stakeholders.

(27) While embarking on this new journey in 2018, we will continue to inherit and carry forward the fine tradition of China Merchants Bank, stay vigilant and forge ahead, carry the banner of "Time-honored China Merchants Bank", firmly fulfill the tenet of "coming from society, repaying society", and cooperate with stakeholders to create a brighter future. (China Merchants Bank, 2017).

The sentimental word "will" is a modal verb expressing future promise, intention and vision. It also indicates subjective, visionary and prospective construction of banks' CSR concepts and images.

Numerous sentimental words categorized as optimism in Chinese banks' CSR reports indicate Chinese banks' active and positive strategies, innovative operating concepts, and optimistic corporate values. Thus, Chinese banks' positive and promising CSR images are constructed. At the same time, the higher Optimism may also indicate the prospective construction of Chinese banks' CSR images.

As for American banks, instead of using many positive and optimistic sentimental words to praise their CSR performance and CSR concepts, they tend to concretely express the profits and welfare they have created for their shareholders, as well as their CSR goals and values.

(28) While not everyone has agreed with what we've said or done, I'm proud of the actions we've taken to define who we are and what we stand for as a company. A firm of our size and scale achieves great and big things when we put our mind to it — but my colleagues also impact the lives of many in small but meaningful ways each day. The ways we help make our communities stronger, provide opportunities to those who need support, protect our environment and celebrate diversity are the truest reflection of our values and the progress we enable around the world. (Citi, 2017)

(29) Our mission is to become essential to our customers by providing differentiated products and services to help them achieve their aspirations. (American Express, 2017)

(30) We have invested in improving controls, including those related to risk, compliance and audit, and our progress in these areas is enabling us to safely run and grow our business. In order to become an indisputably strong and stable company, we must ensure that all our employees, at all levels, are held accountable to the highest standards of ethics and professional behavior. (Citi, 2017)

The above American banks' illustration of their CSR performance and values illustrates concrete, detailed care for their people, and services provided for their stakeholders. However, the diminished use of optimistic sentimental words reveals American banks' steady and conservative development concept over these years, as opposed to the rapid-growth development expressed by Chinese banks. Data about the growth rates of Chinese and American banks' total assets are presented in Chapter 5. They show much higher growth rates in total assets among Chinese banks than among American banks from 2013 to 2017. Thus, American banks tend to use less positive and optimistic sentimental words to state their current stable and conservative development concept in corporate governance and CSR performance.

American banks also use "risk" to objectively express potential problems in their current operations or future development, as well as the inadequacies in their CSR performance.

(31) The top issues identified were <u>ethical conduct, systemic risk and transparency and accountability,</u> all of which are fundamental to our business and citizenship success. (Citi, 2014)

(32) The fast-paced, complex and constantly evolving nature of global financial markets requires that the firm maintain a risk-management culture that is incisive, knowledgeable about specialized products and markets, and subject to ongoing review and enhancement. (Morgan Stanly, 2016)

(33) <u>International investing entails greater risk</u>, as well as greater potential rewards compared to U.S. investing. <u>These risks include</u> political and economic uncertainties of foreign countries as well as the risk of currency fluctuations. (Morgan Stanly, 2016)

To summarize, American banks' CSR reports have less positive and optimistic sentimental words and more negative words than those of Chinese banks. This reflects American banks' conservative development/growth concept and objective construction of their CSR images. The higher Optimism tendency and fewer negative words in Chinese banks' CSR reports reflect Chinese banks' active and expansive strategy, as well as their positive and promising mind CSR images.

6.1.1.3 Chinese and American Banks' CSR Mind Image Construction in Activity

Based on the descriptive analysis in Chap. 5, the sentimental tendencies of Activity in Chinese banks' CSR reports is significantly higher than that of American banks.

According to DICTION's explanation, Activity refers to language featuring movement or change in the implementation of ideas, and the avoidance of inertia. Chinese banks' CSR reports present a high Certainty values since they use many sentimental words from the Aggression, Accomplishment, Communication, and Motion sub-lists. These include "seize", "struggle", "pursue", "develop", "created", "accomplishing", "driving", "explore", "advocate", "actively", "achieve". Less words come from Passivity. These would include words such as "think", "estimation", "idea", "hesitation", "steady". These sentimental words from the wordlist of Aggression, Accomplishment, etc. express their activity and reform in corporate structural adjustment, upgrading business mode, and innovation-driven development strategy in order to improve banks' operating efficiency and support national strategy in a better way under China's supply side reform in the new era. See the example below:

> *(34) As a major cooperative bank for China COSCO Shipping Group Corporation, the Shanghai Branch actively supports the corporation to participate in "Belt and Road" construction. (China Merchants Bank, 2017)*

> *(35) In face of the period of historic opportunities for great achievements, as a large state-owned commercial bank, the Bank will follow Xi Jinping Thought on Socialism with Chinese Characteristics for a New Era, fully implement the spirit of the 19th National Congress of the Communist Party of China, persistently enable advancement through technology, drive development through innovation, deliver performance through transformation and enhance strength through reform… (Bank of China, 2017)*

> *(36) Driven by the wave of Fintech, BOC achieved a number of technological breakthroughs in 2017. (Bank of China, 2017)*

> *(37) We supported the development of small and micro businesses, boosting structural reform on the supply side and powering transformation and upgrading of the real economy to improve quality and efficiency. (Agricultural Bank of China, 2016)*

Combined with the above contexts, Chinese banks use many sentimental words to present stakeholders with the achievements they have gained and their initiative in internal business innovations, products, and structural reforms in order to bring convenience and profits to stakeholders. High Activity can indicate Chinese banks' innovative, technology-driven corporate conceptions and transformation-oriented development strategies. China, as a nation, is the primary stakeholder for Chinese banks. China is experiencing massive transformations in many fields, and thus Chinese banks also need to conduct their own transformations. Their businesses need to be upgraded in order to serve the national financial strategies and the ever-increasing demands of stakeholders. This also coincides with what President Xi advocated in the 19th National Congress of the CPC—modern society's major social contradictions have been transformed into the contradiction between the people's ever-growing needs for a better life and developmental disparities.

Furthermore, under the background of China's "the Belt & Road Initiative", additional financial liberalization, and improved international standing, Chinese banks have adopted the internationalization development strategy in their business operations and structural reforms. This is done in order to serve the opening-up policy, and to improve the internationalization of the Chinese banking industry as a whole.

> *(38) ABC has served free trade zone construction, made more efforts in cross-border financial service innovations, and enhanced the international competitiveness of Chinese enterprises. (Agricultural Bank of China, 2016)*

(39) The Bank has accelerated the internationalization of its operations, setting up overseas institutions in 29 countries and regions and providing cross-region... (China Construction Bank, 2016)

Thus Chinese banks' reformative corporate structures and strategies, their innovation-driven CSR concepts and their active CSR mind images are embedded in the sentimental words of their CSR reports.

As for American banks, instead of using many sentimental words of Motion to express their activity in business modes and business structure reforms, they use more sentimental words from Passivity and Cognitive Terms, such as "maintain", "think", "estimation", "idea", "steady" to describe their current stable development status and mature business mode. They also use them to express their conservative and steady development concepts and CSR mind image.

(40) Morgan Stanley maintains significant market positions in its three business segments—Institutional Securities, Wealth Management and Investment Management. (Morgan Stanley, 2017)

(41) In 2017, our voluntary turnover rates by region continued to remain stable or within expected ranges. A consistent range of employee turnover indicates the stability of our business, balanced by our ability to refresh talent from external sources. (Morgan Stanley, 2017)

(42) Through our involvement, we are demonstrating continued prudent EHS risk management for the firm while supporting the company's growth and the goals of our investors. (Goldman Sachs, 2017)

(43) We have 200 years of experience helping our clients meet the world's toughest challenges and embrace its greatest opportunities. (Citi, 2016)

American banks tend to express their competitiveness and trustworthiness over other banks by stating their long-lasting business structures and the stability of their current business. American banks have existed longer than Chinese banks and bear a long-standing development history. Situated in the U.S.A, the most developed capitalist country and a mature market economy, American banks have achieved an advanced and sophisticated developmental status (i.e. corporate governance, business models, product structures, etc.) Thus, perhaps, there is no need for them to actively reform their business operations as boldly as Chinese banks do. Besides, even though American banks have already recovered from the 2008 financial crisis and achieved stable growth rates, they still maintain the cautious attitude in their business management. All of these current developmental statuses and concepts are conveyed in their CSR reports. American banks intend to win their stakeholders' trust and persuade them to accept their trustworthy, reliable CSR image by stating their mature business modes, stability of business and prudent concepts in corporate development in CSR reports. They do so by using sentimental words which show stability and steadiness instead of activity.

To summarize, there are more Motion and Aggression sentimental words and less Passivity words in Chinese banks' CSR than American banks'. This reflects Chinese banks' corporate structural reform activities and innovation-driven development strategies. Chinese banks' active and innovative mind CSR images are constructed and transmitted to stakeholders in their CSR reports. The lower Activity tendency and fewer Motion words in American banks' CSR reports reflect the stability of American banks' current business operation, as well as their steady and stable development strategies. American banks' conservative CSR image is constructed and transmitted to stakeholders in their CSR reports.

6.1.1.4 Chinese and American Banks' CSR Mind Image Construction in Realism

Based on the descriptive analysis in Chap. 5, and different from the other 4 sentimental indicators, the sentimental tendency of Realism in Chinese banks' CSR reports is significantly lower than that of American banks.

According to DICTION's explanation, Realism refers to language describing tangible, immediate, recognizable matters that affect people's everyday lives. High Realism values indicate a text's detailed and concrete orientation toward familiar objects. Chinese banks' CSR reports present a lower Realism value since they use less sentimental words from the sub-wordlists of Concreteness, Familiarity, Spatial and Temporal Awareness, Present Concern, and Human Interest, such as "regulations", "property", "for", "bring", "live", "give", "woman", "ourselves", "their". They use more words from Past Concerns and Complexity, such as "provided", "achieved". They also use some long words, including long adjectives.

Chinese banks frequently use Past Concern words such as "provided", "achieved" and long sentimental adjectives to express our achievements in supporting national strategies, and their endeavor for these CSR achievements. Examples include:

> *(44) China Construction Bank ("CCB", "the Bank" or "the Group") achieved outstanding results by forging ahead with reforms and striving towards the transformation... (China Construction Bank, 2016)*
>
> *(45) ABC also provided RMB 1,440 billion of agriculture-related loans to 13 major grain producing areas throughout China. (Agricultural Bank of China, 2016).*
>
> *(46) As of the end of 2017, BOC had achieved full outlet coverage of three counties in the Xiongan New Area, contracted 306 service points in 557 natural villages of Xiongan to help farmers. (Bank of China, 2017)*

Meanwhile, American banks tend to use more sentimental words from Present Concern, Concreteness, and Familiarity such as "for", "bring", "live", "give", "woman" to express their specific care and efforts for their people and current CSR behaviors for their shareholders' interests and welfare.

> *(47) Our efforts focus on developing and advancing women and other diverse talent, increasing team member engagement and strengthening our workplace culture, growing our diverse supplier base, implementing inclusive policies and practices, and investing in emerging technologies to meet evolving customer preferences. (Wells Fargo, 2017)*
>
> *(48) The service not only helps48)* bring these small business owners *into the formal banking sector, but also* provides users *the potential for greater economic well-being. (Citi, 2016)*

The above analysis of Chinese banks' higher Certainty value than American banks' illustrates that Chinese banks use many adjectives from Tenacity and Insistence and less Self-reference words to express their authority and the achievements they have made in supporting national strategy. Since this part reflects Chinese banks' CSR contributions to their top stakeholder—the country and the public, the remaining stakeholders who are the mainstream group of CSR report readers (e.g. clients, and shareholders) may feel the unfamiliarity in Chinese banks' CSR reports. Chinese banks' CSR reports present a lower Realism value is also due to their less frequent use of sentimental words from the sub-wordlists Concreteness, Familiarity, and Human Interest, and more frequent use of words from Past Concern. Thus, the sentimental analysis in the Certainty part is the insistence with the Realism value in Chinese banks' CSR reports. Both the higher Certainty value and the lower Realism value in Chinese banks' CSR reports indicate Chinese banks' country-responsible and national strategy-oriented CSR mind image. They are also indicative of American banks' CSR image of profit-creator for employees, and shareholders.

Realism also expresses language's description of tangible and objective facts, rather than the subjective descriptions. Different American banks' factual statement of CSR concepts and behaviors made for their people, Chinese banks have a lower Realism since they prospectively describe CSR commitments to their stakeholders. They also express CSR vision and slogan for the future by positive sentimental words, in order to establish a positive and optimistic CSR image. Examples include:

> *(49) According to the overall deployment of the Three-Year Plan for the construction of the learning and development system, the Company will comprehensively improve training and operational support capabilities to corporate university standards, further strengthen the integration of internal and external resources... so as to continuously achieve cost reduction and efficiency. (Chinese Minsheng Bank, 2017)*
>
> *(50) ABC remains true to our original aspiration and keeps our mission firmly in mind, and applies the guiding principles of the 19th CPC National Congress into all operations and reform. (Agricultural Bank of China, 2017)*

Furthermore, the above analysis of Chinese banks' higher Optimism values than American banks' reflects Chinese banks, besides showing objective and factual construction of CSR image, also express prospective construction of their CSR image. Chinese banks use more positive and optimistic sentimental words to express banks' future commitments, intentions and CSR prospect. American banks use more concrete words to convey their service provided to their stakeholders.

Thus, the sentimental analysis in Optimism also coincidences with the lower Realism value for Chinese banks' CSR reports. Both the higher Optimism value and the lower Realism value in Chinese banks' CSR reports indicate Chinese banks' prospective construction of their CSR mind images.

6.1.1.5 Chinese and American Banks' CSR Mind Image Construction in Commonality

According to DICTION's explanation, Commonality = (Centrality + Cooperation + Rapport)/ (Diversity + Exclusion + Liberation) and Commonality means language highlighting the agreed-upon values of a group and rejecting idiosyncratic modes of engagement. Based on the descriptive analysis in Chap. 5, the sentimental tendency of Commonality in Chinese banks' CSR reports (52.44) is significantly higher than that of American banks (50.56). Both Chinese and American banks use many sentimental words from the Cooperation sub-wordlists, such as "accompanies", "union", "close", "consistent", and from the Rapport sub-wordlist, such as "communities", "incorporated", "joined", "contribution" in their CSR reports. They do this in order to establish a good relationship with their stakeholders.

As for the differences, Chinese banks' CSR reports present a higher value for Commonality since they use more sentimental words from the Centrality sub-wordlist such as "primary", "fundamental", "standard", "core". They use these to express their centralized, collective CSR concept and behaviors in being responsible for country, national strategy and public as well. This is also due to Chinese banks' financial business ranges, which are smaller than those of American banks'. See below for examples.

> *(51) Serving "Sannong" (meaning agriculture, rural areas, and farmers) is not only an important mission given to ABC by the CPC Central Committee and the State Council, but also ABC's fundamental purpose. (Agricultural Bank of China, 2016)*
>
> *(52) Organize CSR training, communication with the core members of head office's CSR team and other activities to discuss CSR standards and spread CSR information, laying a solid foundation for CSR practices. (Bank of Communication, 2016)*

The above context reveals that many Chinese banks' CSR concepts are developed based on national initiatives. The object of their CSR values and performances may be the initiatives of the country and banks' management groups. Thus, their CSR concepts and behaviors, as well as their business services, are standardized and less diverse. Also, Chinese banks are more centralized in their banking services, and therefore less diverse than American banks. Thus, they may use the sentimental words in Centrality, such as core, when they describe their business structures in their CSR reports.

> *(53)* The Bank's core business *is commercial banking, including corporate banking, personal banking and financial markets services. (Bank of China, 2016).*

However, American banks use less sentimental words from the Centrality sub-wordlist. They use more sentimental words from Diversity such as "variously", "diversity", "diversify", "varied", "range", "different", "specifies", "multiplicity", and from Liberation, such as "freedom", "women", "liberation", "radical", "individuals" to express their varied CSR concepts and behaviors, as well as their diversified financial business products and services. Examples are given below.

(54) Collectively, our diversity and inclusion professionals are partnering more closely with our businesses, our employee and business resource groups, and corporate partners and external alliances... drive accountability for our people through a culture of inclusion and innovation. (New York Melon, 2015)

(55) Globally, we invest in a robust range of diversity and inclusion development programs to help recruit, retain and promote women and multicultural talent. (Morgan Stanley, 2017)

(56) To promote ethical conduct and enhance Citi's culture, we focus on both <u>empowering individuals</u> and creating firm wide policies and programs that embed our values throughout the organization. (Citi, 2016)

The examples above show that American banks have internalized the concept of diversity into their CSR values based on their diversity in stakeholder engagement and business services. For the CSR value level, American banks have developed the individualistic service value since they are the value/interest makers for their employee, customer, clients, and shareholders under the capitalist system. Additionally, liberalism and individualism in American society also influence American banks' CSR value cultivation by highlighting the importance of individuals' interests and diversity in racial and gender groups. For the business product and service level, different from Chinese banks' major business in deposits and loans, American banks are comprehensive financial groups. They can provide diversified financial services (i.e. products for both individual and group customers). Many American banks commit to becoming life-long financial experts who can provide the comprehensive financial services for American citizens. Thus, sentimental words contained in CSR reports show that American banks tend to be more diversified and professional than Chinese banks.

To summarize, the higher Commonality value in Chinese banks' CSR reports than that of American banks' reflects Chinese banks' less diversified business lines, and CSR concepts standardized by the requirement of the country and banks' management groups. Thus, the CSR values transmitted by Chinese banks' CSR reports and the public-oriented CSR mind image of Chinese banks are less diversified and collective. Meanwhile, more sentimental words in the Diversity and Liberation wordlists used in American banks' CSR reports convey American banks' diversified and inclusive CSR corporate values, as well as the individual-oriented CSR mind image.

6.1.2 Chinese and American Banks' CSR Mind Image Construction Via Readability

Readability, the reading ease, refers to the extent to which a document is easy to read and understand in terms of its content and text-based writing styles (Courtis, 2004). Previous studies have indicated the relationship between corporate narrative's readability, company's management group's preference and intentions, corporate financial performance and capital market reaction (Li, 2008; Courtis, 2004). These have been guided by the theories of information asymmetry, signaling theory and the obfuscation hypothesis. Due to the information asymmetry between company and stakeholders, management groups have the opportunity and incentives to manipulate the corporate narrative's readability for impression management. The readability of corporate narratives, such as the CSR report, may serve as a signal to the readers and market. It can influence readers' attitudes towards a company's CSR image and the market's expectation of corporate value. Based on the influencing mechanism between banks' CSR reports' discursive features of readability and banks' CSR mind image guided by the signaling theory and behavioral finance, it can be seen that readability in Chinese and American banks' CSR reports influences readers' perspectives and understanding efficiency of CSR reports. Thus readers' attitudes towards banks' CSR concept and CSR mind image are influenced.

This section is based on the outcome of calculations of Chinese and American banks' CSR reports' readability by Coh-Metrix and WordSmith in Chap. 5 and the co-constructive mechanism between readability and banks' CSR mind image. It analyzes how Chinese and American banks' CSR values and CSR mind images are constructed and transmitted by discursive features of readability evaluation (lexical readability, syntactic readability and textual readability) in their CSR reports.

The readability evaluation indicators STTR and mean word length on the lexical level, mean sentence length and all connectives incidence on the syntactic level, the Flesch-Kincaid Grade Level in textual level in Chinese banks' CSR reports are significantly higher than those of American banks. Flesch Reading Ease in Chinese banks' CSR reports is significantly lower than that of American banks. These above readability indicators show that Chinese banks' CSR reports contain more information, longer words, longer sentences and more complex logical relations than American banks' CSR reports.

Since readability is the outcome of textual content and text-based writing styles (Courtis, ibid), this section focuses on Chinese and American banks' CSR reports' different contents and writing or communicating styles which are reflected by discursive features of readability in banks' CSR reports. This is used to examine Chinese and American banks' different CSR concepts and discursively constructed CSR mind images.

Chinese banks' English version CSR reports are difficult to comprehend than American banks' due to their high lexical density, long words and long sentences. Based on the outcome of readability evaluation, concordance and plot view function of Antconc, as well as close reading, it is found that Chinese banks use more notional words, longer words, and longer sentences to express their CSR values and performance in supporting principles of the Party and national strategy, and answering to the requirements of regulatory authorities. Several examples are listed below.

> *(58) 2017 saw the 19th National Congress of the Communist Party of China (the 19th CPC National Congress), a critical period during which the ABC met tough challenges in reform and forged ahead. Adhering to the fundamental principle of serving "Sannong" and the real economy, focusing on the general requirements for promoting development of the economy, and firmly upholding the underlying principle of pursuing progress while ensuring stability, ABC remains true to our original aspiration and keeps our mission*

firmly in mind, and applies the guiding principles of the 19th CPC National Congress into all operations and reforms. (Agricultural Bank of China, 2017)

(59) In the background of national focus on the improvement of quality and efficiency, and the supply side structural reform, with accelerating financial marketization, disintermediation, integration, digitization, internationalization and other processes in China... firmly grasps the essential requirement for finance serving the real economy. (China Industrial Bank, 2016)

The above excerpts show that Chinese banks use long and complex compound sentences to express the initiatives in responding the call of Party policies and national strategies. These parts of CSR information contain many long terminologies which may be difficult for non-Chinese readers, including the international investors.

Additionally, those parts of CSR information are Chinese banks' commitment to their top stakeholder, the country. However, the rest of the stakeholders, such as the customers and shareholders may feel unfamiliar when they read the CSR reports. Thus, these long words and sentences employed in Chinese banks' CSR reports may decrease readers' perceptive and understanding efficiency of CSR information and concepts, as expressed by the CSR reports. The discursive features of higher lexical density and longer words and sentences may distance the bank and their stakeholders. Thus banks' Party policy and national strategy-oriented CSR concept and authoritative, official CSR mind image are transmitted to stakeholders.

As for American banks, instead of using long words and complex sentences, they use plain language to express their CSR concepts and behaviors directly. Furthermore, those CSR concepts and behaviors are about their commitments and values they have made to their various stakeholders. These stakeholders are also the majority of the CSR report readers: customers, employees and shareholders. Thus, the readers can better understand their CSR concepts and behaviors. The effective negotiation between the banks and stakeholders is achieved. Examples are given below.

(60) Citi's mission is to serve as a trusted partner to our clients by responsibly providing financial services that enable growth and economic progress. Our core activities are safeguarding assets, lending money, making payments and accessing the capital markets on behalf of our clients. (Citi, 2016)

(61) Our service is built on a foundation of trust. Our customers trust us to deliver on our promises and make things right if we fall short. They know we've got their backs, and they pay us back with their loyalty. (American Express, 2017)

After the SEC's enactment of the Plain English Rule, American listed companies pay great attention to the readability of their annual report as well as other public corporate narratives, including CSR reports. The CSR information about American banks' individual-oriented CSR values and amiable CSR mind images are transmitted to their stakeholders via CSR reports' plain language.

The writing and communicating styles in banks' CSR reports also influence the stakeholders' understanding efficiency of CSR information and attitudes towards banks' CSR value and CSR mind image. Based on the previous literature about the empirical and theoretical analysis of the relationship between corporate narratives' readability and corporate financial activities, it can be seen that corporate narratives' readability is connected to the management group's intentions and corporate financial performance. Chinese banks' long sentences and complex sentence structure via numerous connectives in CSR reports, as compared to those of American banks, may indicate Chinese banks' management groups' different governance concepts. Below are several examples.

> *(62) 2014 is the critical year to implement the deepened reform as advocated in the third plenary session of the 18th Party Congress and further the reform. In the new year, we will continue along the fundamental principle of seeking growth while ensuring stability, proactively support and promote the activities to comprehensively deepen the reform and transform the way of economic development, truly improve the quality and efficiency of our development, and make new contributions to the sustainable development in economy, society and environment. (Industrial and Commercial Bank of China, 2013)*

> *(63) To show our integrity and determination, we strengthened the top-level design, promoted reform and innovations in key areas including the "Big Sannong", "New Sannong" and "Unique Sannong", enhanced financial services for supply-side agricultural reform and fostered our "No.1 Project" for serving "Sannong", so as to open an economic renaissance for rural areas, better living environment, and prosperous farmers. (Agricultural Bank of China, 2016)*

The above examples of long and complex sentence structure are quoted from the Chairman's Statement in the CSR report of the Industrial and Commercial Bank of China and the President's Statement in the CSR report of the Agricultural Bank of China. They show that Chinese banks' presidents use many connectives for foreshadowing, in order to explain the unwavering perseverance of CSR achievements. Chinese banks' management group report the CSR achievements and CSR reactions to the Party and government in banks' CSR reports. The management group's political government-oriented CSR concept and corporate concept of governance are expressed via these long and complex sentences in CSR reports.

As for how managerial groups' government-oriented corporate concept of governance influence their writing style, reasons can be explained from two aspects. As the most vital state-owned financial enterprises in China, many Chinese banks regard the government as their primary stakeholder to which they need to contribute the most. Chinese banks have the responsibility to coordinate with and to support the country's financial development strategies. Thus, Chinese banks use a long passage to disclose their contributions to government. On the other hand, most of the management groups in Chinese banks, especially high-ranking leader groups, have the dual identities: firstly, government officials, and secondly managers or bankers. This is because they are nominated by the Party and the government. Thus, they will pursue achievements in their official careers in order to gain approval from their superior administrative units and get government and self-political promotions in the end. Under such managerial groups' corporate values, and combined with the specific contexts above, Chinese banks' CSR reports have become the platform for management groups to report their achievements to government and the public.Chinese banks use high lexical density, complex terms, adjectives and adverbs, and long compound sentences in their CSR reports. This indicates that Chinese banks' CSR reports contain official communicative and writing style of administrative documents. The generic features as administrative documents and the national strategy-related content in Chinese banks' CSR reports are expressed by the discursive features in readability evaluation. They reflect the government-oriented CSR concept of Chinese banks' management groups and the official CSR mind image of Chinese banks.

American banks are guided by the SEC's Plain English Rule. The management groups aim to transmit their efforts in value creation to their stakeholders—customers, employees, shareholders—in a straightforward way via short sentence and lucid sentence structure. See below for examples.

> *(64) Today, we have the strategy, stability and scale to grow the business by supporting our clients as they create economic activity, fuel innovation, and secure economic futures for people around the world. (Morgan Stanley,2017)*
>
> *(65) First and foremost, we're guided by our mission to responsibly provide financial services that enable growth and progress. (Citi, 2016)*
>
> *(66) We deliver value for both our business and our communities by investing financial and human resources in ways that address the social, environmental, and economic needs of our communities, customers, colleagues, shareholders, and partners. (American Express, 2017)*

The above examples are quoted from CEO letters of 3 American Banks. Compared with Chinese banks' Statements from their Chairmen or Presidents, sentence length and patterns in American banks' CSR reports' CEO letters are shorter and simpler. American banks' management groups express their efforts made for stakeholders in a more personalized way. This shortens the distance between readers and the bank and enables readers to understand banks' CSR values and behaviors. Different from the state-owned nature of Chinese banks, the equities of American banks are owned by many giant financial groups and banks' equity structure is decentralized. The CEO of American banks is nominated by a board of directors which is composed of the major shareholders, thus American banks' CEOs needs to be responsible to the board of directors. Different from the dual identities of Chinese banks' president: government official and manager, American banks' CEOs are merely the banks' managers who need to create more value for their people, customers, employees and shareholders, in order to achieve the utmost value for the company. This shows that the corporate value-oriented CSR concepts of American banks' management groups are expressed, and pragmatist CSR mind images are constructed, via the discursive features in readability evaluation in American banks' CSR reports.

To summarize, the discursive features of lexical density, word length, sentence length, connectives, Flesch Reading Ease and Flesch-Kincaid Grade Level in readability evaluation of Chinese and American banks' CSR reports influence stakeholders' understanding of banks' CSR concepts, behaviors and CSR mind image.

For CSR reports' content level, the longer terms, adjectives and adverbs, longer sentences and lower reading ease in Chinese banks' CSR reports reflect Chinese banks' national strategy-oriented CSR concept and authoritative and official CSR mind image; American banks' individual-oriented CSR values and CSR mind image are also transmitted by their plain English words in their CSR reports.

For the level of CSR reports' writing and communicative style, the complex sentence patterns and official communicative style of banks president in Chinese banks' CSR reports reflect the government-oriented CSR concept of Chinese banks' management groups and the official CSR mind image of Chinese banks. The corporate value-oriented CSR concept of American banks' management groups, and the pragmatistic CSR mind image of American banks are expressed and constructed by American banks' CEOs' personalized communicative style and lucid sentence patterns in their CSR reports.

6.1.3 A Comparison of Chinese and American Banks' Discursively Constructed CSR Mind Images

Based on the above discursive analysis of various discursive features in sentiment and readability evaluation of banks' CSR reports, Chinese and American banks' different CSR values and CSR mind images have been transmitted and constructed. Tables 6.1 and 6.2 compare Chinese and American banks' discursively constructed CSR mind concepts and images via sentiment and readability evaluation.

Tables 6.1, 6.2 and the detailed qualitative analysis of Chinese and American banks' discursively transmitted CSR concepts and CSR mind images show that the discursive features in different dimensions transmit similar CSR concepts and CSR mind images in both Chinese and American banks' CSR reports. For example, Chinese banks' CSR reports' more Leveling words and less Self-Reference words along the Certainty dimension reflect Chinese banks' authority-pursuing development concept. Readability indicators of high lexical density and long sentence reflect Chinese banks' party policy and national-strategy oriented CSR concepts. Each of them transmits and constructs the Chinese banks' authoritative CSR mind images. Furthermore, the less positive and optimistic words and more words in Present Concern and Concreteness in American banks' CSR reports reflect American banks' objective and conservative construction of CSR mind images.

These findings show that various discursive features along different dimensions may achieve the same communicative purposes—that is they may reflect similar CSR concepts and CSR images. This also indicates the function of multi-dimensional linguistic features in expressing communicative purpose in Biber's register analysis and MDA (Biber & Conrad, 2009). Thus, it can be inferred that banks may adopt different discursive strategies which are realized by different linguistic features in their CSR reports. This enables them to repeat and emphasis their specific CSR values, persuade their stakeholders to accept their CSR values, and enhance their specific CSR images.

According to Tables 6.1 and 6.2, the different CSR values and mind images of the Chinese and American banks are transmitted by the discursive features in their CSR reports.

Chinese banks' CSR reports discursively transmit their authority-pursuing, national strategy-oriented, national project-supporting, collective CSR values. This corresponds to the authoritative, official and country and public-oriented CSR

Table 6.1 Comparison of Chinese and American Banks' discursively constructed CSR mind images via sentiment

		Groups	Discursive Features	CSR Concepts	CSR mind images
Sentiment Evaluation: 5 Dimensional Sentimental Tendencies	Certainty	Chinese Banks	More Leveling words, less self-reference words	High-targeted and authority-pursuing development concept	Authoritative CSR mind image
			More words in tenacity and Insistence	National strategy-oriented and national projects-supporting CSR concept	Country-responsible, national strategy-oriented CSR image; practitioner of national strategy
		American Banks	More self-reference words	Employee-caring and service-oriented CSR concept	Service-oriented CSR mind image
			Less words in tenacity, insistence	Individual-oriented CSR concept	Value-creator for customers, employees, shareholders
	Optimism	Chinese Banks	Numerous sentimental words in Optimism	Active strategy, optimistic corporate value	Positive and promising CSR images; prospective construction of CSR mind image
		American Banks	Less positive and optimistic words and more negative words	Steadfast development/growth concept	Conservative and factual construction of CSR mind image
	Activity	Chinese Banks	More words in Motion and Aggression and less Passivity words	Structure reform and innovation-driven development strategy	Active and innovative CSR mind image
		American Banks	Few Motion words	Steady, conservative development strategy	Conservative and stable CSR mind image

(continued)

Table 6.1 (continued)

		Groups	Discursive Features	CSR Concepts	CSR mind images
	Realism	Chinese Banks	More words in Past Concern, Complexity	Future commitment-oriented CSR value	Prospective construction of CSR mind image
		American Banks	More words in Present Concern, Concreteness	Current individual value-oriented CSR concept	Conservative and and factual construction of CSR mind image
	Commonality	Chinese Banks	More words in Centrality and less words in Diversity	Less diversified and collective CSR value	Public-oriented CSR mind image
		American Banks	More sentimental words in Diversity and Liberation	Diversified and inclusive CSR value	Individual-oriented CSR mind image

Table 6.2 Comparison of Chinese and American Banks' discursively constructed CSR mind images via readability

		Groups	Discursive features	CSR concepts	CSR mind images
Readability Evaluation	Content level	Chinese Banks	Long terminologies, adjectives and adverbs, long sentences and low reading ease	Government policy-driven and national strategy-oriented CSR concept	Authoritative and official CSR mind image
		American Banks	Plain English: less notional words, short words and sentence	Individual-oriented CSR value	Individualistic and amiable CSR mind image
	Writing and communicative style level	Chinese Banks	Complex sentence patterns(more connectives) and official communicative style of banks' president	Management group's government-oriented CSR concept	Authoritative CSR mind image
		American Banks	Lucid sentence patterns and banks' CEO's personalized communicative style	Management group' s corporate value-oriented CSR concept	Pragmatistic CSR mind image

mind images. American banks' CSR reports discursively transmit their individualistic, corporate value-oriented, diversified CSR values. This corresponds with their admirable, individual-oriented, paragmatistic CSR mind images.

Additionally, Chinese banks' CSR reports discursively reflect their expansive strategy and optimistic corporate values, reform and innovation-oriented development strategy, and future prospect-oriented CSR values. This corresponds to the positive, active, innovative CSR image, as well as the prospective construction of CSR mind image. American banks' CSR reports discursively transmit their steadfast growth concepts, conservative development strategies, and individual-oriented CSR values. This corresponds to the steady and conservative CSR mind image, as well as the conservative and factual construction of CSR mind image.

In order to improve and achieve better communication and relationships with stakeholders, especially foreign investors, and to establish an internationalized CSR image under the background of a series of financial opening up policies, Chinese banks may learn from American banks in their discursive CSR value transmission and CSR mind image construction via the adoption of some discursive features in CSR reports. Chinese banks have the CSR values and mind images with their own characteristics, and part of those values and images are the merits and competitiveness of Chinese banks which they need to maintain and carry forward. Examples of this are Chinese banks' public-oriented CSR values, optimistic corporate values, and reform and innovation-driven development strategy.

However, comparing with American banks' awareness in employing discursive strategies to transmit CSR values and mind images, Chinese banks still have room to improve. They need to recontextualize the English versions of their CSR reports, both in composition and translation, via multi-dimensional discursive features. This will enable them to better suit international contexts of CSR information disclosure, and meet the reading conventions and demands of international stakeholders.

Chinese banks' English version CSR reports are composed to communicate with international stakeholders. Thus, they need to re-contextualize when composing or translating CSR reports, according to the international stakeholders' contexts. Recontextualization is vital for their overseas CSR value and image transformations. Corporations need to do some deletions, recombination, additions, and substitutions when they transmit corporate culture overseas via translations (Wu et al., 2016; Wu & Li, 2017). It is better for Chinese banks to write new English versions of CSR reports, based on the international contexts, instead of translating the Chinese versions. If this task is inconvenient for Chinese banks, they also need to recontextualize during translation, based on the context of American banks' CSR reports and their target international readers' sociocultural, political, economic context. Examples of this would be deemphasizing the background and achievement reporting sections, and expressing national strategy-oriented CSR values and behaviors in a lucid way. They also need to react more to individual stakeholders' needs in a causal way, in order to more efficiently construct and transmit their amiable CSR mind images.

Like their American counterparts, Chinese banks also need to use less sentimental words from Certainty and Commonality. They also should disclose more CSR information (concepts and behaviors) targeted at the majority of the CSR report readers:

customers, individual shareholders and employees. Indeed, Chinese banks have done perfectly in endeavoring for peoples' values all the time. However, comparing to their disclosures of government-oriented CSR values and performances, the highlights of the individual-focused CSR values and performance are not eye-catching and fully expressed. Chinese banks need more intimate communication and interaction with the majority of their CSR report readers.

Also, American banks are used to expressing their CSR values and behavior in a subjective way by using less positive and optimistic sentimental words, and more words in realism. Thus, in order to suit the context of English version banks' CSR reports, and meet the demands of the majority of both international and domestic stakeholders, Chinese banks need to use more concrete and concise words. This will enable them to express their CSR values and performances in a direct and subjective way, as well as in certain degree, reduce the usage of CSR future commitment to the country and the public.

Furthermore, unlike their American counterparts, Chinese banks' CSR reports have the generic features of government documents. This is due to the low reading ease at the lexical, syntactic and textual levels. Besides using CSR reports as a platform to report achievements, Chinese banks also need to use less long notional terms, and less long sentences and complex patterns to express their endeavors to gain those achievements. Chinese banks need to use plain English to express their CSR values and behaviors to the majority of their stakeholders. More importantly, Chinese banks need to pay attention to culture and language transfer during the translation and composition of the English versions of their CSR reports.

6.2 The Discursive Construction of Chinese and American Banks' CSR Behavior Images

Banks' CSR behavior images are the outcomes of their CSR behaviors. The analysis of discursive construction of banks' CSR behavior image in CSR reports is realized by the CSR keyword analysis of banks' CSR reports. A text's keyword can present the unique keyword features of the text comparing with another text. Banks' CSR keyword features in CSR relative to the corpus of general English (AmE06 and BE06) can reflect banks' CSR activities at the content level, which are the embodiments of bank's CSR behavior image.

Banks' CSR keywords are calculated based on Antconc' keyword function, and classified into 4 categories: CSR keywords about "community and society", CSR keywords about "employees", CSR keywords about "environment", CSR keywords about "corporate governance" based on famous CSR research databases, CSRhub's classification of commercial banks' CSR and Zhu's (2009) standard framework of commercial banks' CSR performance. Based on the co-constructive mechanism between CSR behavior image and CSR keywords in CSR reports in the theoretical chapter, these 4 categories of CSR keywords can discursively reflect banks'

CSR content, CSR behavior in community and society, employees, environment, and corporate governance, respectively.

According to the quantitative and descriptive analysis in Chap. 5, Chinese and American banks' CSR reports have different CSR keywords features. The 4 CSR keywords evaluation indicators: the percentage of CSR keywords about "community and society" in Chinese banks' CSR reports are significantly higher than in American banks' CSR reports. The percentage of CSR keywords from the "employee", "environment" and "corporate governance" in Chinese banks' CSR reports are lower than American banks' CSR reports. Based on the outcome of the keyword analysis of Chinese and American banks' CSR reports and a comparison of Chinese and American banks' keywords categories via Independent Sample T-test in Chap. 5, this section focuses on how Chinese and American banks' CSR behaviors and CSR behavior images are expressed and constructed discursively by 4 categories of CSR keywords in CSR reports. Chinese and American banks' discursively constructed CSR behavior images are also compared.

6.2.1 Chinese and American Banks' CSR Behavior Image Construction Via CSR Keywords of "Community and Society"

The outcome of the keyword analysis in Chap. 5 shows that the percentage of CSR keywords about "community and society" in Chinese banks' CSR reports is significantly higher than those of American banks. They also contain different keywords concerning "community and society". See Table 6.3.

Table 6.3 shows that Chinese banks disclose more CSR information concerning their CSR contributions to community, and especially to society, than do American banks. The sentimental analysis of Chinese banks' CSR reports also shows that Chinese banks express their national strategy-oriented CSR concept and CSR mind image. Based on the corporate identity system, corporate mind image is the

Table 6.3 Comparison of CSR Keywords of "Community and Society" in Chinese and American Banks' CSR Reports

	Total frequency rate (%)	CSR keywords (%)
Chinese Banks	6.7	Poverty (1.32), micro (0.56), projects (0.54), alleviation (0.48), supporting(0.47), rural (0.41), farmers (0.40), agricultural (0.34), national (0.30), promote (0.29), provided (0.28), implementation (0.26), infrastructure (0.24), donated (0.23), charity (0.20), housing (0.19), urbanization (0.18)
American Banks	1.43	Communities (0.52), veterans (0.32), philanthropic (0.21), volunteer (0.20), housing (0.19)

brain of a company. It guides a company's behavior and behavior image construction. Thus, Chinese banks make more CSR contribution in supporting the national economy and people's livelihoods according to country's strategy. CSR keywords "poverty" (1.32%), "micro" (0.56%), "projects" (0.54%), "alleviation" (0.48%), "supporting" (0.47%), "rural" (0.41%), "farmers" (0.40%), "agricultural" (0.34%), "national" (0.30%), "promote" (0.29%), "provided" (0.28%), "implementation" (0.26%), "infrastructure" (0.24%), and "urbanization" (0.18%) are used to express Chinese banks' CSR behaviors in support of national policies such as poverty alleviation, rural issues, and infrastructure construction under "the Belt & Road Initiative".

> *(67) Serving "Sannong" (meaning agriculture, rural areas, and farmers) is not only an important mission given to ABC by the CPC Central Committee and the State Council, but also ABC's fundamental purpose. (Agricultural Bank of China, 2016)*

> *(68) For 15 consecutive years, we have implemented targeted poverty alleviation work in the four counties of Yongshou, Changwu, Xunyi, and Chunhua in Xianyang City, Shaanxi Province, helping more than 200,000 persons in poverty. (Bank of China, 2017)*

> *(69) Minsheng Bank is an important initiator and promoter of Chinese version of "small business finance revolution." In 2009, the Company initiated the segmented market concept of "micro and small," taking micro and small-sized enterprises as an independent financial service group to conduct in-depth research and practice... (China Minsheng Bank, 2013)*

By conducting numerous CSR behaviors in support of the national development strategy, and less CSR behaviors supporting community, Chinese banks construct CSR behavior image as a supporter and practitioner of national strategy. As for American banks, instead of contributing to national development, they express their specific CSR contributions to community development and specific social issue via the CSR keywords "communities" (0.52%), "veterans" (0.32%), "philanthropic" (0.21%), "volunteer" (0.20%), "housing" (0.19%) American banks' CSR activities, such as community development and voluntary work for their community, are less connected with the overall development of country and society at large.

> *(70) With the right group of organization, we knew we could offer more substantial contributions and provide a platform for improved collaboration that could offer greater value to the community. (State Street, 2015)*

> *(71) As we've done elsewhere, we will also deploy the expertise of our firm's employees through our skills-based employee volunteer program, Service Corps, to help build the capacity of our local partners on the ground. (JP Morgan & Chase, 2017)*

> *(72) With the support of our VETNET ERG, BNY Mellon doubled veteran hires in the U.S. over 2014 levels. (BNY Mellon, 2015)*

By expressing their CSR behaviors in support of communities via a series of CSR keywords concerning community development and specific social issues in their CSR reports, American banks establish their CSR behavior images volunteer for community development.

6.2.2 Chinese and American Banks' CSR Behavior Image Construction Via CSR Keywords of "Employee"

The outcome of the keyword analysis in Chap. 5 shows that the percentage of CSR keywords concerning "employee" in Chinese banks' CSR reports is significantly lower than that of American banks. They also have different keywords and emphases concerning "employee". See Table 6.4.

Table 6.4 shows that American banks disclose more CSR information concerning employee than Chinese banks do in their CSR reports. The CSR keyword "employees" ranks 5th according to keyness value in American banks' CSR reports, and 8th in Chinese banks' CSR reports. CSR keywords "training" (0.54%), "education" (0.34%), "opportunities" (0.33%), "well-being" (0.33%), "gender" (0.21%), and "talent" (0.18%) reflect American banks' comprehensive care for their employees' professional development. They invest in and mentor their employees in all phases of the employees' lifecycles. Some American banks regard their employees as their top stakeholder, with corporate value beginning with them.

(73) Our success as a company us a direct result of the character and talent of our employee. (JP Morgan & Chase, 2017)

(74) It's investing in our employees — ensuring they have the resources to reach their goals at work and at home. (Bank of America,2017)

(75) At Citi, we continually enhance the professional development programs and resources offered globally to support the career progress and work/ life balance of our employees. We're also committed to being a truly diverse company where employees come to work every day at a place that recognizes and celebrates our diverse backgrounds and experiences. (Citi, 2017)

(76) Signatories to the charter pledge to have a designated senior executive accountable for gender diversity, set internal gender diversity targets for senior management. (Citi, 2017)

Analysis of CSR keywords concerning employees reveals that American banks' CSR behaviors include providing professional education and training programs, and also resources, in order to train and mentor their employees. American banks devote more to their employees' professional development and self-actualization than do Chinese banks. Additionally, American banks' CSR behaviors of promoting diversity and inclusion in employee development are also expressed via CSR keywords such as

Table 6.4 Comparison of CSR Keywords of "Employee" in Chinese and American Banks' CSR Reports

	Total frequency rate (%)	CSR keywords (%)
Chinese Banks	1.03	Employees (0.45), training (0.32), welfare (0.25)
American Banks	2.5	Employees (0.58), training (0.54), education (0.34), opportunities (0.33), wellbeing (0.33), gender (0.21), talent (0.18)

"diversity" and "gender". Thus, American banks establish an inclusive and employee-centric and CSR behavior image.

As for Chinese banks, less CSR information concerning employees is disclosed comparing with American banks. They are also less diverse in their "employee" CSR keywords in their CSR reports.

(77) BOC actively guides employees to enhance their knowledge about financial security and improve their service awareness and sensitivity to risks... (Bank of China, 2017).

(78) Adhering to the Minimum Wage Standard and related regulations on basic welfare, the Company provides all employees with basic social insurances for pension, medical treatment, unemployment, work-related injury and maternity. (China Minsheng Bank, 2015)

(79) The Company also democratically selects the trade union chairman to safeguard employees' legitimate rights and interests. (China Minsheng Bank, 2014)

The above context reveals how the CSR reports of Chinese banks convey their CSR behaviors pertaining to training their employees' financial knowledge and service awareness, ensuring employees' basic welfare according to national policy and establishing trade union to protect employees' rights. Chinese banks' CSR behaviors concerning employees are less comprehensive. Chinese banks instead focus on training employee expertise, so that employees can generate more value for banks. Also, their care for employee welfare is conducted according to the national policy and is secured by their trade union. Most of the employee related CSR behaviors of Chinese banks remain on the superficial level of employee caring and development. They are driven by banks' development requirements for employees, rather than employees' personal goals, both in work and in life.

Thus, Chinese banks establish less employee-centric CSR behavior image than their American counterparts. This is based on their insufficient employee-related CSR behaviors transmitted by employee-related CSR keywords in their CSR reports.

6.2.3 Chinese and American Banks' CSR Behavior Image Construction Via CSR Keywords of "Environment"

The outcome of the keyword analysis in Chap. 5 shows that the percentage of CSR keywords about the "environment" in Chinese banks' CSR reports is significantly lower than that of American banks. Chinese and American banks have different keywords and emphases concerning "environment" in their CSR reports. See Table 6.5.

The CSR keyword "environmental" ranked 3rd according to keyenss in American banks' CSR reports, and 14th in Chinese banks' CSR reports based on the descriptive analysis of CSR keyword in Chap. 5. American banks disclose more CSR information in their contributions to environmental protection and sustainable development. Many American banks have internalized environmental protection into their corporate strategies in order to achieve environmental sustainability.

Table 6.5 Comparison of CSR Keywords of "Environment" in Chinese and American Banks' CSR Reports

	Total frequency rate (%)	CSR keywords (%)
Chinese Banks	1.29	Green (0.37), environmental (0.36), energy (0.33), carbon (0.23)
American Banks	2.3	Environmental (0.6), energy (0.45), waste (0.30), carbon (0.29), emissions (0.28), climate (0.22), renewable (0.16)

(80) Our strategic management of environmental resources increases profits, helps manage risk, inspires ways to help our clients succeed and supports our communities around the world. (BNY Melon, 2015)

(81) For more than a decade, Citi has increasingly worked with clients to identify areas where there are business opportunities that also positively impact the environment. (Citi, 2017)

The above context shows how American banks' environmental CSR behavior has become banks' development and corporate culture through which they can benefit their customers, clients and employees. In this way, they also set a good example for them in promoting environmental and social sustainability. In addition, American banks also conduct their own environmental protection CSR behaviors spontaneously.

(82) We will also aim to build on our environmental management performance in such areas as reducing greenhouse gas emissions, renewable energy usage, water conservation, waste and recycling. (BNY Melon, 2015)

(83) We also strive to promote sustainability, including energy efficiency and renewable energy, across our buildings, branches and data center. (JP Morgan & Chase, 2017)

American banks' CSR behaviors of initiatively promoting environmental management strategy and social sustainability, as well as influencing more people in practicing environmental protection spontaneously are conveyed by the "environment" keywords in their CSR reports. Thus, American banks construct the CSR behavior image as the practitioners of environmental protection.

Chinese banks express less and simpler environmental protection CSR behaviors as conveyed via the "environment" keywords. The word "green" (0.37) covers the biggest percentage of "environment" CSR keyword category in Chinese banks' CSR reports.

(84) According to regulatory requirements, the Company issued "China Minsheng Bank Provisional Management Method for Green Credit Management of China Minsheng Bank" as the guiding documents for green credit management, which specifies support to industries such as natural gas, wastewater treatment, solid waste treatment, contract energy management, etc. (China Minsheng Bank, 2016).

(85) In 2016, BoCom continued to increase its support for energy conservation, emissions reduction and environmental protection, and developed green finance mechanisms to support the construction of a green economy. (Bank of Communication, 2016)

(86) We endeavor to facilitate the implementation of the state's macro regulatory policies...and prioritize resources to support the development of low-carbon and environmentally friendly economies in China. (Shanghai Pudong Development Bank, 2016)

The above excerpts show that the environmental keyword "green" in Chinese banks' CSR reports reflects Chinese banks' environmental CSR behavior of conducting green finance by offering loans to environmentally friendly enterprises. Chinese banks' environmental CSR behaviors of conducting green finance and low-carbon finance are reactions to CBIRC regulatory requirements, which has been listed above by China Minsheng Bank. These are not banks' initiatives and spontaneous environmental CSR behaviors as compared to American banks. Thus, based on the above environmental CSR behaviors transmitted by "environment" CSR keywords in CSR reports, Chinese banks construct their CSR behavior images as the financial supporters of environmental policy.

6.2.4 Chinese and American Banks' CSR Behavior Image Construction Via CSR Keywords of "Corporate Governance"

The outcome of the keyword analysis in Chap. 5 shows that the percentage of CSR keywords about "corporate governance" in Chinese banks' CSR reports is significantly lower than that of American banks. Chinese and American banks have different keywords and emphases concerning "corporate governance" in their CSR reports. See Table 6.6.

Table 6.6 Comparison of CSR Keywords of "Corporate Governance" in Chinese and American Banks' CSR Reports

	Total frequency rate (%)	CSR keywords (%)
Chinese Banks	8.06	Loans (1.48), responsibilities (0.59), service (0.57), economy (0,55), customers (0.55), branch (0.54), development (0.48), risk (0.45), innovation (0.40), regulations (0.39), governance (0.31), online (0.30), sustainable (0.30), payment (0.25), strategic (0.24), stakeholders (0.23), technology (0.22), supervisors(0.20)
American Banks	11.91	Our (3.03), we (2.04), customers (0.72), global (0.44), risk (0.62), governance (0.50), clients (0.34), services (0.49), shareholders (0.35), diversity (0.34), development (0.29), sustainable (0.33), solutions (0.25), engagement (0,23), capital (0.42), stakeholders (0.21), investing (0.36), commitment (0.36), suppliers (0.22), culture (0.19), ethics (0.19)

Table 6.6 shows that both Chinese and American banks disclose a variety of CSR information in corporate governance. Thus, both Chinese and American banks perform more CSR activities in the field of corporate governance in order to contribute to their stakeholders and to achieve banks' own sustainable development.

Since stakeholder engagement is a major component of banks' CSR behaviors and banks' corporate governance, stakeholder-related keywords cover a large percentage of keywords concerning corporate governance, both in Chinese and American banks' CSR reports, according to Table 6.6. Also, the stakeholder-related keywords vary in Chinese and American banks' CSR reports. Keywords "our" and "we" are the top two keywords in American banks' CSR reports ranked by keyness, whereas, the above two keywords are not included in the top 50 keywords for Chinese banks. Keywords "customer", "employee" and "shareholders" are the 4th, 5th, and 13th significant keyword in American banks' CSR reports, whereas they are the 12th, 8th, and out of the top 50 significant keywords in Chinese banks' CSR reports. American banks use more stakeholder-related keywords such as "we", "our", "customer", "employee", "shareholders" to express their diverse and inclusive CSR behaviors made for their stakeholders.

> *(87) Our strong capital position and low-risk business model is designed to enable us to meet obligations to clients and shareholders, as well as help protect the stability of the larger financial markets. We also offer products and services to our clients to help protect their financial strength. (BNY Melon, 2015)*

> *(88) As part of <u>our customer-centric approach</u> to communicating with customers in a simple and easy-to understand manner, <u>our</u> Global Consumer Banking's U.S. Branded Cards business continued to deliver targeted video messages in 2017. (Citi, 2017)*

The above context shows that American banks' diverse and inclusive CSR behaviors concern providing effective services for their customers, shareholders, and clients via the stakeholder-related CSR keywords. Thus, American banks' CSR behaviors cover most of the interests of all their different stakeholders. These inclusive CSR behaviors of American banks conveyed by various stakeholder-related CSR keywords reflect American banks' diverse CSR behavior images.

As for Chinese banks, less diversified stakeholder-related CSR keywords are used in their CSR reports. Their stakeholder engagement is more connected with, and centralized in their CSR behaviors in making contributions to the country and society.

> *(89) In view of stakeholders' expectations, ABC determined the eight major issues which include "serving 'Sannong', supporting the real economy, poverty alleviation, improving people's livelihoods, optimizing services, promoting public good activities, and facilitating employee development. (Agricultural Bank of China, 2016).*

Thus, the less diverse CSR behaviors of Chinese banks conveyed by less various stakeholder-related CSR keywords, reflects Chinese banks' less diverse and national strategy-oriented CSR behavior image. This coincides with the sentimental evaluation of Chinese banks' mind concepts and mind images in the previous session.

In addition to the diverse stakeholder-related CSR keywords in the field of corporate governance, American banks use more CSR keywords, such as "risk", "sustainable", "governance", to express their risk management, advancing sustainability and stability in corporate governance.

> *(90) Internal audit, a function independent of the lines of business as well as Risk Management and Compliance, tests and evaluates the firm's risk governance and management, as well as its internal control process. (JP Morgan & Chase, 2017)*
>
> *(91) We have also continued to invest in and focus on compliance, risk management and control functions to help ensure our continued safety and soundness. (BNY Melon, 2015)*
>
> *(92) We value the feedback our stakeholders provide, which helps us improve our service and grow our business in a sustainable way. (Morgan Stanley, 2014)*

The above texts show how American banks express their CSR behaviors in risk management, sound governance, compliance and sustainability in business operations. The above CSR behaviors about American banks' commitment to banks' conservative governance are conveyed by a series of compliance-related CSR keywords that transmit American banks' conservative CSR behavior image.

As for Chinese banks, in addition to some of their CSR behaviors of risk management conveyed by the keyword "risk", they use more keywords, such as, "innovation", "online", "payment", "strategic", "technology" to express their active innovation in business and products under the background of the rapid development of the Internet Industry.

> *(93) In 2017, we set up a bank-level Fintech Committee, established the Fintech Equity Investment Fund, and increased financial investment in Fintech. With the plan of taking 1% of pre-tax profits as Fintech innovation fund each year, we are committed to further improving customer experience through professional services and financial technology advantages, and enhancing our ability to create value continuously. (China Merchant Bank, 2017)*
>
> *(94) Industrial E Financing online financing, the Bank has been carrying out system optimization and upgrading, revision and improvement concerning the "Online Self-service Circulating Loan" ... provide more personalized service solutions for customers. (China Industrial Bank, 2016)*

The above text reveals that Chinese banks combine internet technology with their financial business and products, in order to improve their operational efficiency and meet customers' demands in the digital era. The word "Fintech" is creatively advocated in Chinese banks' CSR reports, and many of them have regarded Fintech as banks' new development strategy. Chinese banks' numerous CSR behaviors of active innovation in business and product via internet and technology reflected by the innovation-related CSR keywords express Chinese banks' innovative attempts at corporate governance reform. Chinese banks' growing and innovative CSR behavior image, as well as the CSR behavior image as an innovative advocator in Fintech, is thus constructed.

6.2.5 A Comparison of Chinese and American Banks' Discursively Constructed CSR Behavior Images

Based on the above discursive analysis of 4 categories CSR keywords in keyword evaluation of banks' CSR reports, Chinese and American banks' different CSR behaviors and CSR behavior images have been transmitted and constructed via the different CSR keywords in "community and society", "employee", "environment", and "corporate governance". Table 6.7 compares Chinese and American banks' discursively constructed CSR behaviors and behavior images.

To summarize, based on the CSR keyword analysis of Chinese and American banks' CSR reports, and primarily CSR performance in "community and society", Chinese banks perform more CSR behaviors in support of social and national development. American banks perform more CSR behaviors in supporting community development.

Furthermore, for "employee" and "environment", American banks focus on the diverse and spontaneous CSR behaviors expression in employee development and environmental protection.

Finally, in "corporate governance", American banks show an inclusive CSR behaviors concern a variety of stakeholders. Chinese banks perform more CSR behaviors of active innovation in business and products, whereas American banks perform more CSR behaviors in pursing sound and conservative governance.

To summarize, many of Chinese banks' CSR behaviors are about "supporting or promoting" national strategy in social development, employee's basic welfare, and the environment. They establish the CSR mind image as the supporter of national strategy, national policy in employee welfare and environmental protection. Many of the American banks' CSR behaviors are initiated by the banks themselves, and American banks internalize these CSR behaviors into their corporate values and corporate sustainable development and strategy. American banks establish their CSR behavior image as the volunteer for community development, environment protection and inclusive CSR behavior image.

Based on Liu's (2008) classification of CSR behaviors: reactive or responsive CSR behavior and strategic CSR behavior, most Chinese banks' CSR behaviors can be categorized as reactive CSR behaviors—they react to and support social and public needs. However, for most American banks, strategic CSR behaviors are conducted and are combined with banks' strategies in order to accomplish banks' sustainable development.

Thus, in order to discursively refine the disclosure of Chinese banks' CSR behavior, improve Chinese banks' CSR behavior image, promote Chinese banks' internationalization and attract more international investors, Chinese banks need to disclose more and comprehensive strategic CSR behaviors in employee development and environmental protection which we have done perfectly by highlighting their initiative consciousness in caring for employees and practicing environmental management. Moreover, since Chinese banks has devoted a great deal to various

Table 6.7 Comparison of Chinese and American Banks' Discursively Constructed CSR Behavior Images

	Group	CSR behaviors	CSR behavior images
Community and society	Chinese Banks	More CSR behaviors in supporting, implementing and promoting country's policy, such as poverty alleviation, "Sannong", credits for small and micro enterprises; Less CSR behaviors in supporting community	Supporter and practitioner of national strategy
	American Banks	More CSR behaviors in supporting community development: Such as doing voluntary work for community, donation, veteran hires	Volunteer for community development
Employee	Chinese Banks	Less expression of initiative employee-related CSR behaviors: Such as ensuring employees' basic welfare according to national policy	Less cultivating CSR behavior image
	American Banks	Comprehensive employee-related CSR behaviors: Caring for their employee's development, ability cultivation and self-actualization	Inclusive CSR behavior image
Environment	Chinese Banks	Less expression of environmental CSR behaviors: Conducting green finance and low-carbon finance according to regulatory requirements	Financial supporter of environmental policy

(continued)

Table 6.7 (continued)

	Group	CSR behaviors	CSR behavior images
	American Banks	More expression of environmental CSR behaviors: implementing environmental management strategy, practicing environmental protection spontaneously	Practitioner of environmental protection
Corporate Governance	Chinese Banks	Less expression of diversified stakeholder engagement, making contributions to country, society	National strategy-oriented CSR behavior image
	American Banks	Diverse and inclusive CSR behaviors concerning providing effective service for their customer, shareholders, clients, suppliers	Diverse CSR behavior image
	Chinese Banks	CSR behaviors of active innovation in business and product via Internet and technology, Fintech	Growing and innovative CSR behavior image as well as the CSR behavior image as an innovative advocator in Fintech
	American Banks	CSR behaviors in pursing stable governance: Risk management, compliance and sustainability in business operation	Sound and conservative CSR behavior image

stakeholder group, they need pay attention on disclosing more diverse CSR behaviors concerning the individual stakeholders (i.e. customers, clients and shareholders). Chinese banks may use fewer words to describe their CSR behaviors as a response to national strategy. Instead, they need to use more words and sentences to express their voluntary internalization of their CSR contributions to society, community, employees, and the environment, with their corporate strategy and bank's sustainable development.

6.3 The Discursive Construction of Chinese and American Banks' CSR Visual Images

Similar to words, visual representation in the discourse is also a kind of visual rhetoric which can represent meanings (informational structure), and construct meanings (rhetoric structure) rhetorically (Yang & Miao, 2017). Kress and Van Leeuwen (1996) constructed a systematic framework of visual grammar based on Halliday's systematic functional grammar to analyze the meanings of image in 3 categories: representational meaning, interactive meaning and compositional meaning. Thus, visualization's function in representation and interaction has been consolidated from the linguistic perspective.

In the field of management, visual emphasis on corporate narratives is a kind of manipulation of the presentation of information under the theory of impression management and signaling theory (Courtis, 2004). Many studies have proven visualization's function in corporate narratives as well as the relations between visual effects and corporate financial performance and market reaction.

Thus, visual expression is an important and effective way for companies to express their corporate concepts and images in order to improve their corporate value. According to the corporate identity system, banks' CSR visual images are designed and displayed based on banks' CSR mind concepts: CSR value and strategy. Banks' visual images reflect their CSR value and behaviors which enhances the stakeholders' perceptions and senses of banks' CSR value and behaviors visually. Stakeholders' perceptions, impressions and attitudes toward banks will be influenced by visual resources. Visual evaluation indicators of CSR reports are measured by the standardized processing of pictures on the cover and in the content of CSR reports.

According to the descriptive study of visual evaluation in Chap. 5, visual indicators in Chinese banks' CSR reports are lower than those of American banks (mean difference: –0.22). The different CSR visual effect may be influenced by Chinese and American banks' different CSR concepts and CSR behaviors.

This section focuses on how the discursive feature, visualization in Chinese and American banks' CSR reports, reflects and enhances banks' CSR concepts and behaviors and constructs banks' CSR visual images. This part of the analysis includes Chinese and American banks' CSR reports' employment conditions in terms of picture number, Chinese and American bank' CSR reports' covers, presidents' photos in Chinese and American bank' CSR reports, as well as the content of pictures in Chinese and American banks' CSR reports. The different CSR visual images of Chinese and American banks are also compared and discussed.

6.3.1 Discursive Construction of Chinese Banks' CSR Visual Images

This section will examine the employment conditions of pictures in terms of picture number, the visual degree of covers, president or chairman's photo, and content of picture in Chinese banks' CSR reports. It will also examine what kind of CSR concepts and behaviors they reflect or enhance and what kinds of CSR visual images they transmit.

As for Chinese banks' CSR reports' employment condition of pictures in terms of picture number, visual value in Chinese banks' CSR reports is lower than American banks' CSR reports. The maximum number of pictures of 50 Chinese banks' CSR reports is 159, and the minimum is 0. According to the standardized processing of numbers of pictures, the CSR visual score/value of each Chinese banks' CSR report = the number of pictures in one CSR report/ 159–0. It can be inferred that Chinese banks show a wide difference in picture employment in their CSR reports, in terms of picture number. American banks have more awareness of the visual presentation of CSR information in their CSR reports.

Some Chinese banks rarely use pictures in their CSR reports. For example, the 2016 CSR report of China Citic Bank contains only 1 picture. The 2017 CSR report of China Citic banks contains no pictures and 2013 CSR report of China Industrial Bank contains 4 pictures. Thus, they express their CSR information in a simple and monotonous verbal form (Fig. 6.1). Some Chinese banks are unaware of visual effects' function in CSR information disclosure and stakeholder negotiation as well as interaction in CSR reports (Figs. 6.2 and 6.3).

According to the result of readability evaluations of CSR reports, Chinese banks' CSR reports are more difficult to read and comprehend than American banks'. Ji et al.' s (2016) empirical research verifies that having a colorful cover and the number of pictures in CSR reports influences the readability of CSR reports and firms' financial performance. Thus, the lesser picture employment in some Chinese banks' CSR reports will increase stakeholders' difficulty in reading CSR reports, and reduce the visual communication and interaction with stakeholders. Chinese banks' less awareness in the visual presentation in their CSR reports also indicates the generic features of government documents and the reports contained in Chinese banks' CSR reports.

Thus, the less awareness in CSR reports' visual presentation reflects Chinese banks' authority-pursuing CSR concepts, and their authoritative, official CSR visual images.

About the Bank

Founded in 1987, the Bank is the largest subsidiary of CITIC Group. It is one of the earliest emerging commercial banks established during China's reform and opening up and also China's first commercial bank participating in financing at both domestic and international financial markets. As a keen contributor to China's economic development, the Bank is renowned at home and abroad for brushing numerous track records in the modern Chinese financial history.

The year 2017 marked the 30th anniversary of the Bank. Over the past 30 years, the Bank's development kept pace with the country's economic development and changed with the times. Its name was changed from "CITIC Industrial Bank" to "CITIC Bank"; it was transformed from a "office building bank" relying on corporate banking to an integrated bank placing equal emphasis on corporate and private banking; it introduced foreign strategic investors, successfully listed its shares on the Shanghai Stock Exchange and The Stock Exchange of Hong Kong Limited, and opened a new chapter in the corporate governance of modern commercial bank, becoming one of the "Top 1,000 World Banks". According to the latest data, the Bank ranked 25th and 22nd among the banks in the world in terms of tier-one capital and brand respectively selected by *The Banker* of the United Kingdom.

In the context of the "new normal" of the economy and financial marketization, the Bank aspires to become "the bank offering the best comprehensive financing services". To attain this strategic development vision, the Bank leverages on the unique competitive advantages of CITIC Group in placing financial and non-financial businesses on an equal footing, and spares no efforts to build an integrated service platform and strengthen its core competence.

The Bank holds firm to the core values of "customer first". For corporate customers and institutional customers, the Bank offers integrated financial solutions in corporate banking business, international business, financial markets business, institutional banking business, investment banking business, interbank business and custody business. For individual customers, the Bank provides diversified financial products and services in retail banking, credit card, consumer finance, wealth management, private banking, going abroad finance and e-banking. As such, the Bank satisfies the needs of corporate and individual customers for comprehensive financial services on all fronts.

The Bank had more than 1,400 outlets in 142 large and medium-sized cities in China, mainly distributed in coastal areas in Eastern China and economically developed cities in Central and Western China. It had over 50,000 employees. The Bank established London Branch in the UK and Sydney Representative Office in Australia. The Bank had four subsidiaries, including Zhejiang Lin'an CITIC Rural Bank Limited and CITIC Financial Leasing Co., Ltd. in Chinese Mainland, and CITIC International Limited and CNCB (Hong Kong (Investment Co., Ltd. (formerly China Investment and Finance Limited) in Hong Kong. China CITIC Bank International Limited had 40 outlets in Hong Kong, Macau, New York, Los Angeles and Singapore, with more than

I. Implementing China's Major Development Strategies

i. Building the "Belt and Road" financial artery

The Bank has made great efforts to accelerate the building of the "Belt and Road" (B&R) financial artery. In 2015, it provided USD28.6 billion loans and followed up on 330 key projects with a loan commitment of USD87 billion. Currently, it has 18 subsidiaries along the Belt and Road, three of which was established in 2015. It also successfully issued the world's first B&R-themed bond.

Case: The Bank successfully issued the world's first B&R-themed bond

In 2015, BOC issued a B&R-themed bond in Dubai, Singapore, London, Hong Kong and Taiwan to raise a total of USD4 billion. The fund raised will be used to meet capital demand of BOC branches along the Belt and Road for funding the projects under the B&R Initiative, including port construction, electricity, transportation and airport construction projects. It's not only the first B&R-themed bond in the international financial market but also BOC's largest bond issue in overseas markets.

Case: Expanding presence to nine ASEAN countries

ASEAN countries are strategically located and crucial to the 21st Century Maritime Silk Road Initiative. At the end of 2015, BOC had presence in nine out of the total ten ASEAN countries. These countries are Singapore, Thailand, Vietnam, Malaysia, the Philippines, Indonesia, Cambodia, Laos and Myanmar. The institutions are Singapore Branch, Bank of China (Thai) Public Company Limited, Ho Chi Minh Branch, Bank of China (Malaysia) Berhad, Manila Branch, Jakarta Branch, Phnom Penh Branch, Vientiane Branch and Rangoon Branch.

Case: Leveraging on joint efforts of domestic and overseas institutions to assist in matchmaking with international trade customers along the Belt and Road and the Chongqing-Xinjiang-Europe Railway

The Chongqing-Xinjiang-Europe Railway is an important vehicle for the participation of Chongqing City in the B&R Initiative. It links Chongqing to Russia, Belarus, Germany and other countries in Eastern and Western Europe. BOC further promoted the establishment the "1 + 1 + 10" "Chongqing-Xinjiang-Europe" domestic and overseas coordination mechanism. The Bank held business matchmaking events in Chongqing and Dusseldorf (Germany) to promote the bilateral trade activities.

Fig. 6.1 Simplex Verbal Disclosure of Chinese Banks' CSR Reports

China Minsheng Banking Corp., Ltd.

Environmental, Social and Governance Report 2016

China Minsheng Banking Corporation Limited

2017 Environmental, Social and Governance Report

Fig. 6.2 Covers in China Minsheng Bank's CSR Reports

Additionally, as for covers in CSR reports, some Chinese banks present only the title of their CSR reports together with banks' logo, without other visual images.

Since covers in CSR reports serve as the face of the CSR report, they provide stakeholders with a first impression of the banks' CSR image. Through the simplex presentation of only CSR report name and banks' logo, Chinese banks lose the chance to negotiate with their stakeholders and transmit their CSR value and corporate images to their stakeholder at the beginning. The less visual effects in Chinese banks'

Fig. 6.3 Chairman/President's Photos in Chinese Banks' CSR Reports

CSR reports covers may be also be the result from government documents' generic features in Chinese banks' CSR reports.

Thus, Chinese banks' authority-pursuing a CSR concepts are reflected and enhanced via the less visual effects of their CSR reports covers. Additionally, Chinese banks' authoritative and official CSR visual images are constructed and transmitted to their stakeholders.

Also, president/chairman's photos in Chinese banks' CSR reports are consistent and most of these photos in the sections on president/chairman's statement are the bank presidents' formal identification photos.

The above photos are of the chairman or president of some biggest banks in China. Both are wearing dark formal suits with ties, and with reserved gestures and minimal facial expressions. Also, the two photos are taken in a long shot and the president/chairman is greatly involved in the photo. This indicates the social distance between the president/chairman and the stakeholders, as well as the impersonal relations between president/chairman and the stakeholders (Kress & Van Leeuwen, 1996).

As mentioned, the president/chairman of most Chinese banks has the dual identities: government official first, banker or manager second. The above analysis of their photos just indicates their identity as the government official. As a government official, the president/chairman of Chinese banks needs to establish and maintain his or her authority and devotion to the country's development. The president/chairman's photos in Chinese banks' CSR reports reflect an authoritative and official image of Chinese banks' leaders. Since leaders' personal image is an important component of corporate image which can reflect and represent companies' corporate image, Chinese banks' authoritative and government-oriented CSR visual images are constructed, enhanced and transmitted to the stakeholders via president/chairman's photos in their CSR reports.

Furthermore, the content of the pictures in Chinese banks' CSR reports' functions to visualize Chinese banks' CSR concepts and behaviors, and Chinese banks' CSR visual images. Thus, pictures need to be located in specific contexts in CSR reports.

Indeed, many Chinese banks use various pictures in their CSR reports to express their CSR information. After the close reading of a picture and the discursive contexts in CSR reports in which the pictures are located, it is found that the majority of the pictures used in Chinese banks' CSR reports are the direct reflection and the repetition of their specific CSR behaviors in the visual mode. See Fig. 6.4.

The verbal content in the first figure is about Bank of China's sub-branches' financial knowledge publicity to less developed countries in order to express their CSR contribution to the public. The picture is the presentation and record of the situation concerning banks employees' face-to-face financial knowledge popularization to villagers. This is also influenced by government document and reports' generic features in Chinese banks' CSR reports and Chinese banks' government-oriented CSR values. Instead of using more visualization to achieve better communication with their stakeholders and shorten the distance between banks and readers, Chinese banks tend to use pictures to record and repeat their CSR behaviors.

Based on the above analysis, pictures in Chinese banks' CSR reports mainly have the function in CSR behavior presentation and few function in stakeholder interaction. Since most of the pictures repeat the Chinese banks' CSR behaviors, less CSR values are reflected or enhanced via visualization. Thus, the repetition function of visualization in Chinese banks' CSR also reflects the responsive CSR behaviors of Chinese banks. Chinese banks' less interactive CSR visual images are constructed and transmitted via the repetitive function of pictures in CSR reports.

To summarize, after the analysis of Chinese banks' CSR reports' employment conditions of pictures, visual degree of covers, president or chairman's photos and content of pictures, Chinese banks tend to use pictures to present their CSR information repetitively. They have less awareness in employing pictures in CSR reports to shorten the distance between banks and stakeholders, have interaction with their stakeholders, or reflect and enhance their CSR values. Chinese banks' authority-pursuing, government-oriented CSR concept and CSR behavior mode are reflected and enhanced, and Chinese banks' authoritative, official CSR visual images are constructed and transmitted to their stakeholders via the visual effects in their CSR reports.

Financial knowledge publicity on campus

In September 2017, Guizhou Branch of BOC came to Guizhou Provincial Economic School to carry out the activity of financial knowledge publicity on campus, hold financial knowledge seminars, demonstrate anti-counterfeit money skills in the forms of exhibition booth, physical comparison, case teaching and scenarios as well as leaflets, and explain the use of bank cards, credit card risk prevention and other related knowledge.

Financial knowledge publicity in the old revolutionary base areas

In September 2017, Hainan Branch of BOC, together with Haikou Central Sub-branch and Chengmai Sub-branch of the People's Bank of China, came to Longchang Village, Gaoshanlang County, to hold a face-to-face financial knowledge class for villagers, answer villagers' questions and teach financial knowledge.

Exploring and Supporting Poverty-Alleviating Ecological Resettlement Project

Guizhou Province launched its poverty-alleviating ecological resettlement project in 2012 and plans to move 2 million very poor farm households away from the concentrated contiguous exceptionally impoverished areas and regions of harsh environment by 2020.

To support the resettlement project, Guizhou Branch drew up the "Measures for Management of the Poverty-Alleviating Loans for Ecological Resettlement Project (For Trial)" in May 2013. By the end of 2013, the branch had completed the examination and approval of RMB 90 million of loans for the ecological resettlement in Cengong County in the southeast of the province.

Fig. 6.4 Content of Pictures in Chinese Banks' CSR Reports

6.3.2 Discursive Construction of American Banks' CSR Visual Images

This section will examine the employment conditions of pictures in terms of pictures number, the visual degree of covers, president or chairman's photo and content of picture in American banks' CSR reports. It will also address what kind of CSR concepts and behavior they reflect or enhance and what kinds of CSR visual images they transmit.

For American banks, the employment conditions of pictures, in terms of pictures numbers and visual value in American banks' CSR reports is significantly higher than that of Chinese banks. Based on the calculation principle of standardized processing of numbers of pictures, it can be inferred that American banks have a strong awareness and are more skilled in visual presentation of CSR information than Chinese banks. This is because the number of pictures in American banks' CSR reports is more consistent and averaged than Chinese banks.

American banks have developed the conventions and are skilled in using pictures to express their CSR information and promote stakeholder negotiation and interaction in the CSR reports. The function of visual effects in American banks' CSR reports is to improve their readability since American banks use pictures to make the layout and structure of the CSR reports more reader-friendly. See Fig. 6.5.

American banks also use pictures to make their CSR reports more colorful and persuasive by employing colorful backgrounds and vivid pictures of people, such as their customers and employees in order to shorten the distance with their stakeholders and increase negotiation and interaction with their stakeholders. See Fig. 6.6.

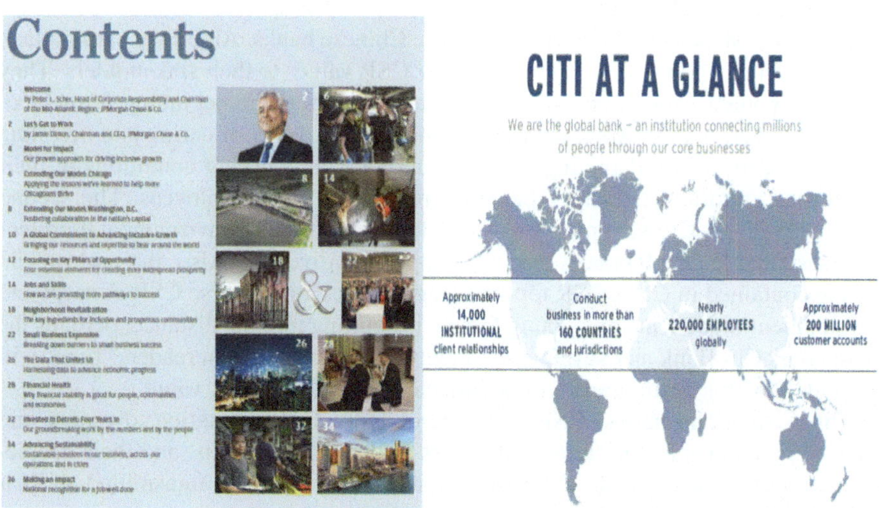

Fig. 6.5 Pictures in American Banks' CSR Reports (Reader-Friendly)

Fig. 6.6 Pictures in American Banks' CSR Reports (Stakeholder Interaction)

The strong awareness and proficient use of visual emphasis via craftily employing pictures for improving CSR reports' readability and achieving better communication with their stakeholders reflects American banks' individual-oriented CSR concepts and CSR behaviors. It constructs American banks' interactive CSR visual images.

As for covers in CSR reports, most American banks use pictures on the covers of their CSR reports, and American banks seize every chance to have visual communication with their stakeholders in order to influence their first impressions of banks' CSR value and CSR image. See Fig. 6.7.

Figure 6.7 shows that different from some Chinese banks, American banks attach great importance to visually expressing their CSR values to their stakeholders. They tend to negotiate with and persuade their stakeholders at the beginning of the text. The first cover vividly expresses BNY Mellon's CSR value of caring and investing in their employees by depicting the cozy and relaxing working conditions of their employees and the satisfactory facial expression of their employees. The second picture expresses Citi's comprehensive CSR commitment to environmental protection, sustainable development, care for people and diversity. Also, the multi-racial people contained in Citi's CSR report covers reflect Citi's diverse CSR concept and development mode. One of a young female is pointing into the distance, perhaps the prosperous Citi Bank and sustainable society in the future. Then readers' focus will be guided by this gesture and will be inflected with Citi's' CSR value.

Thus, American banks' CSR concepts of individual orientation, diversity and inclusion are enhanced in the visual covers of their CSR reports, and their people-focused and inclusive CSR visual image are constructed and transmitted to their stakeholders in the beginning of CSR reports.

Also, photos of CEOs/chairmen in American banks' CSR reports are different from those of Chinese banks. See Fig. 6.8.

Fig. 6.7 Covers in American Banks' CSR Reports

Fig. 6.8 CEOs/Chairmen's Photos in American Banks' CSR Reports

The CEOs/chairmen of American banks wear business suit of many colors which are less formal and more approachable than the dark formal suits. The CEO/chairman of American banks always smile which shortens the distance to stakeholders and leaves them an amiable and easygoing personal impression. Different from the dual identities of Chinese banks' presidents/chairmen, CEO/chairmen of American banks only have one identity—bank manager and they are the representative of the whole company. They are nominated by boards of directors and may be fired by boards of directors when they commit misconducts in bank management. Thus, they need to maintain a good relationship with stakeholders by establishing an amiable and approachable personal image.

Also, the photos of CEOs/chairmen of American banks are taken in a close shot and only their head and the little upper part of the body are involved in the pictures. This indicates the short social distance between CEO/chairman and the stakeholders, as well as the interpersonal relations between presidents/chairmen and stakeholders (Kress & Van Leeuwen, 1996).

The CEO/chairmen' photos in American banks' CSR reports reflect the amiable, caring, easygoing personal image of American banks' leaders. They are the representatives of their companies. Thus, American banks' interactive CSR visual image are constructed, enhanced and transmitted to the stakeholders via CEO/chairman's photos in CSR reports.

Additionally, previous analysis has indicated that the content of the pictures in Chinese banks' CSR reports mainly have the function of representing, recording and enhancing their CSR behaviors. The pictures in American banks' CSR reports can reflect and enhance their CSR values in specific contexts of CSR reports. Most of the pictures in American banks' CSR reports are figurative and metaphorical. This connotes the banks' CSR values to their stakeholders in a vivid way in order to improve the communication efficiency with their stakeholders and rhetorically persuade them to accept and identify with banks' CSR values. See Fig. 6.9.

Figure 6.9 shows that besides presenting CSR behaviors, American banks use pictures to transmit and enhance CSR values. In the first picture, several hands of different colors put together symbolize banks' diverse and inclusive people-oriented service value and CSR concept. In the second picture, the shovel symbolizes banks' nurturing of their customers, communities, and employees. Banks are compared to the gardener and their people are compared to the grass metaphorically. Thus banks' responsibility and CSR concept in contributing to their people are enhanced by this figurative picture. In the third picture, customers' satisfaction and happiness are expressed by the big smile on their faces. Thus, the readers may be infected by banks' customers' gratification, and identify with banks' service value.

Thus, American banks are experts in transmitting and enhancing their CSR values to stakeholders interactively and metaphorically via visual emphasis in their CSR reports. Thus, an effective and interactive communication is achieved. Stakeholders will be infected by banks' discursively transmitted CSR values and CSR images and American banks' interpersonal CSR visual images are established.

To summarize, after the analysis of American banks' CSR reports' employment conditions of picture, visual degree of covers, CEOs/chairmen's photos and content of picture, most American banks tend to use pictures to present their CSR information. However, American banks are good at transmitting and enhancing their CSR values via pictures in which their caring for people and other CSR values are expressed metaphorically. Pictures in American banks achieve the visual function of enhancing and supplementing banks' CSR concepts in a reader-friendly way. American banks have a strong sense of achieving visual communication with their stakeholders, thus the distance between banks and stakeholders is shortened. American banks' individualistic, inclusive CSR concepts are reflected and enhanced, and American banks' interpersonal CSR visual images are metaphorically constructed and transmitted to their stakeholders, via the visual effects in their CSR reports.

Fig. 6.9 Content of Pictures in American Banks' CSR Reports

6.3.3 A Comparison of Chinese and American Banks' Discursively Constructed CSR Visual Images

The above discursive analysis of visual effects in banks' CSR reports show that Chinese and American banks' different CSR visual images are transmitted and constructed via the different employment conditions of the pictures in terms of picture number, the visual degree of the covers, president/chairmen/CEOs' photos and content of picture. Table 6.8 compares Chinese and American banks' discursively constructed CSR visual images.

To summarize, American banks show more awareness in employing pictures in CSR reports to enhance their CSR value and have less interaction with their

Table 6.8 Comparison of Chinese and American Banks' discursively constructed CSR visual images

	Group	Visualization	CSR visual images
Picture employment condition	Chinese Banks	Less awareness in visual presentation of CSR information	Authoritative, official CSR visual image
	American Banks	More awareness and skillful in visual presentation of CSR information: improve the readability of CSR report; More interaction with stakeholders	Interactive CSR visual images
Cover	Chinese Banks	Report title, banks logo	Authoritative CSR visual image
	American Banks	Express their CSR value via cover picture	Individual-focused CSR visual image
President/ chairman/CEO' photo	Chinese Banks	Dark formal suit, less facial expression, long shot	Authoritative, government-oriented and CSR visual image
	American Banks	Business suit, more facial expression, close shot	Interactive CSR visual image
Picture content	Chinese Banks	Presentation, repetition of CSR behavior	Official CSR visual image
	American Banks	Transmitting and enhancing their CSR values interactively and metaphorically	Interpersonal CSR visual images

stakeholders. Also, Chinese banks tend to use pictures to present their CSR information repetitively, and pictures in Chinese banks' CSR reports have the function of representation. Chinese banks' less visualization in CSR reports reflect their authority-pursuing, government-oriented CSR concept CSR behavior. Chinese banks' authoritative, official, CSR visual images are constructed in their CSR reports.

As for American banks, they focus on using pictures to present their CSR information and enhance their CSR values. Pictures in American banks' CSR reports serve as the figurative enhancement and supplement of banks' CSR concepts, which have the function of both representation and interaction. The crafty and metaphorical visual communication between American banks and their stakeholders shortens the distance and improves the interaction between banks and stakeholders. American banks' individualistic, inclusive CSR concepts are enhanced, and interpersonal CSR visual images are metaphorically constructed and transmitted to their stakeholders via the visual effects in their CSR reports.

As can be seen, there are several inadequacies in the visualization of Chinese banks' CSR reports, as well as discursively constructed CSR visual images, when compared with American banks. Thus, in order to improve the visualization in Chinese banks' CSR reports, enable Chinese banks achieve better communication and interaction with their stakeholders and promote the Chinese banking industry's internationalization, Chinese banks need to develop more awareness on the visual emphasis of their CSR reports.

Chinese banks need to emphasize visual effects' functions in stakeholder communication and employ more pictures in every section of their CSR reports to make them more interactive and reader-friendly, including the cover.

Also, Chinese banks need to present more approachable photos of their presidents/chairmen in order to establish an amiable and easygoing leader image and company image.

Furthermore, besides using pictures to present their CSR behaviors, Chinese banks need to use craftier pictures which can connote, enhance and supplement their CSR values, both directly and metaphorically, in their CSR reports.

6.4 Reasons for Chinese and American Banks' Different Discursively Constructed CSR Images

Based on the above multi-dimensional discursive evaluation of Chinese and American banks' CSR reports, Chinese and American banks transmit different CSR concepts and strategies, CSR behaviors, and visual effects of their CSR value and behaviors via various discursive features in sentiment, readability, CSR keywords and visualization in their CSR reports. Chinese and American banks' different CSR mind images, behavior images, and visual images are discursively constructed and transmitted to their stakeholders.

In this session, reasons for Chinese and American banks' different discursively constructed CSR images will be interpreted and explained in light of legitimacy theory and stakeholder theory under Chinese and American banks' different political, economic, cultural, social and regulatory contexts.

Social reporting is an organization's need in order to make their activities acceptable and justified by society and obtain social legitimization (Shocker & Sethi, 1973). Legitimacy theory has been used as the framework to explain organizations' social disclosure practices, including CSR reports (Fuoli, 2012). According to legitimacy theory, since companies need to be considered legitimate in order to exist and develop in society, they have to behave, and are expected to behave, according to social system and rules (ibid). As for banks, they also need to be legitimate citizens and accepted by the public and society. Since language has the function of texturing and constructing social identities and social relations (Fairclough, 1992), disclosing CSR information via CSR reports is a good chance for banks to meet social expectations and establish a legitimate and responsible corporate image. Thus, legitimacy theory can analyze banks' different communicative purposes and motivations behind their CSR values and their CSR performance in their CSR reports, as well as their discursively constructed different CSR images.

Also, social expectations change over time and different organizations have different social systems and social relations. Thus, Chinese and American banks need to be justified and admitted by different social systems by meeting the expectations of different social groups within their own social systems. According to stakeholder theory, stakeholders are individuals and groups that can influence the achievement of an organization's goal (Freeman, 1984). Thus banks' social reporting also needs to meet the demands and expectations of their stakeholder groups. Due to the different social systems between Chinese and American banks, they have different stakeholder groups.

In order to be justified and become a legitimate citizen, Chinese and American banks will have different social reporting in their CSR reports and different discursively constructed CSR images in order to meet the expectations of their different stakeholder groups within their different political, economic, culture, social and regulatory contexts.

6.4.1 Political Context

In CSR reports, Chinese banks enhance their major communicative goals: supporting country development, contributing to society and public by transmitting their national strategy-oriented CSR value, behaviors and establishing their authoritative, public-oriented CSR images via various discursive features in sentiment, readability, CSR keywords and visualization. However, the major communicative goal of American banks' CSR reports is maintaining good relationship with their customers, clients, employees, shareholders and communities in order to improve corporate value. American banks also employ various linguistic features to transmit their individual-oriented, corporate value-oriented CSR values and behaviors as well as discursively establish amiable CSR images.

Reasons for the above different images can be explained from the following 2 aspects concerning China and the USs' different political backgrounds.

In the first place, most Chinese banks are state-owned enterprises under the socialist system with Chinese characteristics and all American banks are non-state enterprises under the capitalist system. Based on the data for Chinese and American banks' different equity structures, government is the biggest equity-owner of Chinese banks and most Chinese banks have the duty to regard government and people as their first and the most vital stakeholder who can influence their operations. They also need to regard the contribution to government and national strategy as the prior CSR commitment. As for American banks, they are owned by non-governmental giant financial groups. Rather than making the biggest contribution to the government, the most important CSR activity that American banks need to perform is to obey national laws and rules and to be legal citizens. Instead, what they need to prioritize is improving corporate value to meet the expectations of their shareholders and prioritizing people in order to make more profits. Shareholders, customers, and employees are the most vital stakeholders to which they need to be the most devoted.

Furthermore, in China, most state-owned enterprises, including many Chinese banks, especially the big banks are under both the leadership of the Communist Party of China (CPC) and the board of directors. However, all the American banks are under the leadership of their boards of directors. All the business operation of American banks need to be responsible to their boards of directors and produce more value for them. American banks' corporate-value oriented CSR concepts and pragmatistic CSR images are discursively constructed in their CSR reports. As for many Chinese banks, we have the dual leadership: the CPC is the first priority and the board of directors is the second priority. The Chinese banks' CSR reports' reading ease under English context is decreased due to banks' CSR information concerning their Party-oriented, national strategy-oriented CSR values and behavior. Also, their authoritative CSR images are discursively constructed and transmitted to the stakeholders, especially international investors.

Chinese banks need to employ suitable discursive features in their CSR reports to make CSR information concerning the Party more easy to understand for international stakeholders in order to make more publicity of our own Chinese characteristics.

6.4.2 Economic Context

China and the US's different discursively constructed CSR images are also the result of the different economic development status. Our research targets are Chinese and American banks' CSR reports from 2013 to 2017. In this period, China experienced rapid growth and have stabled as world's second biggest economic entity. During the same period, the United States experienced more stable and slower growth.

As known, the development of banks is connected with national economic development. As the country's major financial resources allocators, the Chinese banking industry benefits from the country's rapid growth and is willing to take chances to achieve rapid growth. Some Chinese banks' total assets have doubled. Thus, the positive, optimistic sentimental tendencies are shown in Chinese banks' CSR reports through Chinese banks' expansive, positive CSR strategy and values. Also, their positive, promising and active CSR images are expressed and constructed.

As for American banks, since they have experienced the financial crisis, even though they have already recovered, they still regard prudence and compliance as their first operation principle. Also, since the US has experienced slow economic growth, it is hard for American banks to find new and rapid economic growth points. Adhering to their prudent strategy value in the post-financial period, they maintain stable, steadfast strategies and construct steady, reliable CSR images which are reflected by their realistic and less optimistic sentimental tendencies and more CSR keywords concerning risk management and conservative governance in their CSR reports.

6.4.3 Cultural Context

Chinese and American banks' different discursively constructed CSR images are also influenced by their different cultural contexts.

According to Hofstede et al.'s (2010) cultural dimensions in the concept of power distance, China has a high power distance in which power is distributed unequally inequities exist and power relationship is the fundamental facts in Chinese society. People in this kind of culture attach importance on social position, establishment and obeying authority. The communicative and social relation between Chinese banks and stakeholders is comparatively long and unequal. In Chinese banks' CSR reports, the authority-pursuing and government-oriented CSR concept and authoritative, official CSR image are discursively constructed. As for America, it has a low power distance and egalitarianism, and equal right are advocated. The social relation between American banks and stakeholders is comparatively short and American banks attach importance on the interest of each stakeholder. Thus they achieve a closer relationship and more effective negotiation with their stakeholders in CSR reports, their individualist CSR value and approaching CSR images are discursively constructed.

On the basis of Hofstede et al. (ibid), China has high-context culture in which collectivism is advocated. In China, individual's loyalty, even sacrifice to group is encouraged and group interest is higher than individual interest. Chinese banks need to put national interest in the first place which is reflected in their national strategy-oriented CSR value and image. Chinese banks' employees need to put banks' interest in the first place via devoting more which is reflected in Chinese banks' less employee investment CSR behaviors in their CSR reports. As for American banks, they advocate and perform individualism in their business operation. They treasure individual interest, including their customer, shareholder, employee, client, supplier, etc. which is reflected in their individual-oriented CSR value and image in their CSR reports.

Besides, Chinese people emphasize "face", "face work" and the concept of "face" is originated from Chinese sociocultural context which influences Chinese banks' discursively constructed positive and subjective CSR image. Brown & Levinson (1987) regard face as a normal social demand for adults, and their face theory focuses on how to pass language use to mitigate facial threatening behavior and thus protecting the hearers' face. From the perspective of interpersonal pragmatics, Ran and Liu (2015) propose that we need to pay attention to how the communicator cares for "face" via choosing specific language and the influence on interpersonal relationships. Chinese banks use positive, optimistic sentimental words and less realistic sentimental words to express their great CSR achievements and promising future in order to make "face work" and highlight their positive CSR images to their stakeholder, especially the government. Chinese banks' prospective construction of positive CSR image and the achievement-oriented governance concept are resulted from Chinese people's emphasis of "face".

6.4.4 Social Context

China and the US's different discursively constructed CSR images are also a result from their different social structures, which also influence Chinese and American banks' different stakeholder groups and stakeholder rankings.

The mainstream group of American society is the middle class; the rural population is small, whereas, the rural population is the major component of Chinese society. By the end of 2017, China's rural population was 576.61 million, accounting for 41.48% of the country' total population. Issues relating to agriculture, rural areas, and rural people, are the top concern of China's development. Due to the high proportion of the rural population in China, both the country and Chinese banks need to meet their demands and expectations and make more CSR contributions to them. Chinese banks employ many CSR keywords concerning three rural issue to express their CSR behaviors in supporting the national strategy in solving problems in agriculture, rural areas, and peasant and poverty alleviation. Thus, Chinese banks' discursively constructed public-oriented or people's livelihood-oriented CSR image is also influenced by the special social structure of the country.

As for American banks, since the middle class group is the major component of American society, American banks need to meet the demands of the middle class group in pursuing stable and decent living condition by providing excellent, reliable, stable even lifelong comprehensive financial services. Thus, their CSR image as a professional value-creator for customers, shareholders, and employees is discursively constructed via their individual-oriented and inclusive CSR concepts and CSR behaviors.

6.4.5 Regulatory Context

Since our research focus is Chinese and American banks' different discursively constructed CSR images, we cannot neglect the different regulation mechanisms in the Chinese and American banking industry. The banking regulation system in American is comparatively complex. American banks are regulated by Federal Reserve (FED), the U.S. Office of Comptroller of Currency (OCC) and the United States Federal Deposit Insurance Corporation (FDIC). Chinese banks are regulated by China Banking and Insurance Regulatory Commission (CBIRC).

The regulation tightness of Chinese and American banks are different. The regulation policy of American banks is strict and American banks' cost of violation is high. American banks have to pay huge amount fines for irregularities. Due to the high costs of violation, American banks invest a lot of money in their risk management and compliance. Thus, the risk management and compliance have become an essential part of American banks' governance concept and CSR values which guide their CSR behaviors in risk management and compliance. They also construct the conservative, reliable CSR images of American banks. However, the regulation policy of Chinese banks is looser, and has less deterrent effects towards the irregularities. The fine paid for their irregularities is much less than the money they devote to prudent management. Thus, Chinese banks have not developed the systematic prudent government, compliance and risk management awareness that American banks have. Perhaps, Chinese banks' expansive, growth-pursued development strategy and active CSR image are partly influenced by the loose regulation policy of the CBIRC.

Also, the regulation of American banks is part of compliance regulation, whereas regulation of Chinese banks is guiding regulation. To be specific, American regulatory authorities only focus on the compliance of banks' business operations and American banks can conduct any kind of business as long as they obey regulatory laws and rules. Thus, many American banks' CSR behaviors are voluntary and spontaneous. Meanwhile, CBIRC influences Chinese banks' business operations, including their CSR behaviors. The CBIRC regulates Chinese banks' operations. It also leads Chinese banks and requires them to conduct specific businesses by releasing regulatory rules, such as credit for small and micro enterprises, green finance, inclusive finance, and supporting private enterprise for national development. CBIRC is an important stakeholder for Chinese banks. Thus, Chinese banks express some CSR behaviors in their CSR reports as a commitment to the regulatory commission as well as their official and policy-supporting CSR value. Chinese banks' CSR behaviors and CSR image are influenced by the guiding regulation of CBIRC.

Finally, the regulation mechanism of American banks is mixed supervision which means that American banks can conduct a comprehensive business including banking, insurance, securities, investment, and consulting. Thus, American banks express their inclusive and diverse business, serving and producing, as well as the diverse CSR images in CSR reports. However, the regulation mechanism of Chinese banks is dividing supervision. Chinese banks are only qualified to do commercial banking business. This influences Chinese banks' simplex and their less diverse and professional CSR values and images.

6.5 Summary

In this chapter, Chinese and American banks' discursively constructed CSR mind images are explained and compared based on sentiment and readability evaluation of CSR reports. CSR behavior images are explained and compared via CSR keyword evaluation. CSR visual images are explained and compared via visualization in their CSR reports. Chinese and American banks discursively construct different CSR images under their own political, economic, cultural, social and regulatory contexts.

Both Chinese and American banks use discursive features along different dimensions to transmit and enhance similar CSR values, behaviors and CSR images in order to persuade stakeholders and influence their stakeholders' perceptions and attitudes towards their CSR images rhetorically.

First, Chinese banks discursively construct an authoritative, official, national strategy-oriented, less diverse CSR image by employing more sentimental words from Certainty and Commonality, high lexical density, long words and complex sentences patterns, less and simplex visualization and disclose more official CSR behaviors in supporting national development and policies. They also convey less CSR behaviors in employee investment and environmental management in their CSR reports. American banks discursively construct a, pragmatistic, individual-oriented CSR image via using less sentimental words from Certainty and Commonality, plain English, more metaphorical and interactive visual effects and disclosing more CSR behaviors concerning customers, employees, shareholders, communities and the environment.

Also, American banks show the factual construction of CSR image by using less sentimental words showing Optimism and more words expressing Realism. Chinese banks, besides showing objective and factual construction of CSR image, also express prospective construction of their CSR image by using many sentimental words from Optimism and less from Realism.

Furthermore, Chinese banks show active, innovative, positive CSR images by using more sentimental words from Activity and disclosing more CSR behaviors in business structure reform and Fintech innovation. American banks show stable, conservative and reliable CSR images by using fewer words from Activity.

In order to help Chinese banks improve our English CSR disclosure systems, achieve effective and interactive communication with their stakeholders and promote Chinese banking industry's internationalization, Chinese banks need to learn from American banks to employ suitable discursive features that better comply with international stakeholders' economic, cultural, and social contexts. This needs to be done in addition to maintaining the Chinese banks' CSR images with Chinese characteristic.

To achieve such an end, Chinese banks need to use less sentimental words expressing Certainty and Commonality, and less long words and complex sentence patterns. This can make their Party-oriented and national strategy-oriented CSR values and behaviors more reader-friendly. This will enable them to establish a more amiable and interactive CSR image, and also promote the publicity of the Chinese banking industry's own characteristics to international stakeholders.

Also, Chinese banks need to use less sentimental words from Optimism and more words from Realism in order to comply with reading and CSR disclosing system in international contexts.

Furthermore, Chinese banks need to use less sentimental words from Activity and disclose more CSR behaviors concerning risk management and compliance in order to establish a steadier and prudent CSR image.

Additionally, Chinese banks need to disclose more initiative and strategic CSR behaviors in employee investment, environmental sustainability and sound corporate governance.

Finally, Chinese banks need to strengthen their awareness in employing more pictures which contain dual functions of CSR information representation and stakeholder interaction in order to make their CSR reports more interactive and reader-friendly, and to establish interpersonal CSR images.

Chapter 7
An Empirical Study of the Discursive Construction of Chinese and American Bank's CSR Images' Effects on Capital Markets

This chapter answers the third research question: What are the effects of banks' discursive construction of CSR images on capital markets based on the multi-dimensional discourse evaluation? This is addressed based on the description and comparison of the multi-dimensional discursive features in Chinese and American banks' CSR reports in Chap. 5. The explanation and comparison of Chinese and American banks' discursively constructed CSR images through CSR reports' multi-dimensional discursive features in Chap. 6 are also considered.

In this chapter, an empirical study is conducted to explain the actual effects of Chinese and American banks' discursively constructed CSR images that they bring to capital markets. It utilizes the background of previous studies' verification of the relationship between corporate narratives including CSR reports' linguistic features and corporate financial performance, capital market performance. These are brought in from the disciplines of linguistics, management, economics (Li & Wang, 2017; Wang & Bu, 2017; Muslu et al., 2019). Also incorporated is the theoretical support of signaling theory and behavioral finance.

Chinese and American banks' discursively constructed CSR images are transmitted and realized by the multi-dimensional discursive features in sentiment, readability, CSR keywords and visualization in CSR reports, as explained in Chap. 6. Therefore, in this chapter the focus is on the actual effects or influences that multi-dimensional discursive features bring to capital markets or the capital market reaction towards the various discursive features in banks' CSR reports.

Guided by signaling theory, CSR reports' discursive features that are employed by banks to persuade stakeholders and discursively construct their CSR images, serve as the signals in capital markets. They may influence stakeholders', especially investors', attitudes towards banks' CSR images and corporate value. According to behavioral finance, the investors' attitudes or perceptions are part of investors' psychological activity. This can influence investors' investment behaviors and capital market performance.

Firstly, event study is conducted to analyze banks' CSR reports' discursive features' actual effects on markets. This is reflected by CAR in 30 days after

M. Wan, *CSR Image Discursive Construction of Banks and the Effects on Capital Markets*,
https://doi.org/10.1007/978-981-19-6012-3_7

banks disclose CSR reports in order to indicate language's economic value in capital market empirically. Also, the CAR of Chinese and American banks' stock prices are compared and discussed in order to shed light on Chinese banks' CSR disclosure, discursive construction of international CSR image and corporate value enhancement.

Next, based on the empirical results of event study, gray relational entropy analysis is conducted to evaluate the influencing degrees between multi-dimensional discursive features in CSR reports and capital market reaction, in other words, multi-dimensional discursive features' different contribution degrees to the CAR of bank's stock trends.

The higher contribution degree a discursive indicator has, the more it contributes to capital market performance and banks' corporate value enhancement. Additionally, Chinese and American banks' rankings of multi-dimensional discursive features' affecting degree on capital market reaction are compared and discussed. This helps Chinese banks learn from American banks in international corporate image management and corporate value enhancement via the employment of discursive features in CSR reports. It also provides more objective suggestions for Chinese banks to achieve internalization from a linguistic level.

7.1 Event Study of Discursive Features' Effects on Capital Markets

Event study is an empirical research method that uses financial market data, before and after an event, to analyze the impact of that particular event on the value of the company. Due to the advantages of rigorous research theory, clear logic, and simple calculation processes, event study has been used by scholars in many fields to study the impact of specific events on corporate value. In the capital field, event study focuses on the impact of events, including mergers and acquisitions, earnings releases, media press comments, and corporate narrative disclosure on capital markets. This can be reflected in changes in corporate accounting performance, CAR, and changes in trading volumes.

The discursive features in banks' CSR reports can discursively construct banks' CSR images based on the influencing mechanism of CSR reports' discursive features on capital market reaction proposed in this study. They serve as the signals which influence investors' investment behaviors since they can rhetorically influence stakeholders', especially investors' perceptions and attitudes (also psychological activities in behavioral finance) towards banks' CSR images and valuation. This is in accordance with close relationship between CSR disclosure and corporate value, corporate financial performance in previous studies (Shen & Yang, 2008; Shen et al., 2011, Baker and Ameer, 2011). Thus, by regarding banks' disclosure of CSR reports as an event which may bring actual effects on capital markets, event study is used to examine the impact of multi-dimensional discursive features in Chinese and American banks' CSR reports on the CAR of banks' stock prices.

7.1.1 *Empirical Analysis of Event Study*

The empirical analysis of impacts of multi-dimensional discursive features in Chinese and American banks' CSR reports on capital markets (CAR) are conducted according to the calculation steps and formulas of event study in the Research Methods Chapter.

7.1.1.1 Determining Event Windows

The focus of this study is the impact of the CSR reports' discursive features on the stock price of Chinese and American listed banks. Therefore, we use the release date of the CSR report as the event day. Because CSR reports contain a considerable amount of information, the market may take a long time to digest the information. Thus, a long period, 30 days, is set as the event window period (the day of the event day is also included in the event window). A period of 180 days before the event day and 1 day before the event day [−180, −1] is selected as the estimation window for the event. It should be noted that security markets only trade on weekdays. However, considering that the information will be interpreted and analyzed on non-trading days, the natural day is adopted from 180 days before the event day to 30 days after it. Only data for the trading days during this period are used for data processing.

7.1.1.2 Calculating Real Rates of Return and Estimating Normal Rates of Return

The release date of a bank's CSR report is chosen according to the release date in CSMAR and Wind databases, thereby confirming the estimated window period and event window period, and deriving the daily trading data for each stock as well as the Index in the corresponding period. Since the selected Chinese and US listed banks' stocks are weighted stocks in their respective markets, the Composite Index that reflects the overall market trend are not selected. Instead, the CSI 300 Index (Shanghai and Shenzhen 300 index) and the NYSE US 100 Fund Index (New York Stock Exchange US 100 Fund Index) are used. These better reflect the trend of weighted stocks in the Chinese and American stock markets. Based on the obtained data in CSMAR and Wind databases, using the CAPM model and the linear regression method, the real rate of return and the estimated normal rate of return for each bank's stock within 30 days after the release date of the 2013–2017 CSR reports are calculated.

Table 7.1 CAR of Chinese and American banks

	2013	2014	2015	2016	2017	Average
Chinese banks (%)	3.35	−2.40	1.43	−3.04	−2.66	−0.66
American banks (%)	4.73	1.85	4.10	3.35	1.17	3.04

7.1.1.3 Calculating Abnormal Return and Cumulative Abnormal Return

The daily real return rate for each bank is subtracted from the estimated normal rate of return to obtain the abnormal return (AR) of the corresponding trading day. The daily return within 30 days is calculated to obtain the cumulative abnormal rate of return (CAR) of each bank's corresponding annual event window. The arithmetic average of 10 Chinese banks' and 10 American banks' CAR in the corresponding year is taken as the average CAR of the Chinese and American banks. The calculation results of the CAR are shown in Table 7.1.

According the results of CAR in Table 7.1, the CAR for all of the American banks' stock prices from 2013 to 2017 are positive. Meanwhile, the CAR of Chinese banks' stock price is negative for the year 2014, 2016 and 2017 and the average CAR of Chinese banks' stock price is -0.66% which is also negative and smaller than that of American banks (3.04%).

Thus, the discursive features in Chinese banks' CSR reports produce negative impacts on capital market performance. On the contrary, the discursive features of American banks' CSR reports bring positive impacts on capital markets. American capital markets react more to the discursive features in banks' CSR reports than do Chinese capital markets. In other words, the discursive features in American banks' CSR reports achieve an effective function in the discursive construction of banks' CSR images and corporate value enhancement.

7.1.1.4 T-Test

In this study, whether the discursive features in banks' CSR reports can bring significant actual effects on capital markets (banks stock price's CAR) needs to be analyzed in order to examine language's economic value in promoting corporate value.

T-tests are frequently used in statistical tests since they are not limited by sample size, and are suitable for testing the difference between the average values of two small samples.

A simple sample T-test was used as the last step of event study to examine whether the average CAR within 30 days after the release of Chinese and American banks' CSR reports is significantly different from 0. The null hypothesis and the alternative hypotheses are listed below.

H0: The average CAR 30 days after the release of the Chinese and American banks' CSR reports is not significantly different from 0.

Table 7.2 T-test result of Chinese Banks' average CAR from 2013 to 2017

Chinese banks	Mean difference (%)	Variance	T-stat	P-value
2013	3.35	18.751	2.446	0.037
2014	−2.40	8.431	−2.612	0.028
2015	1.43	2.146	3.094	0.013
2016	−3.04	11.800	−2.798	0.021
2017	−2.66	12.884	−2.346	0.044

Table 7.3 T-test result of American Banks' average CAR from 2013 to 2017

American Banks	Mean difference (%)	Variance	T-stat	P-value
2013	4.73	14.037	3.992	0.003
2014	1.85	3.751	3.021	0.014
2015	4.10	8.315	4.496	0.001
2016	3.35	6.694	4.095	0.003
2017	1.17	2.347	2.415	0.039

H1: The average CAR 30 days after the release of the Chinese and American banks' CSR reports is significantly different from 0.

The T-test result of the significance of Chinese Banks' average CAR from 2013 to 2017 is shown in Table 7.2.

The T-test result of the significance of American Banks' average CAR from 2013 to 2017 is shown in Table 7.3.

The above T-test results in Tables 7.2 and 7.3 show that the P values from 2013 to 2017 are less than 0.05. Thus, the null hypothesis can be rejected with 95% confidence. It may be concluded that, the average CAR 30 days after the release of both Chinese and American banks' CSR reports is significantly different from 0. Thus, the multi-dimensional discursive features in Chinese and American banks' CSR reports may have the significant impact on banks' stock price trends, and may cause actual effects on capital market performance.

7.1.2 *Discussion of the Empirical Results of the Event Study*

The empirical results of the event study will be discussed in two aspects: the significance of CAR, and Chinese and American banks stock prices' different CAR values within 30 days after the release of CSR reports.

First, in terms of the significance of CAR, and based on the results of the T-test in the event study, the multi-dimensional discursive features in both Chinese and American banks' CSR reports may have significant impact on capital markets. This is because average CAR 30 days after the release of Chinese and American banks' CSR reports is significant.

This finding verifies discourse's function in social, economic practice (Fairclough, 1995), discourse's function in institutional identity construction (Chen, 2016, 2017), as well as language's function in signaling theory and behavioral finance. Furthermore, it also consolidates the rationale of this study, the discursive construction of bank's CSR image, and its actual effects on capital markets.

Thus, both Chinese and American banks need to highlight the importance of CSR information disclosure in terms of the employment of multi-dimensional discursive features in CSR reports. This can impact capital market performance and corporate value enhancement on the linguistic level. This is because they each have the function in the discursive construction of banks' CSR images and can influence investors' attitudes/expectations towards banks' CSR images and corporate value.

Secondly, in term of CAR values, the average CAR value of Chinese banks' stock prices from 2013 to 2017 is negative, and the average CAR value of American banks' stock price from 2013 to 2017 is positive. American banks stock prices' CAR value in 30 days after the release of CSR reports is higher than that of Chinese banks.

This finding verifies Chinese banks' employment of multi-dimensional discursive features in CSR reports. This is discussed in Chap. 5. Furthermore, this finding also verifies the inadequacies of Chinese banks' discursive construction of CSR images in Chap. 6 comparing with the American banks in order to better comply with the international contexts in which international stakeholders are located, and to internationalize the Chinese banking industry.

The negative CAR value indicates that discursive features in Chinese banks' CSR reports may cause negative impact on capital markets. Reasons can be explained from the following two aspects:

The negative reaction on capital markets may be influenced by Chinese banks' comparatively low quality CSR disclosure systems and inadequate CSR performance relative to those of American banks. Numerous academic studies (Song & Gong, 2007; Shen et al., 2011) and public CSR research centers have pointed out that Chinese companies have less adequate and less effective CSR disclosure systems than their American counterparts. This is due to the less compulsory disclosure policies of company's CSR report given by relevant supervision department in order to improve the Chinese companies' CSR report disclosure quality. Also, Chinese companies started conducting CSR later than their American counterparts. This may have led to their comparatively less awareness of CSR performance. The less CSR behavior activities concerning employee-care and sustainable management in Chinese banks' CSR reports according to previous CSR keyword analysis also reflects Chinese companies' lesser awareness of CSR performance disclosure.

Moreover, multi-dimensional discursive features in Chinese banks' CSR reports couldn't comply with foreign investors' reading conventions and contexts in some degree. This may also lead to their negative impacts on capital markets. For example, the lower reading ease and higher Optimism sentimental tendencies and less visual interaction in Chinese banks' CSR reports may decrease both Chinese and foreign investors' reading efficiency and influence their expectations of banks' corporate value and their investment behaviors in the market.

Thus, Chinese banks also need to learn from American banks to develop and enhance awareness in using discursive features to construct CSR images, attract investors and improve corporate value. To be specific, Chinese banks need to recontextualize their CSR reports. This includes adopting more proper discursive features which suit the foreign contexts in order to better transmit our CSR values and behaviors, and improve our international CSR images from the linguistic level.

To summarize, according to the results of event study of CSR report disclosure's impact on capital market performance, the multi-dimensional discursive features in CSR reports may significantly impact capital markets, for both Chinese and American banks. Importance should be attached to the discursive features in CSR reports, by both Chinese and American banks, in improving their CSR images and corporate value.

Furthermore, Chinese banks need to develop their awareness by using recontextualized discursive strategies in the English versions of their CSR reports. This may influence international investors' investment behaviors and improve corporate value.

7.2 GREA of Discursive Features' Affecting Degrees on Capital Markets

Gray relational analysis is mainly used in multi-factor analysis of gray systems. This dissertation examines the relation degrees between the various discursive features in banks' CSR reports, and the capital market reaction (CAR) after the release of the CSR reports of 10 Chinese and 10 American banks after 30 days. This is a typical small-sample-problem that contains inaccurate and incomplete information, making it a gray system. Thus, it is suitable to use grey system theory to examine the affecting degrees of discursive features in banks' CSR reports on capital markets.

As a multi-factor statistical analysis method, the basic idea of gray relational analysis is to judge how close correlation is according to the similarity degree of the sequences' curve geometries. The closer the curve is, the greater the correlation between the corresponding sequences, and vice versa (Li, 2005). Compared with other traditional multi-factor analysis methods, gray correlation analysis requires less data and less computation. This makes it convenient for a wide array of applications. Usually, this method can be used to analyze the influence of various factors on results, and to solve the problem of comprehensive evaluation with time. The core is to establish the reference sequence with time according to certain rules. It is also important to take each evaluation objects' changes with time as comparison sequences, in order to determine the relation degrees or affecting degrees between each comparison sequence and reference sequence. The results are drawn according to the value of relation degrees from 0 to 1.

Gray relational analysis also has two obvious shortcomings due to its calculation mechanism: partial correlation tendency and loss of personality information (Li, ibid). Thus, some scholars have developed a grey relational entropy analysis method (GREA) based on grey relational analysis (Wen et al., 1998). Compared with the traditional grey relational analysis method, GREA can make full use of the individual information to achieve overall proximity. It can then make the results more scientific and reasonable.

GREA was chosen to measure entropy relation degrees between multi-dimensional discursive features in CSR reports and the stock price trends (CAR) of Chinese and American banks. This is guided by signaling theory and behavioral finance. It is done in order to examine discursive features' different contribution degrees to capital markets and objectively provide more effective discursive suggestions for Chinese banks to improve their CSR images, and to attract more foreign investment and become more internationalized.

7.2.1 Empirical Results of GREA

The empirical analysis of entropy relation degrees between CSR reports' multi-dimensional discursive features and the CAR of Chinese and American banks' stock prices is calculated according to the steps and mathematical model of GREA illustrated in Chap. 4.

7.2.1.1 Determining Analysis Sequences and Variables in GREA

The first step is to determine the reference sequences that reflect the characteristics of the system's behavior and the comparison sequence that affect the behavior of the gray system. Banks' CSR reports' multi-dimensional discursive features' affecting degrees on capital market are examined in this study. The CAR of banks' stock prices can reflect and represent capital market reaction. Thus, the CAR of banks' stock prices is chosen as the reference sequence. The variable value of reference sequence is the average CAR of banks stock price 30 days after the release of their CSR reports, as calculated by event study.

The multi-dimensional discursive features (sentimental tendency in Activity, Optimism, Certainty, Realism, Commonality in sentiment evaluation, lexical density, mean word length, mean sentence length, cohesion, Flesch Reading Ease, Flesch-Kincaid Grade Level in readability evaluation, CSR keyword categories of "community and society", "employees", "the environment", "corporate governance" in CSR keyword evaluation, visualization in the visual evaluation of CSR report) that can influence the behavior of capital market are chosen as the 16 comparison sequences. The variable values of the 16 comparison sequences are the indicator value of 16 discursive features. The analysis sequences in GREA are shown in Table 7.4. X_0 refers to the reference sequence, and X_1-X_{16} refer to the comparison sequences.

Table 7.4 List of analysis sequences in GREA

Sequence type		Sequence	Sequence name
Capital market performance		X_0	CAR
Multi-dimensional discursive features in CSR report	Sentiment	X_1	Activity
		X_2	Optimism
		X_3	Certainty
		X_4	Realism
		X_5	Commonality
	Readability	X_6	Lexical Density
		X_7	Mean Word Length
		X_8	Mean Sentence Length
		X_9	Cohesion
		X_{10}	Flesch Reading Ease
		X_{11}	Flesch-Kincaid Grade Level
	CSR Keyword	X_{12}	Community & Society
		X_{13}	Employee
		X_{14}	Environment
		X_{15}	Corporate Governance
	Visualization	X_{16}	Visualization

7.2.1.2 Calculating Entropy Relation Degrees

CAR within 30 days after the release of the 2013–2017 CSR reports of 10 listed Chinese banks and 10 listed American banks are used as the reference sequence. The 16 discursive features in Chinese and American banks' 2013–2017 CSR reports are used as the corresponding observe sequences. Both reference and observe sequences are time sequences from 2013 to 2017. Since the dimensions or units of variable values in each sequences are different, it is inconvenient to compare them directly. Therefore, when performing GREA, the initial value or the mean value processing is generally used to make indicator values dimensionless. The initial value method for non-dimensionalization is thus selected. After processing, the gray relation coefficients for each comparison sequence are calculated. Next, the entropy relation degrees for each comparison sequences are calculated.

The value of the entropy relation degree is between 0 and 1. The closer to 1, the higher the conformity between the comparison sequences and the reference sequence, the greater the correlation between the comparison sequences and the reference sequence, and the more influence or contribution the comparison sequences have to the reference sequence.

Table 7.5 shows the calculation results of entropy relation degree for the 16 discursive indicators in comparison sequences. E represents the entropy relation degree of the corresponding comparison sequence.

Table 7.5 Results of entropy relation degree for 16 discursive indicators

	E_1	E_2	E_3	E_4	E_5	E_6	E_7	E_8
Chinese Banks	0.9571	0.9566	0.9582	0.9568	0.9572	0.9589	0.9576	0.9627
American Banks	0.9683	0.9668	0.9665	0.9662	0.9673	0.9654	0.9675	0.9726
	E9	E10	E11	E12	E13	E14	E15	E16
Chinese Banks	0.9570	0.9631	0.9567	0.9429	0.9560	0.9499	0.9562	0.9544
American Banks	0.9769	0.9713	0.9823	0.9603	0.9678	0.9682	0.9623	0.9375

Table 7.6 Rankings of discursive indicators' entropy relation degrees

Rank	Chinese banks	American banks
1	Flesch reading ease	Flesch-Kincaid grade level
2	Mean sentence length	Cohesion
3	Lexical density	Mean sentence length
4	Certainty	Flesch reading ease
5	Mean word length	Activity
6	Commonality	Environment
7	Activity	Employee
8	Cohesion	Mean word length
9	Realism	Commonality
10	Flesch-Kincaid grade level	Optimism
11	Optimism	Certainty
12	Corporate governance	Realism
13	Employee	Lexical density
14	Visualization	Corporate governance
15	Environment	Community and society
16	Community and society	Visualization

Based on the mathematical mechanism of GREA, if the entropy relation degree of one comparison sequence is closer to 1, the discursive indicator in that comparison sequence ranks higher and has more effects on capital market performance in the reference sequence. Thus, the rankings of Chinese and American banks' discursive indicators, according to their entropy relation degrees, are listed in Table 7.6.

7.2.2 Discussion of the Empirical Results of GREA

The results of GREA show that the rankings of entropy relation degree for the 16 discursive indicators of Chinese and American banks' CSR reports are different. Reasons for their different entropy relation rankings can be explained from the different political, social, economic, cultural factors of Chinese and American banks.

This will not be explained in detail since this study is focused on the practical insight that the Chinese banks can derive in order to improve their CSR report disclosure, international CSR images, and corporate value, discursively.

One important finding is that most of the discursive indicators for readability evaluation rank high for both Chinese and American banks. Examples include Flesch Reading Ease, mean sentence length, lexical density, mean word length in the Chinese banks and Flesch-Kincaid Grade Level, cohesion, mean sentence length, and Flesch Reading Ease in the American banks. Thus, discursive features that realize the readability of Chinese and American banks' CSR reports have higher entropy relation degrees with the CAR of banks' stocks prices. In order words, the readability of Chinese and American banks' CSR reports has more impact on capital markets, and it contributes the most to capital market performance.

According to the descriptive analysis of readability evaluation of banks' CSR reports, discursive indicators along the readability dimension all reflect that Chinese banks' CSR reports are more difficult to read and comprehend than American banks'. This is due to the typical generic features of government documents in Chinese banks' reports, the terms about Party and national projects and long notional words. These include adjectives, adverbs, nouns and complex sentence patterns concerned with insistent and unwavering CSR commitment to the government and national strategy. Also, the culture and language transfer and the neglect of foreign contexts during the translation of Chinese banks' English versions CSR report also decrease their reading ease.

Combined with the negative CAR value of Chinese banks' stock prices 30 days after the release of CSR reports calculated by event study in the previous session, it can be inferred that the discursive features that realize the low reading ease of Chinese banks' CSR reports may contribute more to the development of the negative CAR values of banks' stock prices. This is because discursive indicators in readability have higher degrees of entropy relation.

Additionally, the discursive indicators of readability also have more influence on American banks' stock price performance in capital markets. Stakeholders, especially investors, are more sensitive to the readability of CSR reports when they make investment decisions. Thus, the above 2 aspects show that Chinese banks need to prioritize improving English version CSR reports' reading ease when they compose or translate them. This can improve foreign investors' reading efficiency and their attitudes towards banks CSR images and corporate value.

Also, in order to comply with foreign contexts in CSR reports to transmit better CSR images and enhance corporate value, Chinese banks also need to prioritize the discursive indicators that have higher entropy relation degrees and contribute more to capital markets in the American context, but have lower entropy relation degrees and contribute less to capital markets in the Chinese banks' CSR reports. These discursive indicators closely connected with banks' CSR images and corporate value in foreign investors' concerns. Examples such as the CSR keywords concerning the "environment" and "employees". Their influential degree to capital market performance is higher in the American banks' CSR reports than in the Chinese banks' CSR reports. Thus, it is suggested that Chinese banks need use more CSR keywords in CSR reports to disclose more initiative CSR behaviors in employee-training and environmental management. This is also analyzed in Chap. 6.

To summarize, the empirical results of GREA indicate that most discursive indicators that realize the readability of CSR reports have more influence on capital market performance than other discursive indicators. This is true for both Chinese and American banks. Thus, Chinese banks should prioritize reading ease improvement when they compose or translate their English version CSR reports. This will help them better comply with international contexts.

Thus, since CSR keywords concerning "employees" and the "environment" have more influence on the development trends of banks' stock prices, Chinese banks should disclose more CSR behavior by using more CSR keywords pertaining to initiatives, comprehensive employee care, and environment protection. This will enable them to meet the expectations of international investors and internationalize Chinese banks' CSR images.

7.3 Summary

This chapter examines the discursive construction of Chinese and American banks' CSR images' actual effects on capital markets. Guided by signal theory and behavioral finance, it utilizes event study to examine whether multi-dimensional discursive features of CSR reports can significantly impact the CAR of banks' stock prices and verify discourse's function in image construction and capital market performance. Then, the GREA method is used to examine the entropy relation degrees between multi-dimensional discursive features in Chinese and American banks' CSR reports and capital market performance in order to objectively provide more suggestions for Chinese banks to learn from American banks by using discursive features to improve CSR images and corporate value.

Based on the result of the event study, this study finds that the multi-dimensional discursive features in CSR reports may lead to a significant impact on capital market performance in both Chinese and American banks. Discursive features in American banks' CSR reports bring more influence to capital market compared with Chinese banks.

Based on the results of GREA, this study finds that the readability indicators of Chinese and American banks' CSR reports contribute more to capital market performance. In international contexts, investors and markets are more sensitive to CSR keywords concerning "employees" and "environment".

Thus, in order to discursively construct CSR images that better comply with international contexts and fasten the speed of Chinese banks' internalization via CSR reports, Chinese banks should:

Firstly, pay more attention to using discursive features to construct CSR images and improve corporate value, since they may significantly impact capital markets.

Also, improve banks' disclosure strategies through recontextualization in CSR reports' composition and translation. This will help them develop the awareness and habits of using discursive features in CSR reports to improve banks' CSR images and corporate value.

Finally, prioritize reading ease, and use comparatively more CSR keywords concerning "employees" and "environment" to express more initiative CSR behaviors in employee-training and environmental protection during the recontextualization of English versions of CSR reports, as the above two areas contribute more to corporate value enhancement in international contexts.

Chapter 8
Conclusion

In the concluding chapter, the major findings concerning the 3 research questions of this study will be summarized. Suggestions for the Chinese banks to discursively improve their CSR images and corporate value via the employment of multi-dimensional discursive features in CSR reports are offered. The contribution of this study to the acceleration of the internalization of Chinese banking industry under China's series of opening-up policies in the financial sector and the interdisciplinary integration of business discourse research and other disciplines will be highlighted. Limitations of this study will be presented and suggestions for future studies will be put forward at the end of this chapter.

8.1 Major Findings

Under the theoretical background of Fairclough's three-dimensional model, Biber's register analysis, and based on Chen's (2017) framework of discursive construction of institutional identity, and the corporate identity system, this study integrates a multi-dimensional discourse evaluation framework to examine various discursive features along 4 dimensions: sentiment, readability, CSR keywords, and visualization in Chinese and American banks' CSR reports. It also explores banks' discursive construction of CSR images in 3 dimensions: CSR mind image, CSR behavior image and CSR visual image, based on the multi-dimensional discourse evaluation framework.

Then, guided by signaling theory and behavioral finance, an empirical study of event analysis and GREA is conducted to examine banks' discursively constructed CSR images' effects on capital market performance. This is done to verify language's function in economic practices and objectively provide more advice for the Chinese banks so they can improve their international CSR image and influence on capital markets.

M. Wan, *CSR Image Discursive Construction of Banks and the Effects on Capital Markets*,
https://doi.org/10.1007/978-981-19-6012-3_8

The major findings will be stated in the following 3 aspects, in terms of the 3 research questions in this study.

8.1.1 Different Discursive Features in Chinese and American Banks' CSR Reports

This study analyzes and compares CSR reports' multi-dimensional discursive features along 4 dimensions: sentiment, readability, CSR keywords, visualization based on a corpus and linguistic computational tools: Anctonc, WordSmith, DICTION, and Coh-Metrix.

The descriptive and quantitative analysis in Chap. 5 presents the different discursive features of the 4 dimensions: sentiment, readability, CSR keywords, and visualization in Chinese and American banks' CSR reports from 2013 to 2017.

On the sentimental evaluation level, sentimental indicators in Chinese banks' CSR reports Activity (50.97), Optimism (54.84), Certainty (50.81) and Commonality (52.44) were found to be significantly higher than those of American banks, Activity (49.54), Optimism (50.79), Certainty (49.31) and Commonality (50.56). The sentimental indicator of Realism in Chinese banks' CSR reports (40.35) was significantly lower than that of American banks' (41.75). In general, Chinese banks' CSR reports show a higher sentimental tendency than American banks' CSR reports.

On the readability evaluation level, the readability indicators STTR (43.99) and mean word length (5.46) on lexical level, mean sentence length (30.91) and all connectives incidence (105.67) on syntactic level, Flesch-Kincaid Grade Level (12.885) on textual level in Chinese banks' CSR reports were found to be significantly higher than those of American banks' CSR reports: STTR (40.49) and mean word length (4.96), mean sentence length (27.41) and all connectives incidence (88.16), Flesch-Kincaid Grade Level (10.172). Flesch Reading Ease (32.593) in Chinese banks' CSR reports was significantly lower than that of American banks' CSR reports (45.416). In general, all these readability indicators show that Chinese banks' CSR reports contain more information, longer sentences and more complex logical relations. Thus, Chinese banks' CSR reports are comparatively more difficult to read.

On the CSR keyword evaluation level, the percentage of CSR keywords about "community and society" (6.7%) in Chinese banks' CSR reports was found to be significantly higher than American banks' CSR reports (1.43%). The percentage of CSR keywords categories of "employee" (1.03%), "environment" (1.29%) and "corporate governance" (8.06%) in Chinese banks' CSR reports were significantly lower than those of American banks: "employee" (2.5%), "environment" (2.3%) and "corporate governance" (11.91%). In general, Chinese banks disclose more CSR information about their contributions to society and public, whereas American banks disclose more CSR concerns for employees, customers, the environment and corporate governance.

On the visual evaluation level, it was found that visual value in Chinese banks' CSR reports (0.32) is significantly lower than that of American banks (0.54). In general, American banks have a stronger sense of visual presentation of CSR information than Chinese banks. Pictures in Chinese banks' CSR reports have the function of visual representation of CSR information. However, pictures in American banks' CSR reports have dual functions of visual representation of CSR information and stakeholder interaction.

In general, Chinese banks' CSR reports show a higher sentimental tendency than American banks' CSR reports; English version Chinese banks' CSR reports are comparatively more difficult to read; Chinese banks disclose more CSR contributions to society and public, whereas American banks disclose more CSR concern for employees, the environment and corporate governance; American banks prefers to employ pictures in CSR reports to persuade and interact with their stakeholders.

8.1.2 Different Discursively Constructed CSR Images of Chinese and American Banks

Guided by the CIS system, the theory of information asymmetry, the theory of discourse and institutional identity and linguistic theories behind the discursive features, this study analyzes Chinese and American banks' discursive construction of CSR images along 3 dimensions by multi-dimensional discourse evaluation of their CSR reports.

The cross-disciplinary interpretation and explanation in Chap. 6 present Chinese and American banks' different discursively constructed CSR mind images, CSR behavior images and CSR visual images.

It is found that CSR reports' various linguistic features along different dimensions reflect the same CSR values, transmit the similar CSR behaviors and are rhetorically employed to persuade stakeholders to identify with banks' particular CSR value and behaviors. They also enhance banks' CSR images in certain aspect. For example, more sentimental words in Leveling and less words in Self-Reference are used in the sentimental evaluation of Certainty in Chinese banks' CSR reports. This reflects the authoritative CSR images of Chinese banks; Readability indicators of high lexical density and long sentence reflect the Chinese CSR reports' generic features of government documents by which the official CSR mind image areas constructed; more CSR keywords concerning CSR contributions to government and society also convey the society and public-oriented CSR behavior image of Chinese banks. This finding also indicates the multi-dimensional linguistic features' function in expressing the same communicative purposes as in Biber's register analysis (Biber and Conrad 2009).

At the level of CSR mind image construction, it was found that Chinese banks' authoritative, country and public-oriented CSR mind images are constructed via their higher sentimental tendencies in Certainty, Optimism, and Commonality. This is also constructed via high lexical density, long terminologies, sentences and complex sentence pattern in Chinese banks' CSR reports. Through these features, Chinese banks' authority-pursuing, national strategy and public-oriented, optimistic CSR value are reflected; American banks' individualistic, pragmatistic, corporate value-oriented CSR mind images are constructed via the lower sentimental tendencies in Certainty and Commonality, higher sentimental tendencies in Realism and plain English.

Chinese banks' active and innovative CSR mind images are constructed by their higher sentimental tendencies of Activity and Optimism. This is because they reflect Chinese banks' positive, innovation-driven development strategy; American banks' steadfast and conservative CSR images are constructed by the lower sentimental tendency in Activity and Optimism, as they reflect American banks' corporate governance concept of stability and compliance.

At the level of CSR behavior image construction, it was found that most Chinese banks' CSR behaviors are official CSR behaviors, and most American banks' CSR behaviors are individualistic CSR behaviors.

Chinese banks disclose more CSR performance in supporting social and national development and less CSR information in employee-training and environmental protection. Thus, Chinese banks discursively construct a CSR behavior image as the supporter of national strategy and the national policy of basic employee welfare and environmental protection. Meanwhile, American banks disclose more CSR performance in community commitment and more CSR information about the comprehensive and initiative employee investment and environment management. Thus, American banks construct a CSR behavior image as the volunteer for community development and environment protection; Chinese banks disclose less diversified stakeholder engagement and more innovative reforms in business and products. Thus, Chinese banks discursively construct a national-strategy oriented, innovative CSR behavior image. American banks disclose more CSR performance in diverse stakeholder concerns and conservative governance. Thus, American banks discursively construct an inclusive and prudent CSR behavior image.

At the level of CSR visual image construction, it was found that Chinese banks' authoritative and official CSR visual images are constructed via the repetitive and less interactive visual effects in their CSR reports; American banks' individualistic and interpersonal CSR visual images are constructed via the interactive and metaphorical visual effects in their CSR reports.

In general, Chinese banks construct authoritative, national strategy-oriented, society and public-oriented CSR images. American banks construct pragmatistic and individual-oriented CSR images; American banks show objective and factual construction of CSR image; Chinese banks, besides showing objective and factual construction of CSR image, also express prospective construction of their CSR image.; Chinese banks convey active, positive, innovative CSR images. American banks transmit stable and conservative CSR images.

8.1.3 Discursively Constructed CSR Images' Effects on Capital Markets

Event study is conducted in order to scientifically examine Chinese and American banks' discursively constructed CSR images' actual effects on capital markets, and to verify language's function in economic practices.

Based on the **event study's empirical results**, it was found that multi-dimensional discursive features in both Chinese and American banks' CSR reports may bring significant CAR to banks' stock prices and capital market performance. Multi-dimensional discursive features in Chinese banks' CSR reports bring more negative influence, unlike the positive impact of those of American banks. Chinese banks' need to emphasize the use of discursive features to improve corporate images and enhance corporate value. Furthermore, these findings also consolidate the rationale of this study, the discursive construction of bank's CSR image, and its actual effects on capital markets.

GREA was conducted to rank the discursive features' contribution degrees to market performance. This was done in order to examine the multi-dimensional discursive features' different affecting degrees on capital markets. It also provides Chinese banks with more scientific advice in discursive image construction and internationalization.

The **results of GREA** showed that readability indicators in Chinese and American banks' CSR reports contribute the most to capital market performance. CSR keywords concerning "employees" and "environment" have higher affecting degrees to capital markets in the foreign context.

In general, discursive features in CSR report that discursively transmit and construct banks' CSR images can significantly impact capital market performance. Chinese banks need to pay more attention to reading ease improvement in English context as well as disclose more CSR information pertaining to "employees" and "environment" in discursively CSR images construction since they may bring more effects on capital market performance.

8.2 Suggestions and Countermeasures

Based on our findings and research objectives, several suggestions are proposed, on the discourse level, to help Chinese banks improve their international image and enhance China's international image in financial sectors.

Firstly, the regulating organization of the Chinese banking industry, CBIRC, needs to guide Chinese banks in CSR information disclosure by enacting systematic and uniform formats and principles for banks' CSR reports disclosure. CBIRC is suggested to add the quality of banks' English CSR reports into the evaluation indicators of their annual supervision.

Also, Chinese banks need to reconstruct and recompose their English version CSR reports based on the Chinese version CSR reports, instead of rigidly translating them. Recontextulization is suggested during their composition of their English versions in order to comply with foreign stakeholders' reading conventions as well as international contexts.

Another suggestion is that Chinese banks need to emphasize the economic effects that discursive features in CSR reports bring. They need to improve the ease of reading of their CSR reports' since readability is international stakeholders' top concern. It also contributes the most to capital market performance. Chinese banks also need to focus on the CSR information concerning "employees" and "environment," since these are greatly emphasized by foreign stakeholders and international markets.

Moreover, Chinese banks need to disclose their CSR contributions to the government and the Party in a concise and straightforward way in order to weaken their authoritative CSR images. This can also better transmit the CSR values and behaviors of China's own characteristics to foreign stakeholders.

Chinese banks are suggested to decrease the sentimental tendency in Optimism and increase the sentimental tendency of Realism in their CSR reports in order to better comply with international contexts.

Finally, Chinese banks need to pay attention on the visual effects in their CSR reports and use pictures to achieve visual interaction and persuasion with stakeholders, metaphorically.

8.3 Implications of This Study

Under the background of China's financial reform and the series of opening-up policies implemented since the 19th National Congress of the CPC, it is urgent for Chinese banks to establish an international CSR image in order to attract more foreign investment. This can also expand China's international influence in the financial sector. This study has the following implications.

8.3.1 Practical Implications

Firstly, by integrating a cross-disciplinary and multi-dimensional discourse evaluation framework of banks' CSR reports, the deficiencies of Chinese banks' employment of discursive features in discursive image constructions have been pointed out, by comparing them with those of the American banks. This study contributes to the improvement of the Chinese banks awareness in CSR disclosure and the quality of the CSR disclosure system. It also contributes to the establishment of Chinese banking industry's international images.

Additionally, by conducting empirical research via event study and GREA, advice has been provided for Chinese banks to discursively influence investors' attitudes towards banks' CSR images in order to improve Chinese banks corporate value and performance in capital markets.

Also, since more and more Chinese companies from different sectors are choosing to list overseas, the findings in this study also have practical implications for their information disclosure, the discursive construction of international images, and corporate value enhancement through corporate narratives, such as annual reports and IPO prospectuses. In other words, this study contributes to the internalization of Chinese companies from the discourse level, thus more effectively telling "Chinese stories" and spreading China's national image.

Finally, since the corporate identity system has been used to examine the corporate image construction of many institutions, the analytical model of this study has practical implications for the discursive construction of various institutions, such as university image construction via websites, and national image construction via publicity materials.

8.3.2 Theoretical Implications

The multi-dimensional discourse evaluation framework for discursive construction of banks' CSR images and the influencing mechanism of discursive features on capital market reaction proposed in this study promotes the inter-disciplinary integration of linguistic theories, management theories and financial theories.

Also, the multi-dimensional discourse evaluation framework for discursive construction of banks' CSR images integrated in this study is a cross-disciplinary attempt in institutional identity research. It extends Chen's (2017) framework of discursive construction for institutional identity, and contributes to the development of cross-disciplinary research on institutional image construction.

Furthermore, this study is an innovative and inter-disciplinary trial of the relations between corporate narratives and corporate images. It reveals the problem-solving function of discourse which sheds light both on theoretical research of both corporate governance and business discourse.

Finally, this study verifies language's function in image construction and capital market performance since the discursive features in CSR report serve as signals that can influence investors' psychological activities in their investment behaviors. Thus, it provides a discursive approach to address pivotal questions in capital market research, and sheds light on behavioral finance.

8.3.3 Method Implications

This research employs the corpus method and computational linguistic method to explore the discursive features of Chinese and America banks' CSR reports. This makes the quantitative analysis of corpus more comprehensive and scientific. The computational linguistic tools used in this study, such as DICTION and Coh-Metrix, can be used to analyze the multi-dimensional sentimental tendencies, and the lexical, syntactic, textual features and cohesion in business discourse.

Also, this research adopts the empirical models of event study in the financial field, and GREA in the mathematical field in business discourse analysis. This is done in order to scientifically examine and verify discursive features' actual effects and influential degrees on capital market performance. The event analysis and GREA used in this study provide cross-disciplinary and empirical methods to examine language's function in economic practices. This can be used in future cross-disciplinary business discourse research.

8.4 Limitations of the Present Study

As a cross-disciplinary attempt in the field of business discourse, corporate image construction and capital market performance, this research has at least 3 limitations.

The range of Chinese and American banks' CSR reports is limited to 5 years. This is due to the Chinese banks' short history and less awareness of disclosing English versions of CSR reports. More CSR reports, over a longer time frame, may make the discursive features calculated by corpus and computational linguistic tools more comprehensive. Discursive features' effects on capital market performance calculated by empirical research could also be more scientific and accurate.

Additionally, the multi-dimensional discursive features used for banks' CSR image construction are not comprehensive enough. For example, metaphors in CSR reports that can also implicitly reflect banks' CSR concepts and discursively construct and transmit banks' CSR mind images have yet to be analyzed.

Finally, a grading system concerning the discursive quality of banks' CSR reports, based on the multi-dimensional discursive evaluation of CSR reports for more companies to check the quality of their CSR reports and improve CSR disclosure system, has yet to be established.

8.5 Suggestions for Future Studies

The above limitations provide several research orientations and directions for future studies.

Firstly, future studies can add the CSR reports of other companies in financial sectors, such as insurance companies and security companies as the research objects. This could help them discursively construct their international CSR images, and improve China's international influence and status in financial sectors comprehensively.

Also, more discursive evaluation indicators need to be proposed and added to the multi-dimensional discursive evaluation framework for corporate CSR image construction. This would make the discursive exploration of CSR reports more comprehensive and fully achieve language's function in economic practice.

Moreover, a grading system concerning the discursive quality of CSR reports, based on the multi-dimensional discursive evaluation of CSR reports for CSR image construction and corporate value improvement, should be established. This could provide companies with a scientific, convincing and comprehensive system to improve the quality of their CSR reports. It could also help improve their international corporate images and enhance their corporate value.

Finally, the multi-dimensional discursive features of CSR reports can be connected with banks' actual CSR performance via empirical research in order to examine the consistency between "CSR" companies have said, and "CSR" companies have actually accomplished. It could also provide more suggestions for the improvement of companies' CSR disclosure and CSR performance.

References

Abraham, S., & Shrives, P. J. (2014). Improving the relevance of risk factor disclosure in corporate annual reports. *British Accounting Review, 46*(1), 91–107.

Adams, C. A., & Harte, G. (1998). The changing portrayal of the employment of women in British banks' and retail companies' corporate annual reports. *Accounting Organizations & Society, 23*(8), 781–812.

Aiezza, M. C. (2015a). We may face the risks ... Risks that could adversely affect our face. A corpus-assisted discourse analysis of modality markers in CSR reports. *Studies in Communication Sciences, 15*(1), 68–76.

Aiezza, M. C. (2015b). *BRIC by BRIC. The CorSus of corporate social responsibility. A corpus-assisted discourse analysis of sustainability reports.* Ph.D. dissertation, Università degli studi di Napoli Federico II.

Akerlof, G. A. (1970). The market for "lemons": Quality uncertainty and the market mechanism. *The Quarterly Journal of Economics, 84*(3), 488–500.

Austin, J. (1962). *How to do things with words.* Oxford University.

Bakar, A. S. A., & Ameer, R. (2011). Readability of corporate social responsibility communication in Malaysia. *Eco-Management and Auditing, 18*(1), 50–60.

Baker, P. (2006). *Using corpora in discourse analysis.* Continuum.

Balmer, J. M. T. (2008). Identity based views of the corporation: Insights from corporate identity, organizational identity, social identity, visual identity, corporate brand identity and corporate image. *European Journal of Marketing, 42*(9/10), 879–906.

Banerjee, S. B. (2008). Corporate social responsibility: The good, the bad and the ugly. *Critical Sociology, 34*(1), 51–79.

Bargiela-Chiappini, F., Nickerson, C., & Planken, B. (2007). *Business discourse.* Palgrave Macmillan.

Beattie, V., McInnes, B., & Fearnley, S. (2004). A methodology for analyzing and evaluating narratives in annual reports: A comprehensive descriptive profile and metrics for disclosure quality attributes. *Accounting Forum, 28*(2004), 205–236.

Bebbington, J., Larrinaga, C., & Moneva, J. M. (2008). Corporate social reporting and reputation risk management. *Accounting Auditing & Accountability Journal, 21*(3), 337–361.

Betts, E. A. (1949). Readability: Its application to the elementary school. *Journal of Educational Research, 42*(6), 438–459.

Bhatia, A. (2012). The corporate social responsibility report: The hybridization of a "confused" genre (2007–2011). *IEEE Transactions on Professional Communication, 55*(3), 221–238.

Bhatia, V. K. (2002). Applied genre analysis: A multi-perspective model. *Ibérica, 4*, 3–19.

Bhatia, V. K. (2004). *Worlds of written discourse: A genre-based view.* Continuum.

Bhatia, V. K. (2005). Generic patterns in promotional discourse. In H. Halmari & T. Virtanen (Eds.), *Persuasion across genres: A linguistic approach* (pp. 213–228). John Benjamins.

M. Wan, *CSR Image Discursive Construction of Banks and the Effects on Capital Markets*,
https://doi.org/10.1007/978-981-19-6012-3

Bhatia, V. K., Flowerdew, J., & Jones, R. H. (Eds.). (2008). *Advances in discourse studies*. Routledge.
Biber, D., & Conrad, S. (2009). *Register, genre, and style*. Cambridge University Press.
Biber, D. (1988). *Variation across speech and writing*. Routledge.
Bloomfield, R. J. (2002). The "incomplete revelation hypothesis" and financial reporting. *Accounting Horizons, 16*(3), 985–988.
Brown, N., & Deegan, C. (1998). The public disclosure of environmental performance information—A dual test of media agenda setting theory and legitimacy theory. *Accounting & Business Research, 29*(1), 21–41.
Brown, P., & Levinson, S. C. (1987). *Politeness: Some universals in language usage*. Cambridge University Press.
Burman, E., & Parker, I. (1993). *Discourse analytic research: Repertoires and readings of texts in action*. Routledge.
Campbell, D., Craven, B., & Shrives, P. (2003). Voluntary social reporting in three FTSE sectors: A comment on perception and legitimacy. *Accounting Auditing & Accountability Journal, 16*(4), 558–581.
Carroll, A. B. (1991). The pyramid of CSR: Toward the moral management of organizational stakeholders. *Business Horizons, 34*(4), 39–48.
Carroll, A. B., & Shabana, K. M. (2010). The business case for corporate social responsibility: A review of concepts, research and practice. *International Journal of Management Reviews, 12*(1), 85–105.
Catenaccio, P. (2012). *Understanding CSR discourse: Insights from linguistics and discourse analysis*. Arcipelago Edizioni.
Chen, J. (2016). Comparative studies of the discursive construction of the institutional identities of Chinese and western universities. *Foreign Languages in China,* (4), 29–39. [陈建平. (2016). 中外大学机构身份话语建构比较研究. *中国外语,* (4), 29–39].
Chen, J. (2017). A comparative study of the discursive construction strategies of the institutional identities of Chinese-British-American universities. *Modern Foreign Languages, 40*(1), 28–40. [陈建平. (2017). 中英美大学机构身份的话语建构策略比较. *现代外语, 40*(1), 28–40].
Chen, L., Srinidhi, B., Tsang, A., & Yu, W. (2016). Audited financial reporting and voluntary disclosure of corporate social responsibility (CSR) reports. *Journal of Management Accounting Research, 28*(2), 53–76.
Chen, X. (2014). Current research on identity from the pragmatic perspective: Key issues and main approaches. *Modern Foreign Languages, 37*(5), 702–710. [陈新仁. (2014). 语用学视角下的身份研究——关键问题与主要路径. *现代外语, 37*(5), 702–710].
Cheng, R., & Zhang D. (2017). Multimodal discourse analysis in China: Taking journal articles as an example. *Foreign Languages in China,* (3), 36–44. [程瑞兰、张德禄. (2017). 多模态话语分析在中国研究的现状、特点和发展趋势——以期刊成果为例. *中国外语,* (3), 36–44].
Chou, J. R., & Tsai, H. C. (2009). On-line learning performance and computer anxiety measure for unemployed adult novices using a grey relation entropy method. *Information Processing & Management, 45*(2), 200–215.
Clatworthy, M. A., & Jones, M. J. (2006). Differential patterns of textual characteristics and company performance in the chairman's statement. *Accounting Auditing & Accountability Journal, 19*(4), 493–511.
Courtis, J. K. (2004). Color as visual rhetoric in financial reporting. *Accounting Forum, 28*(3), 265–281.
Croft, W., & Cruse, D. A. (2004). *Cognitive linguistics*. Cambridge University Press.
D' Andrea, A., Ferri, F., Grifoni, P., & Guzzo, T. (2015). Approaches, tools and applications for sentiment analysis implementation. *International Journal of Computer Applications, 125*(3), 26–33.
Dai, G. (2012). *Business stylistics*. Shanghai: Shanghai Foreign Language Education Press. [戴桂玉. (2012). *商务英语文体学*. 上海: 上海外语教育出版社].
Das, S. R., & Chen, M. Y. (2007). Yahoo! for Amazon: Sentiment extraction from small talk on the web. *Management Science, 53*(9), 1375–1388.

Davis, A. K., Piger, J. M., & Sedor, L. M. (2012). Beyond the numbers: Measuring the information content of earnings press release language. *Contemporary Accounting Research, 29*(3), 845–868.

Davis, A. K., Ge, W., Matsumoto, D., & Zhang, J. L. (2015). The effect of manager-specific optimism on the tone of earnings conference calls. *Review of Accounting Studies, 20*(2), 639–673.

Deegan, C. (2002). Introduction: The legitimizing effect of social, and environmental disclosure—A theoretical foundation. *Accounting Auditing & Accountability Journal, 15*(3), 282–311.

Deegan, C., Rankin, M., & Voght, P. (2000). Firms' disclosure reactions to major social incidents: Australian evidence. *Accounting Forum, 24*(1), 101–130.

Degano, C. (2010). Linguistic perspectives on image construction and moral identity: The case of banks. In P. Evangelisti—Allori, & G. Garzone (Eds.), *Discourse, Identities and Genres in Corporate Communication* (pp. 235–261). Bern: Peter Lang.

De Fina, A., Schiffrin, D., & Bamberg, M. (2006). *Discourse and identity*. Cambridge University Press.

Deng, J. (1990). *A course in gray system theory*. Wuhan: Huazhong University of Science and Technology Press. [邓聚龙. (1990). *灰色系统理论教程*. 武汉: 华中理工大学出版社].

Deng, X., Kang, J. K., & Low, B. S. (2013). Corporate social responsibility and stakeholder value maximization: Evidence from mergers. *Journal of Financial Economics, 110*(1), 87–109.

Dhaliwal, D. S., Li, O. Z., Tsang, A., & Yang, Y. G. (2011). Voluntary nonfinancial disclosure and the cost of equity capital: The initiation of corporate social responsibility reporting. *The Accounting Review, 86*(1), 59–100.

Dhaliwal, D. S., Radhakrishnan, S., Tsang, A., & Yang, Y. G. (2012). Nonfinancial disclosure and analyst forecast accuracy: International evidence on corporate social responsibility disclosure. *The Accounting Review, 87*(3), 723–759.

Drago, C., Ginesti, G., Pongelli, C., & Sciascia, S. (2017). Reporting strategies: What makes family firms beat around the bush? Family-related antecedents of annual report readability. *Journal of Family Business Strategy, 1*(1), 1–8.

Du, H., & Cai, J., (2013). A Coh-Metrix-based model of linguistic features predicting argumentative writing quality of EFL learners. *Modern Foreign Languages,* (3), 293–300. [杜慧颖、蔡金亭. (2013). 基于Coh-Metrix的中国英语学习者议论文写作质量预测模型研究. *现代外语,* (3), 293–300].

Eccles, R. G., Ioannou, I., & Serafeim, G. (2014). The impact of corporate sustainability on organizational processes and performance. *Management Science, 60*(11), 2835–2857.

Fairclough, N. (1992). *Discourse and social change*. Polity Press.

Fairclough, N. (1995). *Critical discourse analysis: The critical study of language*. Longman Group.

Fan, H. (2013). The strategy for national image building and communication. *Journal of Tsinghua University(Philosophy and Social Sciences),* (2), 141–152. [范红. (2013). 国家形象的多维塑造与传播策略. *清华大学学报(哲学社会科学版),* (2), 141–152].

Feldman, R. (2013). Techniques and applications for sentiment analysis. *Communications of the ACM, 56*(4), 82–89.

Feng, D., & Peter, W. (2011). Intertextual voices and engagement in TV advertisements. *Visual Communication, 10*(4), 565–588.

Fombrun, C. (1998). Indices of Corporate Reputation: An analysis of media rankings and social monitors' ratings. *Corporate Reputation Review, 1*(4), 327–340.

Forceville, C. (1999). Educating the eye? Kress and Van Leeuwen's Reading images: The grammar of visual design (1996). *Language & Literature, 8*(2), 163–178.

Franco, G. D., Hope, O., Vyas, D., & Zhou, Y. (2015). Analyst report readability. *Contemporary Accounting Research, 32*(1), 76–104.

Freeman, R. (1984). *Strategic management: A stakeholder approach*. Pitman Publishing Inc.

Fuoli, M. (2012). Assessing social responsibility: A quantitative analysis of appraisal in BP's and Ikea's social reports. *Discourse & Communication, 6*(1), 55–81.

Gazdar, K. (2007). *Reporting nonfinancials*. Wiley.

Goss, A., & Roberts, G. S. (2011). The impact of corporate social responsibility on the cost of bank loans. *Journal of Banking & Finance, 35*(7), 1794–1810.

Graesser, A. C., Mcnamara, D. S., Louwerse, M. M., & Cai, Z. (2004). Coh-Metrix: Analysis of text on cohesion and language. *Behavior Research Methods Instruments & Computers, 36*(2), 193–202.

Graesser, A. C., & Mcnamara, D. S. (2011). Computational analyses of multilevel discourse comprehension. *Topics in Cognitive Science, 3*(2), 371–398.

Gray, E. R., & Balmer, J. M. T. (1998). Managing corporate image and corporate reputation. *Long Range Planning, 31*(5), 695–702.

Gray, R., Kouhy, R., & Lavers, S. (1995). Corporate social and environmental reporting: A review of the literature and a longitudinal study of UK disclosure. *Accounting, Auditing & Accountability Journal, 8*(2), 47–77.

Gu, X., & Li, Y. (2007). Language and identity construction: Literature review. *Foreign Language Research*, (6), 105–112. [谷小娟、李艺. (2007). 语言与身份构建: 相关文献回顾. *外语学刊*, (6), 105–112].

Gui, S. (2009). *A corpus-based analysis of the register of English linguistics*. Beijing: Foreign Language Teaching and Researching Press. [桂诗春. (2009). *基于语料库的英语语言学语体分析*. 北京: 外语教学与研究出版社].

Hall, S. (2011). Introduction: Who needs identity. In S. Hall & P. Du Gay (Eds.), *Questions of Cultural Identity* (pp. 1–17). Sage Publications Ltd.

Halliday, M. A. K. (1998). Things and relations: Regrammaticizing experience as technical knowledge. In J. R. Martin & R. Veel (Eds.), *Reading Science: Critical and Functional Perspectives on Discourses of Science* (pp. 185–235). Routledge.

Halliday, M. A. K., & Hasan, R. (1976). *Cohesion in English*. Longman.

Halliday, M. A. K., & Hasan, R. (1985). *Language, context, and text: Aspects of language in a social-semiotic perspective*. Deakin University Press.

Halliday, M. A. K., & Matthiessen, C. M. I. (2004). *An introduction to functional grammar*. Arnold.

Han, J. C. Y. (1994). Empirical research in earnings forecasts. *Accounting Review, 28*, 79–102.

Henry, E. (2008). Are investors influenced by how earnings press releases are written? *Journal of Business Communication, 45*(4), 363–407.

Hofstede, G., Hofstede, G. J., & Minkov, M. (2010). *Cultures and organizations: Software of mind*. McGraw-Hill.

Hooghiemstra, R. (2000). Corporate communication and impression management—New perspectives why companies engage in corporate social reporting. *Journal of Business Ethics, 27*(1/2), 55–68.

Hu, C. (2014). A corpus-based study of "Bubble" metaphor. *Journal of PLA University of Foreign Languages, 37*(1), 18–30. [胡春雨. (2014). 基于语料库的泡沫隐喻研究. *解放军外国语学院学报, 37*(1), 18–30].

Hu, C. (2015a). Keyword analysis and its applications in business discourse studies. *Journal of Guangdong University of Foreign Studies, 26*(3), 48–53. [胡春雨. (2015a). 主题词分析及其在商务话语研究中的应用. *广东外语外贸大学学报, 26*(3), 48–53].

Hu, C. (2015b). Corpus stylistics approaches to the characteristics of English for business contracts. *Journal of PLA University of Foreign Languages, 38*(5), 10–19. [胡春雨. (2015b). 语料库文体学视域下的英文商务合同研究. *解放军外国语学院学报, 38*(5), 10–19].

Hu, C., & Fan, L. (2016). A study of conflict talks in business communication. *Foreign Language Education, 37*(2), 12–16. [胡春雨、范琳琳. (2016). 商务交际中的冲突性话语研究. *外语教学, 37*(2), 12–16].

Hu, Z. (2007). Cross-disciplinary trend in linguistic studies. *Foreign Language Teaching and Research, 39*(6), 403–408. [胡壮麟. (2007). 谈语言学研究的跨学科倾向. *外语教学与研究, 39*(6), 403–408].

Huang, X., Teoh, S. H., & Zhang, Y. (2014). Tone management. *The Accounting Review, 89*(3), 1083–1113.

Huang, X., & Zhu, W. (2017). Chinese corporations' conception of sustainable development: An innovative view of corpus analysis. *Chinese Management Studies, 11*(1), 180–190.

Hummel, K., & Schlick, C. (2016). The relationship between sustainability performance and sustainability disclosure—Reconciling voluntary disclosure theory and legitimacy theory. *Journal of Accounting & Public Policy, 35*(5), 455–476.

Hunston, S., & Sinclair, J. (2000). A local grammar of evaluation. In S. Hunston & G. Thompson (Eds.), *Evaluation in text: Authorial stance and the construction of discourse* (pp. 74–101). Oxford University Press.

Hwang, B. H., & Kim, H. H. (2017). It pays to write well. *Journal of Financial Economics, 124*(2), 373–394.

ICBC Green Finance Research Group. (2017). A study of ESG green rating and green index. *Finance Forum,* (9), 3–14. [中国工商银行绿色金融课题组, 张红力、周月秋、殷红、马素红、杨荇等. (2017). ESG绿色评级及绿色指数研究. *金融论坛,* (9), 3–14].

Ji, L., Zhang, L., & Tian, J. (2016). An analysis on the readability of the CSR information disclosed by the Chinese listed companies: A perspective from managerial power and restraint mechanism. *Journal of Accounting and Economics,* (1), 21–33. [吉利、张丽、田静. (2016). 我国上市公司社会责任信息披露可读性研究——基于管理层权力与约束机制的视角. *会计与经济研究,* (1), 21–33].

Jiang, J., & Xu, J. (2015). A corpus-based multi-dimensional analysis of business English registers. *Foreign Language Teaching and Research,* (2), 225–236. [江进林、许家金. (2015). 基于语料库的商务英语语域特征多维分析. *外语教学与研究,* (2), 225–236].

Kearney, C., & Liu, S. (2014). Textual sentiment in finance: A survey of methods and models. *International Review of Financial Analysis, 33*(3), 171–185.

Koller, V. (2009). Brand images: Multimodal metaphor in corporate branding messages. In C. Forceville & E. Urios-Aparisi (Eds.), *Multimodal metaphor* (pp. 45–47). De Gruyter.

Kothari, S. P., Li, X., & Short, J. E. (2009). The effect of disclosures by management, analysts, and business press on cost of capital, return volatility, and analyst forecasts: A study using content analysis. *The Accounting Review, 84*(5), 1639–1670.

Kress, G. (1993). Against arbitrariness: The social production of the sign as a foundational issue in critical discourse analysis. *Discourse & Society, 4*(2), 169–191.

Kress, G., & Van Leeuwen, T. (1996). *Reading images: The grammar of visual design*. Rutledge.

Kroskrity, P. V. (1999). Identity. *Journal of Linguistic Anthropology, 9*(1/2), 111–114.

Kushal, S. J. (2011). *Business communication*. New Delhi: V. K. Global Publications.

Lahtinen, K. D., & Shipe, S. (2017). Readability of financial advisor disclosures. *Journal of Empirical Finance, 44*, 36–42.

Laksmana, I., Tietz, W., & Yang, Y. W. (2012). Compensation discussion and analysis (CD&A): Readability and management obfuscation. *Journal of Accounting & Public Policy, 31*(2), 185–203.

Lang, M., & Stice-Lawrence, L. (2015). Textual analysis and international financial reporting: Large sample evidence. *Journal of Accounting & Economics, 60*(2–3), 110–135.

Langacker, R. W. (1987). *The foundations of cognitive grammar, Vol.1: Theoretical prerequisites*. Stanford: Stanford University Press.

Langacker, R. W. (2001). *Grammaticalization and cognitive grammar*. Oxford University Press.

Lei, X., & Yang, H. (2001). Corpus-based approaches and the MD/MF model in stylistic study of English for academic purposes. *Contemporary Linguistics, 3*(2), 143–151. [雷秀云、杨惠中. (2001). 基于语料库的研究方法及MD/MF模型与学术英语语体研究. *当代语言学, 3*(2), 143–151].

Lemke, J. L. (1998). Resources for attitudinal meaning: Evaluative orientations in text semantics. *Functions of Language, 5*(1), 33–56.

Leung, S., Parker, L., & Courtis, J. (2015). Impression management through minimal narrative disclosure in annual reports. *British Accounting Review, 47*(3), 275–289.

Lev, B., Petrovits, C., & Radhakrishnan, S. (2010). Is doing good good for you? How corporate charitable contributions enhance revenue growth. *Social Science Electronic Publishing, 31*(2), 182–200.

Li, C., & Ran, Y. (2015). A survey of identity construction within interpersonal pragmatics: Its present state, theoretical principles and new directions. *Foreign Languages in China*, (2), 47–54. [李成团、冉永平. (2015). 身份构建的人际语用学研究: 现状、原则与议题. *中国外语*, (2), 47–54].

Li, F. (2008). Annual report readability, current earnings, and earnings persistence. *Journal of Accounting & Economics, 45*(2), 221–247.

Li, F. (2011). Textual analysis of corporate disclosures: A survey of the literature. *Journal of Accounting Literature, 29*, 143–165.

Li, H., Li, P., & Zhang, J. (2009). A study on determinants of customer-company identification: Evidence from the retailing banking industry. *Science of Science and Management of S. & T.*, (12), 169–177. [李惠璠、李鹏、张金成. (2009). 顾客—企业认同的驱动因素研究. *科学与科学技术管理*, (12), 169–177].

Li, L. (2016). A corpus-based structural equation modeling study of appraisal markers in business discourse. *Foreign Language Teaching and Research*, (3), 370–381. [李琳. (2016). 基于语料库的商务话语评价建模研究. *外语教学与研究*, (3), 370–381].

Li, L., & Wang, L. (2017). A structural equation modeling study on three dimensional appraisal features in UK and US CEOs' risk discourse. *Foreign Language Education, 38*(4), 7–12. [李琳、王立非. (2017). 英美CEO风险话语的三维评价特征建模研究. *外语教学, 38*(4), 7–12].

Li, Y. (2005). Grey relation entropy analysis of logistics development affecting factors. *Journal of Highway and Transportation Research and Development, 22*(2), 142–145. [李玉民. (2005). 物流发展影响因子的灰关联熵分析. *公路交通科技, 22*(2), 142–145].

Liu, D., & Lei, L. (2018). The appeal to political sentiment: An analysis of Donald Trump's and Hillary Clinton's speech themes and discourse strategies in the 2016 US presidential election. *Discourse, Context and Media, 25*, 143–152.

Liu, Y. (2017). A corpus-based textual readability study of classical texts—Taking the English translation of *Master Sun's Art of War* as an example. *Journal of Mudanjiang University, 26*(5), 21–23. [刘毅. (2017). 基于语料库的典籍译本语篇可读性研究——以《孙子兵法》英译为例. *牡丹江大学学报, 26*(5), 21–23].

Liu, Z. (2008). *Corporate social responsibility and corporate image construction*. Beijing: China Financial and Economic Publishing House. [刘兆峰. (2008). *企业社会责任与企业形象塑造*. 北京: 中国财政经济出版社].

Livesey, S. M. (2002). The discourse of the middle ground: Citizen Shell commits to sustainable development. *Management Communication Quarterly, 15*(3), 313–349.

Lo, K., Ramos, F., & Rogo, R. (2017). Earnings management and annual report readability. *Journal of Accounting & Economics, 63*(1), 1–25.

Loughran, T., & Mcdonald, B. (2011). When is a liability not a liability? Textual analysis, dictionaries, and 10-Ks. *Journal of Finance, 66*(1), 35–65.

Loughran, T., & Mcdonald, B. (2014). Measuring readability in financial disclosures. *Journal of Finance, 69*(4), 1643–1671.

Lys, T., Naughton, J. P., & Wang, C. (2015). Signaling through corporate accountability reporting. *Journal of Accounting & Economics, 60*(1), 56–72.

Mahon, J. F., & Wartick, S. L. (2003). Dealing with stakeholders: How reputation, credibility and framing influence the game. *Corporate Reputation Review, 6*(1), 19–35.

Malinowski, B. (1923). The problem of meaning in primitive languages. In C. K. Ogden & I. A. Richards (Eds.), *The Meaning of Meaning* (pp. 451–510). Kegan Paul.

Margolis, J. D., & Walsh, M. J. P. (2003). Misery loves companies: Rethinking social initiatives by business. *Administrative Science Quarterly, 48*(2), 268–305.

Martin, J. R., & White, P. R. R. (2005). *The language of evaluation*. Palgrave Macmillan.

Martin, J. R., & Rose, D. (2007). *Working with discourse: Meaning beyond the clause*. Continuum.

Melewar, T. C., & Jenkins, E. (2002). Defining the corporate identity construct. *Corporate Reputation Review, 5*(1), 76–90.

Meng, Y. (2011). *Coherent construction in English learning advertising in China: A multimodal perspective*. Ph.D. dissertation, Peking University. [孟艳丽. (2011). *中国英语学习广告中的连贯构建: 多模态视角*. 北京大学博士学位论文].

Merkl-Davies, D. M., & Brennan, N. M. (2007). Discretionary disclosure strategies in corporate narratives: Incremental information or impression management? *Journal of Accounting Literatures, 26*(3), 116–196.

Meyer, C. (2002). *English corpus linguistics*. Cambridge University Press.

Mishra, D. R. (2017). Post-innovation CSR performance and firm value. *Journal of Business Ethics, 140*(2), 1–22.

Muller, M. G., Kappas, A., & Olk, B. (2012). Perceiving press photography: A new integrative model, combining iconology with psychophysiological and eye-tracking methods. *Visual Communication, 11*(3), 307–328.

Munday, J. (2012). *Evaluation in translation: Critical points of translator decision-making*. Routledge.

Muslu, V., Mutlu, S., Radhakrishnan, S., & Tsang, A. (2019). Corporate social responsibility report narratives and analyst forecast accuracy. *Journal of Business Ethics, 154*(4), 1119–1142.

O' Halloran, K. L. (2005). *Mathematical discourse: Language, symbolism and visual images*. Continuum.

O' Keeffe, A., McCarthy, M., & Carter, R. (2007). *From corpus to classroom: Language use and language teaching*. Cambridge University Press.

Pan, F. (2012). MF and MD analysis of written texts produced by Chinese non-English major undergraduates and graduates. *Foreign Language Teaching and Research*, (2), 220–232. [潘璠. (2012). 中国非英语专业本科生和研究生书面语体的多特征多维度调查. *外语教学与研究*, (2), 220–232].

Perrini, F. (2011). Building a European portrait of corporate social responsibility reporting. *European Management Journal, 23*(6), 611–627.

Price, M. K., Doran, J. S., Peterson, D. R., & Bliss, B. A. (2012). Earnings conference calls and stock returns: The incremental informativeness of textual tone. *Journal of Banking & Finance, 36*(4), 992–1011.

Ramanna, K. (2013). A framework for research on corporate accountability reporting. *Accounting Horizons, 26*(2), 409–432.

Ran, Y., & Liu, P. (2015). The study of relation from the interpersonal pragmatic perspective. *Foreign Language Education, 36*(4), 1–7. [冉永平、刘平. (2015). 人际语用学视角下的关系研究. *外语教学, 36*(4), 1–7].

Reisigl, M., & Wodak, R. (2014). The discourse-historical approach (DHA). In R. Wodak & M. Meyer (Eds.), *Methods of Critical Discourse Analysis* (pp. 87–121). Peking University Press.

Rezaee, Z., & Tuo, L. (2017). Voluntary disclosure of non-financial information and its association with sustainability performance. *Advances in Accounting, 39*, 47–59.

Richards, K. (2006). *Language and professional identity: Aspects of collaborative interaction*. Palgrave Macmillan.

Rindova, V. P., & Fombrun, C. J. (1999). Constructing competitive advantage: The role of firm-constituent interactions. *Strategic Management Journal, 20*(8), 691–710.

Roberts, R. W. (1992). Determinants of corporate social responsibility disclosure: An application of stakeholder theory. *Accounting, Organizations and Society, 17*(6), 595–612.

Rohdin, M. (2009). Multimodal metaphor in classical film theory from the 1920s to the,. (1950s). In C. Forceville & E. Urios-Aparisi (Eds.), *Multimodal metaphor* (pp. 403–428). De Gruyter.

Rutherford, B. A. (2005). Genre analysis of corporate annual report narratives: A corpus linguistics-based approach. *Journal of Business Communication, 42*(4), 349–378.

Scollon, R. (1996). Discourse identity, social identity, and confusion in intercultural communication. *Intercultural Communication Studies, 6*(1), 1–16.

Scott, M. (1996). *Wordsmith tools manual*. Oxford University Press.

Scott, M. (2004). *Wordsmith tools version 4*. Oxford University Press.

Sethi, S. P., Martell, T. F., & Demir, M. (2017). An evaluation of the quality of corporate social responsibility reports by some of the world's largest financial institutions. *Journal of Business Ethics, 140*(4), 787–805.

Sheehy, B. (2015). Defining CSR: Problems and solutions. *Journal of Business Ethics, 131*(3), 625–648.

Sheldon, O. (1923). *The philosophy of management*. Sir I. Pitman.

Shen, H., & Yang, Y. (2008). Research on value correlation of corporate social responsibility information disclosure—Evidence from Chinese listed companies. *Contemporary Finance & Economics,* (3), 103–107. [沈洪涛、杨熠. (2008). 公司社会责任信息披露的价值相关性研究——来自我国上市公司的经验证据. *当代财经,* (3), 103–107].

Shen, H., Wang, L., & Wan, T. (2011). Can corporate social report and assurance be effective signals—An analysis based on reputation theory. *Auditing Research,* (4), 87–93. [沈洪涛、王立彦、万拓. (2011). 社会责任报告及鉴证能否传递有效信号?——基于企业声誉理论的分析. *审计研究,* (4), 87–93].

Shi, X., & Wan, W. (2018). A study of the research methods in Business English studies published in CSSCI and SSCI journals from 2007 to 2017. *Foreign Language World*, (2), 20–28. [史兴松、万文菁. (2018). 国内外商务英语研究方法探析(2007—2017). *外语界,* (2), 20–28].

Shiller, R. J. (2003). From efficient markets theory to behavioral finance. *The Journal of Economic Perspectives, 17*(1), 83–104.

Shocker, A. D., & Sethi, S. P. (1973). An approach to incorporating societal preferences in developing corporate action strategies. *California Management Review, 15*(4), 97–105.

Smith, H. P., & Dechant, E. V. (1977). *Psychology in teaching reading*. Prentice Hall.

Smith, M., & Taffler, R. J. (2000). The chairman's statement—A content analysis of discretionary narrative disclosures. *Accounting Auditing & Accountability Journal, 13*(5), 624–647.

Song, X., & Gong, M. (2007). Assessment on the quality and decision value of the social responsibility disclosures: A content analysis of the financial annual reports of list companies. *Accounting Research,* (2), 37–43. [宋献中、龚明晓. (2007). 社会责任信息的质量与决策价值评价——上市公司会计年报的内容分析. *会计研究,* (2), 37–43].

Spence, M. (1973). Job market signaling. *The Quarterly Journal of Economics, 87*(3), 355–374.

Stone, P. J. (1966). *The general inquirer: A computer approach to content analysis.* M. I. T. Press.

Suchman, M. C. (1995). Managing legitimacy: Strategic and institutional approaches. *Academy of Management Review, 20*(3), 571–610.

Sun, S. (2013). *Design and research of a century Chinese brand visual image.* Ph.D. dissertation, Suzhou University. [孙绍军. (2013). *百年中国品牌视觉形象设计研究.* 苏州大学博士学位论文].

Sun, Y., & Zhang, Y. (2013). The discursive construction of organizational identity: A case analysis of Beijing university's prospectus on the web. *The Journal of Chinese Sociolinguistics,* (1), 66–74. [孙咏梅、张艳斌. (2013). 从"北大简介"看大学身份的话语建构. *中国社会语言学,* (1), 66–74].

Tang, J. (2008). The pragmatic perspective of modal verbs. *Foreign Languages and Their Teaching,* (9), 19–21. [汤敬安. (2008). 情态动词的语用综观性. *外语与外语教学,* (9), 19–21].

Tang, X. (2015). *Sentiment analysis of Er Ma and its four English versions: An appraisal theory perspective.* MA thesis, Beijing Foreign Studies University. [唐宣超. (2015). *评价理论视角下《二马》及四个英译本的情感分析.* 北京外国语大学硕士学位论文].

Tetlock, P. C. (2007). Giving content to investor sentiment: The role of media in the stock market. *Journal of Finance, 62*(3), 1139–1168.

Tilling, M. V., & Tilt, C. A. (2010). The edge of legitimacy: Voluntary social and environmental reporting in Rothmans' 1956–1999 annual reports. *Accounting, 23*(1), 55–81.

Tinker, T., Neimark, M., & Lehman, C. (1991). Falling down the hole in the middle of the road: Political quietism in corporate social reporting. *Accounting Auditing & Accountability Journal, 4*(2), 28–54.

Tversky, A., & Kahneman, D. (1974). Judgment under uncertainty: Heuristics and biases. *Science, 185*(4157), 1124–1131.

Twedt, B., & Rees, L. (2012). Reading between the lines: An empirical examination of qualitative attributes of financial analysts' reports. *Journal of Accounting & Public Policy, 31*(1), 1–21.

Ullmann, A. A. (1985). Data in search of a theory: A critical examination of the relationships among social performance, social disclosure, and economic performance of U. S. firms. *The Academy of Management Review, 10*(3), 540–557.

UNEP-FI, & Mercer (2007). *Demystifying responsible investment performance—A review of key academic and broker research on ESG factors*. Jointed report by United Nations and Environment Programme Finance Initiative (UNEP-FI) and Mercer.

Vilanova, M., Lonzano, J. M., & Arenas, D. (2009). Exploring the nature of the relationship between CSR and competitiveness. *Journal of Business Ethics, 87*(1), 57–69.

Wang, L., & Bu, H. (2017). Multidimensional evaluation and comparative analysis of discourse sentimental tendency in Chinese and American companies. *Foreign Languages Research,* (4), 16–21. [王立非、部寒. (2017). 中美企业话语情感倾向多维评价测量与对比分析. *外语研究,* (4), 16–21].

Wang, L., & Bu, H. (2018). An introduction to textual analysis tool DICTION and its application in sentiment analysis. *Foreign Language and Literature,* (1), 67–74. [王立非、部寒. (2018). DICTION文本分析工具及其在情感分析中的应用. *外国语文,* (1), 67–74].

Wang, L., & Han, F. (2015). A contrastive move analysis between Chinese and English corporate annual reports. *Journal of PLA University of Foreign Languages, 38*(5), 1–9. [王立非、韩放. (2015). 中英文企业年报体裁的语轮对比分析. *解放军外国语学院学报, 38*(5), 1–9].

Wang, L., & Li, Z. (2018). A comparative study on measuring English discourse complexity of Chinese and US bank reports. *Foreign Language and Literature Research,* (1), 93–99. [王立非、李喆玥. (2018). 中美金融报告语篇复杂度测量与对比研究. *外国语文研究,* (1), 93–99].

Wang, L., & Zhang, F. (2016). Conceptualizing and theorizing business English as a sub-discipline. *Foreign Language Research,* (3), 63–66. [王立非、张斐瑞. (2016). 论商务英语二级学科的核心概念及理论基础. *外语学刊,* (3), 63–66].

Wen, K. L., Chang, T. C., & You, M. L. (1998). *The grey entropy and its application in weighting analysis*. Paper presented at the IEEE International Conference on Systems, Man, and Cybernetics, San Diego, CA, USA.

Wu, J., Huang, S., & Zheng, R. (2016). Recontextualization and transformation in media discourse: An analysis of the first-instance judgment of the Peng Yu case. *Discourse & Society, 27*(4), 441–466.

Wu, J., & Li, X. (2017). Recontextualization and the transmission of enterprise culture: A case study on the translation of the websites of Fortune Global 500. *Journal of Foreign Languages,* (2), 90–96. [武建国、李昕蒙. (2017). 重新语境化与企业文化的传播——以世界五百强企业的网页翻译为例. *外国语,* (2), 90–96].

Wu, N., & Zhang, J. (2019). Discursive strategies for the construction of Chinese and American corporate identities. *Modern Foreign Languages, 42*(2), 220–230. [乌楠、张敬源. (2019). 中美企业机构身份的话语建构策略. *现代外语, 42*(2), 220–230].

Wu, X. (2017). A study on syntactic complexity and text readability of international journal articles by Chinese scholars. *Journal of PLA University of Foreign Languages, 40*(5), 11–19. [吴雪. (2017). 中国学者国际期刊论文句法复杂度与文本可读性研究. *解放军外国语学院学报, 40*(5), 11–19].

Xiang, Y. (2009). A review of identity construction. *Social Science Research,* (5), 188–192. [项蕴华. (2009). 身份建构研究综述. *社会科学研究,* (5), 188–192].

Xiao, R. (2010). Multidimensional analysis and the study of world Englishes. *World Englishes, 28*(4), 421–450.

Xiao, Z., & McEnery, A. (2005). Help or help to: What do corpora have to say? *English Studies, 86*(2), 161–187.

Xiao, S., & Shao, Y. (2014). Can commercial banks fulfillment of social responsibilities create value? —Evidence from stakeholders of US banking industry. *Jinan Journal(Philosophy & Social Science Edition),* (12), 30–39. [萧松华、邵毅. (2014). 商业银行履行社会责任能创造价值吗?——来自美国银行业利益相关者的证据. *暨南学报 (哲学社会科学版)*, (12), 30–39].

Xiao, H., Zhan, L., & Wang, Z. (2016). A review of foreign empirical research on accounting text information and prospects. *Foreign Economics & Management, 38*(9), 93–112. [肖浩、詹雷、王征. (2016). 国外会计文本信息实证研究述评与展望. *外国经济与管理, 38*(9), 93–112].

Xu, S., & Huang, J. (2014). Market reaction to the disclosure of corporate social responsibility information: Based on the event study of social responsibility reports. *Collected Essays on Finance and Economics,* (5), 45–51. [徐珊、黄健柏. (2014). 社会责任信息披露的市场有效性——基于发布社会责任报告的事件分析. *财经论丛,* (5), 45–51].

Xu, X. (2010). The extensive reference of first-person plural pronouns in English and Chinese. *Shandong Foreign Language Teaching Journal, 31*(5), 21–24. [徐欣. (2010). 英汉第一人称代词复数的虚指. *山东外语教学, 31*(5), 21–24].

Yang, Z., & Miao, X. (2017). A review of the studies on the layout structure of multimodal discourse. *Foreign Language Research,* (6), 24–29. [杨增成、苗兴伟. (2017). 多模态语篇布局结构研究述评. *外语学刊,* (6), 24–29].

Yekini, L. S., Wisniewski, T. P., & Millo, Y. (2015). Market reaction to the positiveness of annual report narratives. *British Accounting Review, 48*(4), 415–430.

You, H., & Zhang, X. (2009). Financial reporting complexity and investor under reaction to 10-K information. *Review of Accounting Studies, 14*(4), 559–586.

Zhai, L. Y., Khoo, L. P., & Zhong, Z. W. (2009). Design concept evaluation in product development using rough sets and grey relation analysis. *Expert Systems with Applications, 36*(3), 7072–7079.

Zhang, Q., Guo, X., & Deng, J. (1996). Grey relation entropy method of grey relation analysis. *Systems Engineering—Theory & Practice,* (8), 7–11. [张岐山、郭喜江、邓聚龙. (1996). 灰关联熵分析方法. *系统工程理论与实践,* (8), 7–11].

Zhang, W. (2004). The construction of modern city image and marketing concept. *Journal of Zhongnan University of Finance and Economics,* (3), 103–108. [张卫宁. (2004). 现代城市形象的塑造与营销学理念. *中南财经政法大学学报,* (3), 103–108].

Zhang, X. (2013). Study on the market efficiency of information releasing and delivering of corporate social responsibility performance. *Collected Essays on Finance and Economics,* (4), 81–87. [张绪娥. (2013). 企业社会责任绩效信息传递市场有效性实证研究. *财经论丛,* (4), 81–87].

Zhao, X. (2011). New development of conceptual metaphor studies: Multimodal metaphor. *Foreign Languages Research,* (1), 1–10. [赵秀凤. (2011). 概念隐喻研究的新发展多模态隐喻研究兼评 Forceville & Urios—Aparisi《多模态隐喻》. *外语研究,* (1), 1–10].

Zheng, W. (2018). *A comparative study on corporate image building in CSR reports of insurance and banking industry from the perspective of attitude system.* MA thesis, Sichuan International Studies University. [郑文娟. (2018). *态度系统视角下保险业与银行业企业社会责任报告中企业形象建构对比研究.* 四川外国语大学硕士学位论文].

Zhou, H. (2004). Views about the introduction of CIS strategy into college. *Journal of Tongji University (Social Science Section), 15*(2), 76–80+123. [周宏武. (2004). 高校导入CIS策略刍议. *同济大学学报(社会科学版), 15*(2), 76–80+123].

Zhu, W. (2009). *On the Criteria and Mechanism for Commercial Banks' CSR.* Beijing: Economy and Management Publishing House. [朱文忠. (2009). *商业银行企业社会责任标准与机制研究.* 北京: 经济管理出版社].

SPRINGER NATURE

GPSR Compliance

The European Union's (EU) General Product Safety Regulation (GPSR) is a set of rules that requires consumer products to be safe and our obligations to ensure this.

If you have any concerns about our products, you can contact us on ProductSafety@springernature.com

In case Publisher is established outside the EU, the EU authorized representative is:

Springer Nature Customer Service Center GmbH
Europaplatz 3
69115 Heidelberg, Germany

The manufacturer's authorised representative in the EU is Springer Nature Customer Service Centre GmbH, Europaplatz 3, 69115 Heidelberg, Germany. If you have any concerns regarding our products, please contact ProductSafety@springernature.com

Printed and bound by CPI Group (UK) Ltd, Croydon, CR0 4YY
30/09/2026
02225320-0006